BY ROBERT ORNSTEIN

On the Experience of Time

On the Psychology of Meditation (with Claudio Naranjo)

The Psychology of Consciousness

The Nature of Human Consciousness

Common Knowledge

Symposium on Consciousness

The Mind Field

The Amazing Brain (with Richard Thompson and David Macaulay)

Psychology: The Study of Human Experience

Multimind

The Psychology of Consciousness: The Classic Edition Completely
Revised and Updated

The Healing Brain (with David Sobel)

Psychology: The Biological, Mental and Social Worlds

New World, New Mind (with Paul Ehrlich)

Healthy Pleasures (with David Sobel)

The Healing Brain: A Scientific Reader (with Charles Swencionis)

Psychology: The Study of Human Experience, Third Edition
(with Laura Carstensen)

THE EVOLUTION OF CONSCIOUSNESS

*Of Darwin, Freud, and Cranial Fire:
The Origins of the Way We Think*

ROBERT ORNSTEIN

LINE ILLUSTRATIONS BY TED DEWAN

A TOUCHSTONE BOOK
Published by Simon & Schuster
New York   London   Toronto   Sydney   Tokyo   Singapore

TOUCHSTONE
Simon & Schuster Building
Rockefeller Center
1230 Avenue of the Americas
New York, New York 10020

1   3   5   7   9   10   8   6   4   2

Library of Congress Cataloging-in-Publication Data
Ornstein, Robert E. (Robert Evan)
    The Evolution of Consciousness: Of Darwin, Freud, and Cranial
Fire: The Origins of the Way We Think/Robert Ornstein; illustrations
by Ted Dewan.
        p.   cm.
    Includes bibliographical references and index.
    1. Genetic psychology. 2. Neuropsychology. 3. Consciousness.
    4. Adaptability (Psychology)   I. Title.
    BF701.076   1991
    155.7—dc20   91-11306
                                                        CIP

ISBN 0-671-76751-8
ISBN 0-671-79224-5 (pbk)

For Alan, Rachel, Jessie, Jeanne, and Sally
and for the memories of
Jack Mallam and David Ornstein

ACKNOWLEDGMENTS

I'd like to thank so many people here but can mention only a few. Sally Mallam Ornstein bore with me during the intense time of writing this book and survived to help criticize the draft instead of burning it. Sally also did the first renderings for many of the anatomical drawings in the book. Ted Dewan, he of the long-gone magic Bakelite and pen world, did much more than illustrate this book: He re-created it in a new language.

So many readers read the book, it is difficult to remember them all; everyone had something to add. Among them are Sallye Leventhal, Ramsay Wood, David Widdicombe, Brent Danninger, Evan Nielsen, David Sobel, Shane de Haven, Sally Mallam Ornstein, Fred Zlotnick and Linda Garfield, Christina Lepnis, Doris Lessing, Laura Carstensen, Alan Parker, Tony Cartlidge, Sara Forni, Alvin Mungo Thompson, Alan Ornstein, and Rachel Hawk. Many others have asked to remain anonymous—I thank them here.

The book could not have been done without the generous research work of Lynne Levitan and Christina Lepnis, both of whom contributed so very much, under so much time pressure, to the finished work.

The theme of the book is the accidental nature of our life, and the accidents that led to my working with Prentice Hall were welcome. Gail Winston and I had a conversation on another subject, which led to a discussion of current projects. Liz Perle graciously gave up her time, sitting in front of a telephone near a men's room, to discuss the details of our publishing arrangements. Later I found myself indeed fortunate to have collaborated with an admirable editor in Gail and the spark-in-your-face vivacity of Liz. Their skill and enthusiasm are much appreciated.

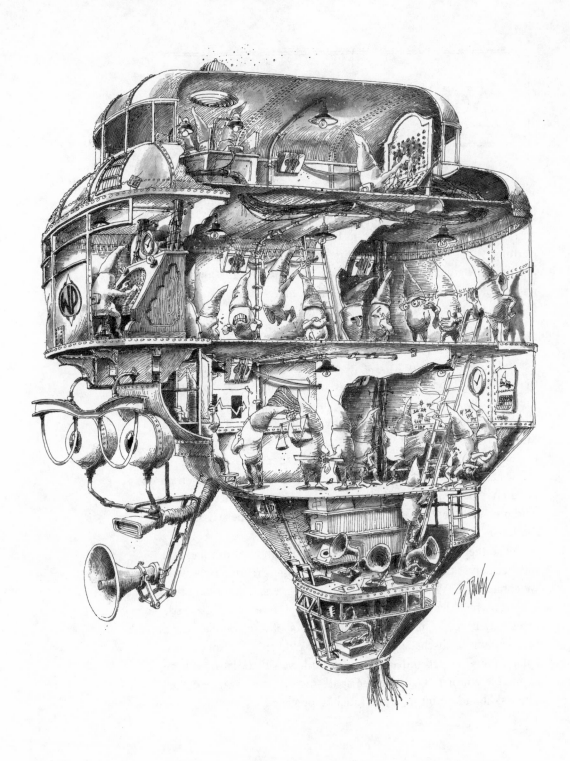

The world-processing system.

CONTENTS

PREFACE

In 1971 I wrote *The Psychology of Consciousness* to present new evidence on the capacity of consciousness and conscious change. In it I tried to show that human consciousness arises from brain organization but must be developed in each of us. I pointed to the similarities between our current scientific analyses of the mind and those of other cultures, noting that thinkers and observers in many societies all over the world had discovered the same things about the human animal. I proposed that, just as we exported scientific knowledge to all parts, perhaps we could import some knowledge about ourselves, our minds, our souls that was lacking in our own society.

In the twenty years since that book, the attitudes toward human action have radically changed. Where many of us once felt that technology could help transform the world, we now know its costs. We once breathed free; now we are choking ourselves off from the air. Now we are cooking ourselves. Now we are crowding ourselves out of the limited food supply. Now we understand other cultures insufficiently. Now we understand our heritage much less. Now we understand our future much less.

The world has changed, even in these twenty years, and so has our place in it. We need to revise, radically and rapidly, our idea of how our mind developed, what is central to the human mind, and how that assessment changes. In this, we need to enlist the revolutionary work from brain and consciousness research, cognitive science, evolutionary biology, and psychology. These disciplines, for the first time, provide a picture of the way the mind evolved from the earlier (unconscious) action-routines of other animals, and how many of these still reside in ourselves.

These nonconscious routines of the mind lead us automatically, and thus unconsciously, along lines of thinking without our ever directing them. Our ordinary actions and reactions were established by our ancestors and work in routines evolved to adapt us to the world. Loud noise—we run or become alert. Ripe fruit—we like it. Sexy look—we are attracted. The different centers of the mind, which I call, only slightly jokingly, "simpletons," have "minds of their own," evolved to handle specific and limited situations, and are all bunched together inside the mind. They seem to run themselves, without—or outside of—consciousness.

I haven't changed my views on the importance and the possibilities of consciousness. But it is difficult to change consciousness while fighting millions of years of evolved adaptations. Then why try? Because many of the important adaptations of the mind are appropriate to a world that is long gone. Biological evolution shaped us to suit a world that disappeared long, long ago, and we are failing to adapt to the modern world. This failure lies at the root of the ecological catastrophes that may well await us, the misdirection of effort in medicine and education, and the constant failure to understand peoples from different parts of the world.

The signals in the world are different now, the dangers greater, and our old system of unconscious adaptation has reached its limits. We haven't needed to direct our minds consciously all that much until now, and we haven't really understood the delicacy and the absolute necessity of doing so—until now.

January 1991
Los Altos, California

I

The Work
of
the Mind

Squadron of simpletons.

1

Aristotle
Is a Hamburger

Originally you were clay. From being mineral, you became vegetable. From vegetable, you became animal, and from animal, man. During these periods man did not know where he was going, but he was being taken on a long journey nonetheless. And you have to go through a hundred different worlds yet. There are a thousand forms of mind.

—Jallaludin Rumi

The mind is a squadron of simpletons. It is not unified, it is not rational, it is not well designed—or designed at all. It just happened, an accumulation of innovations of the organisms that lived before us. The mind evolved, through countless animals and through countless worlds.

Like the rest of biological evolution, the human mind is a collage of adaptations (the propensity to do the right thing) to different situations. Our thought is a pack of fixed routines—simpletons. We need them. It is vital to find the right food at the right time, to mate well, to generate children, to avoid marauders, to respond to emergency quickly. Mental routines to do so have evolved over millions of years and developed in different periods in our evolution, as Rumi noted.

We don't think of ourselves as of such humble origins. The triumphs that have occurred in the short time since the Industrial Revolution have completely distorted our view of ourselves. Hence, the celebrated triumph of humanity is its rationality: the ability to reason through events and act logically, to organize business, to plan for the future, to create science and technology. One influential philosopher, Daniel Dennet, wrote recently: "When a person falls short of perfect rationality ... there is no coherent ... description of the person's mental states."

Yet to characterize the mind as *primarily* rational is an injustice; it sells us short, it makes us misunderstand ourselves, it has perverted our understanding of our intelligence, our schooling, our physical and mental health. Holding up rationality, and its remorseless deliberation, as the model of the mind has, more important, set us along the wrong road to our future. Instead of the pinnacle, rationality is just one small ability in a compound of possibilities.

The mind evolved great breadth, but it is shallow, for it performs quick and dirty sketches of the world. This rough-and-ready perception of reality enabled our ancestors to survive better. The mind did not evolve to know the world or to know ourselves. Simply speaking, there has never been, nor will there ever be, enough time to be truly rational.

Rationality is one component of the mind, but it is used rarely, and in a very limited area. Rationality is impossible anyway. There isn't time for the mind to go through the luxurious exercises of examining alternatives. Consider the standard way of examining evidence, the truth table, a checklist of information about whether propositions are correct or not. To know whether Aristotle is a hamburger, you would look up "Aristotle" or "hamburger" in this table. Now think of the number of issues you immediately know well—what Yugoslavia is, whether skateboards are used at formal dinners, how chicken sandwiches should taste, what your spouse wore this morning—and you will see that your own truth table, if entered randomly, would have millions of entries just waiting!

How much time would it take to search through all the evidence? Consider a computer about as fast as theoretically possible, so fast that it can look up an entry in the truth table in the time that it takes a light ray to cross the diameter of a proton. Suppose, as a new book, *Minimal Rationality*, has it, "This computer was permitted to run twenty billion years, the estimated time from the 'big bang' dawn of the universe to the present. A belief system containing only 138 independent [statements] would overwhelm the time resources of this 'supermachine.'"

Now, this is a little exaggerated, I grant you. We'd never

consider 138 logically independent propositions, nor even a dozen. On the other hand, truth changes constantly. The proposition "Donatello is a turtle" would have had no more meaning than "Aristotle is a hamburger" a few years ago. But that was before the Ninja Turtles landed in pop culture. Even with fixed truths, considering but two logical propositions like this would take 200 million years of this supercomputer's time, a mite longer than we usually take for life-and-death decisions. Imagine an organism that searched through evidence as a tiger approached. What is this expanse of yellow in my visual field? Is this friendly? Take a look at those ears. Such an organism would not contribute any of its genes to succeeding generations.

Obviously we don't search out all alternatives in an attempt to gain knowledge; instead, we use a few simple strategies and analyze everything this way. We have a very simple rough justice here in the mind. The mind works in the overwhelmingly large part to do or die, not to reason or to know why. Most of our mental reactions are automatic, not so automatic, perhaps, as removing one's hand from a hot stove, but stored in fixed routines, as in a military exercise.

We know only what we need for the rough-and-ready reality and are ignorant of things we see all the time because we don't need to know about them. What are the letters on the telephone next to the 7? They are surprisingly difficult to remember because you don't normally need to know the link. You know all the letters and numbers, but you can't easily put them together. This happens all the time. Presumably you know the months of the year, and you know alphabetical order. First say the months in order. Takes about ten seconds or less. Now try them in alphabetical order. How smart are you at this?

We look quickly at the world and compute a rough and likely judgment. How much is $8 \times 7 \times 6 \times 5 \times 4 \times 3 \times 2 \times 1$? Now, how much is $1 \times 2 \times 3 \times 4 \times 5 \times 6 \times 7 \times 8$? Obviously the products are the same. Still and all, when people are asked to assess one or another, the estimate for the first is 2,250; the second, 512? Why? Because we look at only the first few numbers and rough out the answer. Usually these vague estimates work well.

Our mind did not spring from a designer, nor from a set of ideal and idealized programs. Otherwise, we'd certainly not make the mistakes above. Instead, it evolved on the same adaptive basis as the rest of biological evolution, using the processes of random generation and selection of what is so generated.

The primary billet of the mental system is not self-understanding, self-analysis, or reason, but adaptation to the world, to get nourishment and safety, to reproduce and so pass on descendants. The human mind evolved a fantastic set of adaptations to operate within and to mesh with the small world or local environment in which each of us finds ourselves. It works to gain a quick fix on reality and guide action.

This mental system has, or had, good justification; it presents priorities for action via consciousness. However, it doesn't show us the action "behind the scenes" of the mind or even tell us which special-purpose analyzer is working at any time. In the normal course of affairs, we would have no need to observe the mind's actions. We only know what is *on* our mind, rarely what is *in* our mind.

The story of the orgins of the mind lies in many accidents and many changes of function. It begins long ago, with the nerve circuits of the first living beings. Later evolution carried the same primate brain structure found in the tarsier through the gibbon and, most recently, the chimp, gorilla, and orangutan. Thus, many of the mind's units were well worked out and firmly in place before the first human beings ever saw light. The general plan of our mental operation and action was in place before rationality was a glimmer in the eyes of the first farmers in the Levant, 11,000 years ago.

The finishing touches on our mind were complete tens of thousands of years before the rise of modern science, before the American Revolution in 1776, before the steam engine, before electricity, before Agincourt, before Christ, before Egypt, before the first Ice Age settlements in Jutland, before the cave painters of Lascaux.

In our ancestors evolved a mental system in which many of the mind's standardized short-circuit reactions were organized to simplify choices, to improve adaption to a stable world, a world where one's grandparents and grandchildren would be facing the same problems with the same tools. Enhancing one's attention and reaction to short-term changes was important in the world in which we were refined.

Human beings have adapted amazingly, to the Himalayas, to the desert, to the forest, to the seashore, to São Paulo, to Prague. This extraordinary diversity is why our mind is so disorganized, so full of conflict, so diverse. And so difficult to analyze simply.

I hope the tour of the mind in this book will contribute to the current evaluations many are making about education and the way our society can adapt to the future. One implication is that we would look at current failures in education, in judgment, in politics not as failures of rationality or of cultural literacy but as *failures of adaptation*.

If we think of ourselves as rational, our ideas for improvement go along mistaken, though well-established, lines. One is knowing many facts. I've opened E. D. Hirsch, Jr.'s, recent *Cultural Literacy* to his famous list of what one needs to know to be culturally literate. First, I want to say this book contains a very good analysis of how we develop our understanding of the world, how we think and act. Yet the prescription for how to improve is weirdly typical of current thought.

I decided to look at *T* by chance. Here is the list for the first page: tabula rasa; tactics/strategy; Taft, William Howard; Taipei; Taj Mahal; take-home pay; take me out to the ball game (song); telltale; Tampa, Florida; tangent; tango; Tantalus; Taoism; taproot. Nothing on this list will help anybody adapt well to the world, understand what we are doing to the planet, or know how to work.

If we think of the mind as adaptive, we realize that during infancy every baby "picks up," with their mother's milk, the basics of life—language, accent, customs, food preferences, ideas of family and behavior, and identification with sex and tribe. The mind does so, without rational intervention, because it evolved to mesh the individual in a safe world.

If we understand that the adaptations of most "tribes" are now out of date in the modern world, yet we still have the same system, then changing our minds may well be much easier than we think. It will be a prescription much different from the cultural-literacy-type prescribed remedy. Humanity needs a new kind of adaptation to a world that is unprecedented.

I don't want to make mincemeat out of Aristotelian thought, but we cannot make the right kinds of changes in ourselves and in our education, our medicine and our society, without knowing where we came from. And knowing what we came from and how we came to be the way we are. We need to know how human beings came to think, feel, believe, and know the way we do, and how so much of it is firmly based on routines that happened to be around.

People can consciously redirect their minds, but, like learning to read or to do math, this ability doesn't come naturally. It has to be nurtured. We have to know who is in there to order around.

The mind isn't any one thing. Like an army, it has its master builders, its accountants, its dullards, its stooges, its wild spirits, its dreamers especially. The mind contains separate systems of thought, emotion, and ideas, and these *transfer* from one situation to another. Sigmund Freud elaborated on an important mental routine in his analysis of transference, but it isn't specific to the therapeutic encounter. Minds come into consciousness and transfer reactions all the time. This swapping of reactions leaves our consciousness unaware of how a new and different "mind in place" is determining our reactions.

This complicated internal system should have forewarned us that the mind isn't designed to be understood as we might a software routine. It is, basically, just another organ to help a person operate in the world, to stay out of trouble, to eat, sleep, and reproduce. So why should human beings ever have evolved the ability to know what their mental system is doing, any more than we know what our pancreas is doing? And we have not done so. Our natural view of our mental state is deeply distorted.

About This Book

It is time to begin to produce a modern synthesis of Rumi's perspective on the operation of the mental system and the modern information of how the mind evolved over millennia and how the many bytes and pieces of the mind work. If we are to make any real change in the way we do things, we need to understand first where the mind came from and upon what it is based.

This book has several parts. The next one, part 2, begins way back in our biological history, because the same life processes that produced the wing and the eye also produced the cortex in the fish and, finally, the human mind. Understanding how the simple processes of evolution worked over eons will make some of the mind's moves clear, for the mind, like all else on earth, evolved.

We first consider Charles Darwin's displacement of the religious-oriented "designer being" manner of thinking of the nineteenth century—in which organisms were seen to operate the way they do because of a Supreme Being who made them the way they are.

Later in this part we look at whether the human mind is, in part, an accident. Its evolution turns around a central question: Why is our brain so big? Why have a brain capable of not only chess when there was no game, but of building guided missiles when there was no metal or chemistry or writing? For the brain (which is the most "costly" neural material in the body) ballooned up radically 2 million years ago, and the "usual suspects" for this expansion don't seem to have primary responsibility. It was not language, it was not tools, it was not bipedalism alone. The brain seems to have increased in size before all the organized societies, cooperation, and language would have had any call for such a development.

This is the central mystery of the mind: It is difficult to see why we are so advanced relative to our nearest ancestors. We aren't just a slightly better chimp, and it's difficult, on reflection, to figure out why. This gigantic cortex has given us our adaptability as well as the extra capacity to adapt to the heights of the Himalayas, the Sahara Desert, the wilds of Borneo, even to central London.

I've encountered some surprises in doing the work for this book: It seems that some of the physical changes necessary to adapt to the upright position of our ancestors lit a fire within the brain, which ignited the modern mind; and there is evidence that the collage of different "selves" within the brain fight for control and decide what we are going to do on their own.

Part 3, "The Inner Workings of the Mind," follows the mind as it works in the different worlds in which people live. We're able to live all over the earth because the mind gets wired up differently in different territories. The human mind contains a phalanx of adaptations to circumstances, many of which we will never encounter. We learn one or at most a few of the languages on earth, eat but one of a style of foods, learn to behave in a way appropriate to our culture. And we lose many of the possible abilities we possess during development. An individual's evolution moves through several "worlds," as Rumi put it.

Through the enormous brain growth during evolution, the human baby has been oversupplied with a "thousand forms of mind"; it babbles all the sounds of the world during development and then loses some as the individual world selects those minds the baby needs to survive. There are separate, independent abilities, few of which become activated in a person. Your ability to speak Togalog is unused, as is the ability to leap or to live at 10,000 feet above sea level; nevertheless, they are there.

When the nervous system gets organized, it has a lot of potential, a thousand forms of mind. As we get older, a few of the many potential abilities are put into service; most disappear. We see this in a child's ability to dance, to draw, to dazzle in many ways, ways that are often gone by adolescence. This process happens through biological, cultural, linguistic selections early in life. The world in which we find ourselves actually wires up the brain differently because of experience. The world selects what's needed. For example, people develop to digest the food of their region. A fellow graduate student of mine, born in Japan, had to leave the room if Velveeta were even opened, so sick did he become at the smell of rotten milk. (I always wanted to give him blue cheese to see what would happen.) The mind gets customized for each locale.

This part introduces us to how the earliest mental routines, which developed for quick action and survival, later were recruited to make mental judgments. This is why we evaluate war as we do marriage; estimate tiny changes in brightness as we do gigantic changes in government expenses, and why millions shift their travel plans because of one terrorist murder, unaware that more Americans are killed each day with handguns than have been killed in toto by all the terrorists. Same old brain, that SOB.

Part 4 discusses how the brain evolved its specialized centers of action. The large cortex developed into specialized cerebral hemispheres, which contain different kinds of thought. And the specialization goes deeper. Different centers of the mind seem to act independently of consciousness, so that something inside us, for instance, decides how and when to move long before our consciousness knows about it. Our consciousness seems largely to have negative options, to stop one of the simpletons from acting.

The next part concerns our experience and how the mind produces it. We seem to have evolved two kinds of routines for

1-2

Parallels.

understanding the world: One operation gathers information, the second interprets. This is why memories, dreams, and imagination are all the same process, for the mind uses the same interpretations whether it is dreaming at night, recollecting infancy, or imagining a new home. What we think of as our memory is an illusion, as are our dreams. And, surprisingly, so is the sight you see now.

Human beings are broad in that we can live anywhere, but shallow, in that we act the same way. And we are so because of the amazing breadth and lack of depth of the mind. This part of the book, and in a sense, the whole book, is about that dream of the world, and the different dreamers within.

Part 6 goes on to consider how the self is a small isolated part of the mind, sometimes called into play by consciousness, most often on the sidelines. And we as readers try, all through, to see if in our history, our biology, our development, there are sights and insights that we can make use of. This part attempts to show how larger routines get recruited in and out of place. The love we seek makes us vulnerable to cults—shifts our mind, sometimes in a helpful way, sometimes in a dangerous way.

I use the concept of "mind in place" to show how we recruit the same routines to handle different situations. A set of minds swings in and out: One system, then another, then a third takes hold of consciousness. Once recruited for a purpose, the mind in place performs as if it had been there forever, then steps aside, to be replaced with another "actor," one with different memories, priorities, and plans. And "we," our conscious self, rarely notice what has gone on.

This is one reason why we don't we act the way "we" want ourselves to. Since minds shift, "we" are not the same person from moment to moment, not the same "self" at all. The idea most people have that they are consistent in the diverse situations of their lives in an illusion, one caused by the structure of the brain. The self is, itself, just one of the simpletons, with a small job.

Part 7 deals with the question of how we can redirect the mind, if it evolved to work so well in the world. In a sense, it will be easier than we might believe, since the mind contains many different kinds of adaptations awaiting their wake-up call, by experiences in childhood, in learning, in the information surrounding us.

The mind is the way it is because the world is the way it is. The evolved systems organize the mind to mesh with the world. This ancestral arrangement of adaptations can work when the world is stable. And it is this stability that is so changed in the modern world. The world we adapted to is now gone.

In modern urban life, with modern media, education, and information and the movement of people, our ancestral adaptations conflict with the needs of the modern world. And while we are overprepared for some conflicts, such as the sexual, we have no basis for understanding a world of billions of people. How could we ever perceive that our acts of cooling, transportation, and waste disposal could cause a hole in the ozone layer of the planet?

The mechanisms that we use to judge such simple events are the same that we use to judge those that are complex. And we are limited by our mental design, which works better in a world that is stable. Accidents get us excited and move the mind, so that many of our personal and public "policies" are exceedingly sensitive, not to reasoned analysis, but to an overreaction to accidents. An "unforeseen" oil spill in Alaska suddenly focuses the world's attention on what we're doing to the environment. But scientists unanimously warned that this exact kind of spill would happen. How long must we await ever more serious accidents before we act? Until there is a nuclear war?

Our predicament now is not a matter of more information, more critical thinking, becoming more like a logic machine. These are failures of adaptation, not rationality. Our potential to change is great if we look in the right direction, calling up the mind's other adaptations.

The last part proposes that just as humanity has progressed from biological evolution through neural and cultural evolution, we now need to begin a process of conscious evolution. We find unexpected allies in this arena, in modern spirituality and modern science. We need a new kind of ethic, many say; a new kind of religion, others say. This new viewpoint will have to become the province of each person, not just something one learns on Sunday. We are no longer living in tribes with a small horizon; our minds need to encompass a view that has been limited to an elite group: a truly modern reconciliation of the scientific and the spiritual. I believe it can be done, since both spheres, understood best, are about the same animal—us.

We don't want a world of 15 billion people in the next century if 75 percent of them are going to starve. We don't want a world where gangsters have nuclear weapons. We don't want a world where people don't know how their minds work, or know about major new facts of life, their identity, their society, the fate of the earth.

This is an era of reeducation, a time when we will either take our evolution into our own hands or do far worse than we can imagine. There will be no more biological evolution without conscious evolution. It is not a matter of those not knowing history being condemned to repeat the mistakes of our past: Our own history is no longer prologue to our future. Understanding who we are and how we can adapt anew is prologue to our future. And the mind is the focal point of the future.

But now, the past.

II

The Long View:
The Physical
Evolution
of the Mind

The drafting table of God.

2

The Designer
and the Mind

> To study metaphysics as they have been studied appears
> to me to be like puzzling at astronomy without me-
> chanics. . . . Experience shows the problem of the mind
> cannot be solved by attacking the citadel itself—the
> mind is a function of body. . . . We must bring some
> *stable* foundation to argue from.
>
> —CHARLES DARWIN, *The N Notebook*

As a rule, we consider a limited set of candidates to explain why the mind acts as it does: the conflicts between our parents, a love, our inspirational third-grade teacher who engrossed us in oceanic exploration, learning English but not Dutch or Sanskrit. Perhaps it is the way our society encourages men to act in one way and women another. Social sciences and history widen the view to consider how society—our laws, government, attitudes toward sex, life-styles, cooking habits, houses, languages—affects us. Where would we be without mathematics, the Magna Carta, the American Revolution, Gutenberg, Kepler, Copernicus, and all our physics and medicine?

Civilization has certainly informed our lives: We eat produced foods, we wear ready-made clothes, we read accumulated wisdom, or we just go to the movies. We communicate instantly with others all over the world—indeed, our well-developed technology allows us to view Jupiter and the heavens beyond.

Language, family, and culture escort thought to precise tar-gets. While I was giving talks in France on the nature of the mind and brain, one woman, a brain scientist, inquired how I could possibly propose an analysis of the mind in which contempt did not take center stage. Another noted that there is no word for consciousness in French and puzzled why there should be such a word anyway. Neither of these concerns or thoughts are like any I experienced in twenty-five years of lecturing to English-speaking audiences, where discussions of contempt, anyway, are rarely on the list of the central qualities of humanity.

It's difficult for us to understand the Malay *amok*, a recognized social condition in which a person acts crazily for a period and then calms down. We'd offer lithium for it. The notion of worshipping a sacred cow in India seems the ultimate irrationality, yet anthropologist Marvin Harris, in his excellent *Cows, Wars, and Witches*, explains its place in the Indian ecosystem. The peasants don't eat the cow, and "irrationally" lose the value of the meat, but eating the cow would deprive the poor of fuel from the dung and power for plowing, which have more value than the meat does.

The French, not to focus too sharply on their penchants, have constant *crise de foie*—"liver crises"—that threaten lives. Although alcoholism is endemic, the liver to the French is clearly different than it is to us. Similarly, the Chinese acupuncture meridians are not what Westerners consider communication channels in the body.

While culture, family, and education are important, I want to step back and consider a different time frame, one that is not short term, not even historical: a panorama on mind that is almost geological. From that perspective, matters appear differently, as a slow-motion film of the seasons changes the way we see growth and transformation. The brain and mind grew along with the rest of the body in geological time, over millions of years.

The information base on human evolution, biology, brain, consciousness, and cognition should, taken together, reset our view of our real history. Modern human beings, even highly advanced women and men who sell short their stocks, who go to the theater, who commute to offices, who design and work on computers, were complete biologically before the modern world was ever imagined. Our brains reached their current state millennia ahead of the agricultural revolution eleven or so thousand years ago.

Our body and nervous system are formatted on a basis far far older than that. Daily, we all put into service nervous-system

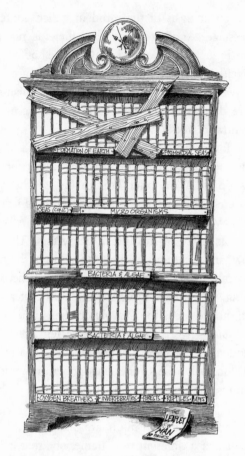

2-2

If we had a bookshelf
containing the history
of earth, human
history would fill
but a tiny leaflet.

routines that began with the first animals, and these recruited
neural arrangements that evolved long before there were vertebrates.

Most of our history is not recorded in bound tomes in librar-
ies, nor in illustrated books on the sequence of Mediterranean
dynasties or the development of perspective in Western painting.
It is our own perspective that needs development: *All* recorded
history is less than one millionth of earth's history.

Perhaps this is far too extreme a view at one slice, and it is
true that for a billion of those years, the pace of change was so
slow that little came to pass that affected our structure. Given that,
let us advance to the last tenth of 1 percent of life on earth. Even if
we restrict ourselves to this most recent 5 million years, our
normal viewpoint would still expand greatly.

Before this era, cows, goats, and deer did not exist, merely a
common ancestor. And as for humanity, all the history that we've
painstakingly recorded and about which we educate ourselves, the

archives of the accomplishments of civilized (and uncivilized!) humanity since Egypt, includes less than two-ten-thousands of the time since our first human ancestors appeared.

During that 99.98 percent of the time of the modern era, the human brain reached its current state of evolution—long before the cave paintings, long before our ancestors domesticated animals or planted crops, long before the pyramids. Those nomads were us, those cave painters were us. Their brain was our brain; our cortex, enormous, was as massive in our remote ancestors. Their visual sensibility, the delicacy of skilled movements in painting, was the same as ours. And their mind, too, was the same as ours.

Our real history is "written," in our blood, in our bones, and in our nerve circuits. And it was written before there were writers.

The mind's beginnings are found in the dazzling variety of adaptations (the adjustments an animal makes to flourish in its world) of countless living beings, striving to survive on earth. At earlier times it was customary to analyze the mind without knowing its history, but doing so was well described by Darwin as missing the underlying mechanism. Now we need to consider the long view of the mind. Doing so will direct us to different events than the usual personal history, life traumas, or culture, in considering the mind.

A few of the most important modern discoverers have overturned our conventional views of the world, even though a given view may be compelling. It is a daily observation of billions that the sun revolves around the earth. But it does not.

It is similarly obvious that biological systems in plants and complex animals must have been brought about by some variety of Supreme Being. The gastrointestinal system extracts those nutrients the body requires from coarse foodstuffs; the eye extracts a few wavelengths of the radiant electromagnetic spectrum and transforms them into sight; the intricate mechanics of locomotion combine to purposive movement; the delicate bones in the middle ear serve to amplify the tiny vibrations in the air so to be read by specialized cells in the cortex as sound. There are so many parts, so carefully and brilliantly articulated!

The archdeacon William Paley, a British theologian, in his *Natural Theology; or, Evidences of the Existence and Attributes of the Deity collected from the Appearances of Nature* (1802), gave the most effectual argument for the existence of a Supreme Being who knew what he was doing.

> In a crossing a heath suppose I pitched my foot against a *stone* and were asked how the stone came to be there; I might possibly answer that for anything I knew to the contrary it had lain there for ever: nor would it perhaps be very easy to show the absurdity of this answer. But suppose I had found a *watch* upon the ground and it should be imagined how the *watch* came to be in that place. I should hardly think of the answer which I had before given, that for anything I knew the watch might have always been there.

After Archdeacon Paley notes the difference between natural objects and watches, he goes on: If we had come upon the watch, even if we didn't know anything about it, we would think that "the watch must have had a maker: that they must have existed at some time, and at some place or other, an artificer or artificers, who formed it for the purpose which we find it actually to answer, who comprehends this construction and designed its use." Watches did not happen by accident—in an old-fashioned watch, the gears mesh to move the hands, which glide over numerals. Looking at the numerals alone tells nothing, but looking at how the mechanism works makes sense if you comprehend its purpose.

Dissect an animal, Paley points out, and one would bring to light signs of watchlike, not stonelike faculties. Of the eye he says, "There is precisely the same proof that the eye was made for vision as there is that the telescope was made for assisting it." And the human organism is far more complicated than any telescope. "Design must have a designer. That designer must have been a person. That person is God," Paley wrote in 1802.

This "designer being" model is the one most of us use to understand our everyday world—all actions have a purpose. It is the one most biologists, until Darwin, used to understand the natural world. We still believe there is a design, in someOne's mind, for mind.

To Paley, our creator made us a fixed machine, like a watch. In the present view, it is a creative machine, one with a little randomness programmed in, like a computer made by somebody in one of the techno-nirvanas in Silicon Valley—designed as parallel processor, designed as a neural net that can learn, designed as a connection machine.

Suppose, following Paley, we had come upon, not a stone, not a watch, but a computer on the ground. Would we believe it had arrived there by chance? Nah. The modern argument from design is the idea that the mind is like a computer. Hominid, homonoid, Hominerd.

Surely the mind can be thought to be similar to a computer: it operates in binary, it processes information, has input and output, serial and parallel ports, random and fixed connections. We compute distance, the likely shape of an object, the similarity of the red of the tomato in bright light with that in a salad in a candle-light dinner, though that salad red may be blacker than a black book at noon. But to say that the mind computes isn't to say that the mind *is* only a computer. A car is for travel. A car has several computers (up to thirty-six separate ones for analyzing transmission shift points in different programs, fuel-air mixtures to be optimized for reduced fuel consumption, maintenance monitors). Yet a car is not a computer. Where one is likely to drive on a Saturday night isn't self-evident from the fuel-air mixtures, nor is it understandable from the maintenance schedule.

Indeed, on prescientific observation, like the earth's position vis-à-vis the sun, the argument from design seems convincing, even obvious. Anything as intricate as the eye is more complex than Paley imagined: it contains hundreds of millions of receptors and far more complex interconnections. The network of nerve connections leaving the retina is so intricate as still to defy a complete analysis, even with thousands of electrophysiology studies. The optic tract, the nerve exiting the eye, is brilliantly crafted, brilliantly designed, it would seem, to do its job as it traverses a well-calculated route to the brain, with passage through distinct nuclei in the cerebrum where the world's elements, such as color and form, are processed.

This complexity and dedication of purpose—should—surely lend credence to the idea that life is designed for a purpose by someone, or some entity, who knew what she was doing. Even if one concedes that some animals act reflexively, surely the marvelous capacities of human nature prove design by a creator with a purpose.* It is difficult to accept the idea that this most intricate instrument could arise by blind chance, random adaptation, and accident.

*By the way, if you think this is creationism, no such luck; that is an altogether different fishy kettle, one far less sophisticated in argument, even two centuries after Paley.

3

How Evolution Works: The Discovery of the Process and the Beginning of the Modern Era

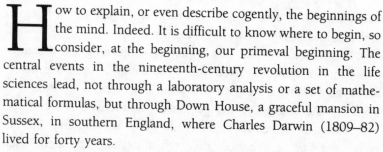

How to explain, or even describe cogently, the beginnings of the mind. Indeed. It is difficult to know where to begin, so consider, at the beginning, our primeval beginning. The central events in the nineteenth-century revolution in the life sciences lead, not through a laboratory analysis or a set of mathematical formulas, but through Down House, a graceful mansion in Sussex, in southern England, where Charles Darwin (1809–82) lived for forty years.

Darwin was chronically ill, too ill to undergo the strains of London, let alone scientific combat, so he lived in seclusion for the most productive decades of his life, observing and thinking. Perhaps it was just this seclusion that enabled him to see the obvious. Perhaps it was the time at which he entered natural science and the base of knowledge available at the time. Perhaps it was his own genius.

Before Darwin, many, if not most, biologists would answer the question "Why do creatures act in a purposive way?" with something like, "God created all species of living creatures perfectly formed, and these species have not changed since creation." Living beings were regarded as separately created for specific, fixed niches. Humans, then, had always existed and had no ancestors but humans; gorillas similarly developed only from other gorillas; sloths were created as sloths. Nothing ever changed in this static world populated by a multitude of living beings. The fossil record was held, not to show progression, but to separate remains of enduring species.

However, in the eighteenth and nineteenth centuries, archaeologists began to dig up fossil remains of creatures that looked like us but no longer lived. One had a head somewhat between a human and an ape; another a leg bone that indicated walking, as do modern human beings, yet a skull similar to that of a chimp. How did scientists explain these fossils?

The great majority of biologists then embraced *catastrophism*. Instead of conceiving that species evolved one from the other and that fossils were the remains of extinct creatures, biologists imagined that God had created the world a number of separate and distinct times. The fossil record is therefore a history of these distinct creations. (This version, bastardized, is the soul of modern creationism.) However, it's a little difficult to believe that God changed her mind so much. If she were so smart, why go through a long process of development and mistakes? It just didn't fit either with the idea of God or with the fossil record.

We now know that this argument concerning the design of organisms is spurious. Even the most complex organs evolved, albeit they changed very slowly over long periods of time. We need a radically different perspective to comprehend this concept. The answer to the central riddle of life, about how different species come in to being and how they might decline, appeared when Darwin published his watershed book, *On the Origin of Species*, in 1859. *Origin* contained his theory of how adaptation occurs, a theory he had developed over more than thirty years.

Although there were many exceptions, in the mid-nineteenth century, most scientists began to recognize that all existing life previously had other forms. They accepted the premise stated by Rumi: Evolution happened, and we developed from earlier forms of life.

But one reason for the lack of acceptance was that no mechanism had been identified that could explain how evolution could operate. How could organisms change shape and grow new organs? Jean-Baptiste Lamarck's theory of inheritance of acquired characteristics was the most plausible. It assumed that animals that underwent changes passed their changes on to their offspring: The giraffe ancestors stretched their necks to get food, and such a stretch would stretch as well to the innate biology of the progeny. Muscles that were built up due to strain, similarly, would pass on to the children. This is the kind of story parents tell their children about why things happen the way they do: The giraffe stretched and stretched his neck until. . . . And it might have been true.

However, no one succeeded in producing a whelp with stronger muscles, no matter what its parent did; nothing done to an animal during its life would affect the nature of the brood. (Some extreme events can affect the progeny, accidents that influence genetic material, such as swallowing poisons, and in the modern world, the exposure to unprecedented hazards such as radiation. Nonetheless, the birth defects so inherited aren't acquired characteristics passed down.) Inheritance of acquired characteristics is one of those perfect and brilliant ideas that anyone can understand. More than that, one can fall completely in love with it. I believed it for years when I was young, and it is the only scientific idea that made me cry when I found out it couldn't be true.

But if you think about it in our ordinary way, the problem is perplexing: How could human beings have ever developed, or "descended;" from apes? How could apes have ancestors in rodents, let alone reptiles? Could the eye just have happened? Could the wing? Could the mind? It seems impossible, even to many people today. There must be a design, there must be a designer, there must be a specific creator. We're too magnificent for it all to be an accident.

How living beings evolved remained a mystery until Darwin made his revolutionary observations which, together with the modern understanding of genetics, underlie the modern theory of evolution and modern life sciences. *Origin* established two important principles: evolution was taking place on earth, and it was driven by natural selection.

The proposition Darwin made is wonderfully uncomplicated, especially considering the complexity and profundity of the natural world. Imagine coming up with it. I must say I am still boggled that he was able to do it.

He understood that the mechanism for growth and change was not to be found within God's directed design, nor in anyone's design, but involved countless organisms adapting to the specific locale in which they lived over immense time. Key to this idea is the huge time scale over which adaptations occur.

The fundamental insight, around which the modern era in life science and human psychology pivoted, is that the procedure of adapting lay inside normal reproductive life. Let's follow his logic: For an animal population to thrive, each generation must replace itself through sexual reproduction. He wrote in one of his notebooks: "The mind of a man is no more perfect than instincts of animals . . . our descent then is the origin of our evil passions!! —the devil under form of baboon is our grandfather!—" (*The M Notebook,* p. 123).

While Darwin was finishing these notebooks, he happened to read Thomas Malthus's *Essay on the Principle of Population* and began to develop his theory of natural selection. He writes in his autobiography: "In October 1838, that is, fifteen months after I had begun my systematic enquiry, I happened to read for amusement Malthus on *Population,* and being well-prepared to appreciate the struggle for existence which everywhere goes on from long-continuing observation of the habits of animals and plants, it at once struck me that under these circumstances favourable variations would tend to be preserved and unfavourable ones destroyed. Here, at last, I had got a theory by which to work." Malthus showed that populations increase geometrically but are always held in check by "hostile factors of nature," such as famine, wars, disease, and other difficulties. This gave Darwin the first major insight: in a natural state where food and other resources are limited, the struggle for existence must be intense. We then need to focus on the special characteristics of who survives—a theory by which to work.

Almost any organism generates far more successors than are needed to replace itself. One salmon lays thousands of eggs; a cat can give birth to several litters of six to seven in her lifetime; a woman can have ten or more children. But animal populations usually remain at a fairly constant size from one generation to the next. There must be a means for selecting who survives and who does not. Mark well the concept of selection here, and note Darwin's second important concept: Individuals differ in height, weight, digestion, hair and eye color, physical and mental prowess. At times it seems that everyone we know and even every animal we know is unique—I don't know that much about goldfish, but have you ever met two cats with the same personality?

This uniqueness is the force of both evolution and diversity. For if everyone were the same, evolution would stop. Somebody has to make it, and someone has to lose. Somebody reproduces offspring that are the most "fit" for success, and the individuals who survive must be more "fit," better able to adapt to their environment. "Fitness" in these particular biological terms isn't physical prowess or strength or sleek muscles but *a match between the traits of a population and its environment.*

How does it happen? Sexual reproduction and the occasional mutation yield offspring that are combinations of two different individuals, not exact copies. Differences that permit the offspring to adapt better, to reproduce, would be likely to be passed on to the next generation, and that generation would change, or evolve. For Darwin, populations are collections of unique individuals, but in the biological world, there is no typical animal or typical plant. Ears of corn, as you will notice, differ from each other, ears of individuals differ in size similarly; tomatoes vary in size, and redheads do as well.

Darwin considered how animal breeders select characteristics. Poodles could be miniaturized because with each litter a breeder can select the smallest female and male to mate and then select the smallest offspring of succeeding matings. Repeat this process, and each succeeding generation, on average, will be smaller than the previous one by this artificial selection. And many characteristics can be selected: the collie's long nose, the color of the Irish setter's coat, the amount of wildness in wolf hybrid dogs. Over the past two decades, breeders have selected Burmese cats' faces to peak out to a point and then recede to a bulldog countenance.

Here is where Darwin proposed the mechanism that could rework living beings over time. The real survival advantage is not something that happens in an individual's life but exists in succeeding generations. The process works in this way: Certain individuals are born with characteristics that enable them to better adapt to their circumstances, and thus they survive longer, to reproduce more successfully. They therefore pass on these characteristics to their progeny. The greater the fitness, the more surviving offspring.

Through natural selection species become more "fitted" to

their circumstances. Predators remove those creatures that are slower, less alert, or less sociable (thus less likely to cling to the pack, becoming more vulnerable), and over time the quarry evolve. So organisms change, adapt, and get selected by their world. Selection is impersonal, slow, and natural.

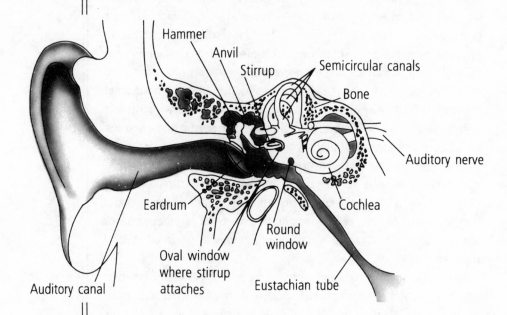

Apply this theory of small changes selected to fit the environment to the miracles of physiology—to the mammalian eye, to the delicate bones hidden within the inner ear that convey the sounds from the air, to the wing, to the mind. How could the eye, with hundreds of millions of neurons, come about? When would it have started? And how would an intermediate eye ever develop? Where would it start? One percent eye doesn't seem likely. How could the wing have come about? The middle ear? The mind?

But these structures were not specially created by a divine watchmaker, following a grand design. They developed over billions of years of adaptation: not to be perfect, but to flourish under particular conditions. Let's think about the wing.* Don't do this experiment yourself at home, but think about it: Cut off 90 percent of each of the wings of a bird. You would thus destroy 100

---

*Here I am indebted to Richard Dawkins's analysis as well as for the lines of the discussion of Paley.

percent of its ability to fly: A tenth-wing can do little, and even 25 percent of a wing would do nothing, it seems. Even one (Zen-type) wing flapping doesn't help much, so we'd have little to go on if we assumed that a single wing could arise, join with another one, and produce flight. But the small dinosaurlike ancestors of the bird didn't go from walking to flying in one soaring leap. If that had happened, we'd have to change our ideas, either of genetics or of evolution.

Could the wing have come to pass all at once? Just popped up atop a small dinosaur, who thence could swoop around and eat everything in sight? No. But could it have happened gradually? Very gradually? If so, from what did it develop? Many animals brachiate, that is, leap back and forth from bough to bough in the trees. Sometimes, especially in small animals, the whole body catches the air and assists the leap. If an animal were to develop slight appendages on the limbs, those extra surfaces would act like an airfoil or sail. So any animal that increases its surface area to weight might leap longer. In time, the growth of larger and larger appendages, "flaps" or ailerons, might well have helped certain animals in certain circumstances. And these first bumps and sails could then project farther for longer leaps. And we have the beginnings of the wing. It simply doesn't all have to happen on a modern schedule.

2-4

The first wing
attempt?

Darwin proposed we consider how organisms come into being in evolutionary, not personal or historical, time. When you look at a slow-motion film of a plant growing, you can see radical changes in its form, invisible to you in any normal time frame. We don't perceive the shoots, the buds, and the flowers, the fruit, the shedding, and the dormancy all as a cycle but as static situations, just as early biologists saw species as static.

We can't perceive the growth cycle of ancient trees such as the giant sequoias in the Sierra Nevada, trees that live a thousand years. And geologic time is still more, well, geological, comprising events over hundreds of millions of years. During this time the original continent, Pangea, divided into the land masses of earth that we know today. Since a life span of a human being has no need for such a perspective, we can't even conceive of this kind of time frame, but it is close to the slow-motion geologic time in which humanity developed. Physical evolution has had thousands of millions of years to "work"—thousands upon thousands, sometimes millions of generations. And we moderns are fewer than one hundred generations away from the time of Christ.

Working in such boundless time, all evolution needs is a tiny and consistent advantage at any point for things to add up. If a small increase in the airfoil helps an animal leap slightly farther and survive without falling, perhaps attain a bit more food, escape a few more predators, and reproduce better, then later increases might help more. These physical adaptations then add up exponentially, since they build upon each other.

In millions of years, and with a generation time of five years, there is an immense time for adaptations to tally up in prehumans. And, in living beings who reproduce quickly (in animals, generation times are only three or four years, and in bacteria, almost no time), major changes can occur in only a few thousand years. *E. coli,* the bacterium of choice for research, has a generation cycle of hours.

Granted so much time, and selection for advantages, all the biological miracles have had *plenty* of time and *plenty* of chance to have happened. After all, a common ancestor spawned both the chimpanzee and us in a few million years, and farther back, we and bacteria have common roots. The offshoots of bacteria that led to us thus had billions upon billions of generations in which to evolve, since for the great majority of life on earth and the great majority of organisms, generation time was very short.

Given enough time, can major changes really happen this simply? Let's assemble a simplified case of how changes can add up in evolutionary time. Consider a trait, something simple and linear such as enhanced height, a characteristic that may have made it possible to see over the horizon, among many possible advantages.

Assume the advantage is slight. Consider one group of prehumans that grows slowly, 1.0001 times faster than another group that doesn't grow at all. Two no-growth one-footers mating produce 1-foot-tall offspring, and two slow-growth one-footers would produce, on average, offspring who are 1 foot and 1/10,000 inch tall.

Assume for this oversimplified example that the slow-growers each mate, as do the no-growers, and that each generation accumulates change. That is to say, the first offspring of the slow-growers would be 1.0001 feet tall and the next would be 1.0001 times 1.0001 feet tall, or 1.00020001 feet tall, not 1.0002 feet (each generation's height multiplies the gain of the previous generation).

These two weird-looking ancestors begin at almost the same size. But after 1 million years, there is quite a difference—the one on the right will be 484 million times taller!

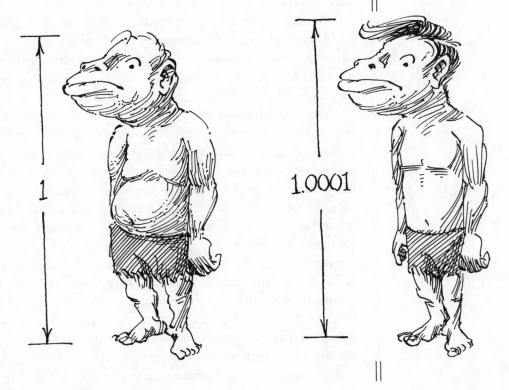

1

1.0001

Now let's get exponential: In a brief period of evolutionary time, say 1 million years, only 1/5,000 of earth's history, and with a fairly typical prehuman generation every five years (giving us 200,000 generations in which to develop) notice the difference in height of the average no-grower slow-grower.

In only 1 million years, the slow-growers would be 484 million times as tall as the others.

This exponential growth, infinitesimal over one generation or one hundred, adds up. If we took time-lapse photographs of the two groups, we would see slow growth over time, more than enough to produce a surging wing, especially with generation times of much less than five years. In 125,000 years, the difference is twelve times; in 250,000, about 148 times; and in 500,000 years, the difference is about 22,000 times.

Slender differences in reproductive success, if consistent, can create enormous changes in a group of animals through exponential growth. If the change had accumulated linearly, adding only .0001 foot to each generation, the slow-growers would be twenty-one times as tall—a great increase to be sure, but hardly close to the exponential increase.

Consider again the eye. Clearly the modern eye as we know it could not have sprung up completely new from the earth. And of what use would a part of an eye be? But possibly there were primitive mechanisms that would have helped living beings in their own right, having, as they say, potential.

One way to answer this question requires us to repair below ground in the Near East. Subterranean moles in that part of the world, christened *Spalax ehrenbergi,* are blind, due to their dark cave life. *Spalax's* eyes are rudimentary, deeply concealed under hair and heavy layers of skin. No neurological reaction measures on electrode implants in the brain when these animals are exposed to intense light stimuli. *Spalax* is as blind as a mole. Of what use are her eyes? If she doesn't see with them, is there another use for the apparatus of the eye, usage that could give us clues to an earlier adaptation? Consider that seeing the world as we do isn't completely necessary as a beginning point, because any kind of sensing what is going on in the world is adaptive. Knowing something about the cycle of the seasons is important in determining when to seek food, when to store it, when to remain underground permanently. Differentiating day from night would certainly be a great advantage. An organism that could sense this could avoid predators and forage better. It would not take much nerve tissue to communicate this information

Spalax's retina helps her recognize seasons by detecting changes in periods of light rather than changes in temperature. In vertebrates the pineal gland buried deep inside the brain secretes melatonin in reaction to shifts in amount of light (which of course signals the seasons), the pineal receiving its stimulus from the retina. So this "eye" seems to enable the mole to sense light changes and thus make seasonal adaptations. Might save a life, or adapt an animal, this 1 percent eye.

The advantage is not just moles', either. Blind people who still have light-dark vision can avoid dangers, they can find their way through a door, they can avoid hitting walls or objects. People with better eyesight who are still legally blind can nevertheless negotiate through the world, with vision that can't be more than 30 percent of normal. It's reasonable, then, at an early stage of evolution, to assume that an animal that had only simple light-dark sensing would have had an advantage.

Light-dark sensing could progress, as well: Instead of just light and dark, gradations of tone could be perceived, such that an increase in darkness might mean a predator approaching, for instance. A frog's eye can perceive such changes.

With enormous time, more and more features can accumulate, if each has an advantage. The ability to see colors, a radical expansion of vision in monkeys, apes, and humans, offers extra information, which helps adaptation. We and our predecessors can, for example, find food more efficiently: Ripe red fruit looks similar to the dark green foliage on a bush if seen in black-and-white but is vivid in color.

And, during these long periods, some of our most important traits were "recruited" from structures developed for another use. As in a real army, it doesn't matter much if the raw recruits are unsuitable; given enough training, they are pushed into shape. Birds and bats recruited the bones of their front limbs to make the wing. Many of the functions of these limbs on the ground—digging, fighting—were taken over by the beak. The "thumb" of the panda is really a wrist bone, conscripted to strip leaves from bamboo.*

*For the discussion of the *Spalax* eye, as well as this thumb and the following ear example, I am indebted to the work of Stephen Jay Gould.

This process happens in daily life as well. You may have a computer at work to do spreadsheets, but it might run games quite well. You may play something on it, get hooked, and find yourself using the computer mostly for games. You might even develop a new game and get recruited into a career as a computer-game designer.

This is what happened with our beautiful middle-ear bones. It is quite easy to think that the ingenious design and impressive functioning of our ears were God's goals and that they represent the most desirable instrument of hearing possible. The ear is, after all, a marvelous physical system of great complexity. It includes a wide-range sound wave analyzer, an amplification system, a two-way communication system, a relay unit, a multichannel transducer that converts mechanical energy into electrical energy, and a hydraulic balance system. All this is compressed into 2 cubic centimeters.

Rolls of pressure roll sound waves down the auditory canal to the eardrum, causing it to vibrate. The vibration of the eardrum causes the three bones of the middle ear (ossicles) to vibrate. These bones, named for their shapes, are the hammer (malleus), the anvil (incus), and the stirrup (stapes). Their vibrations match the original signal in frequency but are of greater amplitude (twenty-five times greater). The pressure of that amplification forces the waves into the inner ear, where they are transduced into electrical energy in the nerve cells. And in the brain we hear Mozart, the sound of waterfalls, poetry, and the complaints of our neighbors.

But we would not have the magnificent ears we do if our reptilian ancestors had not responded to sound waves with their jaws. Fish "hear" by sensing sound waves through the motion of water along their sides. When land creatures began to evolve, the waves received as sound had thence to be received through air, a medium much less dense than water, which can thus convey less pressure.

This change in medium required a new method of hearing: Fish do not need to amplify sound waves as we do. Land vertebrates channel only faint sound waves to the eardrum, sound that is then sent to the inner ear (and on to the brain) via the angelic bones of the middle ear—the malleus, incus, and stapes.

How did this come to pass? it's a long story (and I am sure you know that I mean it by now!), but gill openings behind the mouths of early jawless vertebrates (agnathans) evolved bone supports, or gill arches, two bones hinged together. Jaws need mooring, so the upper bone of the gill arch directly behind the jaw took on the role of buttress (becoming the hyomandibular), attaching the jaws to the braincase for support. Thus "recruited," the bone then evolved to be thicker and sturdier.

But because of the hyomandibular's closeness to the inner ear, it would be recruited again: It lay against a tube leading to the ear, and as bone is capable of conducting sound, it began to amplify sound waves. "Recruited" for hearing, it is called the stapes.

When it supported the jaw, its billet for 100 million years, the stapes was thick and robust. Eventually the cranium and jaw joined permanently in vertebrates, and the stapes shifted its job, as an army recruit may have to, because of changed circumstances, and adapted to hearing. It became a finer, slimmer bone.

The mind too has had its recruits. Structures that evolved for one purpose later changed their function. The cerebellum of the brain began hundreds of millions of years ago as a movement controller in organisms such as crocodiles. In human beings the function changed, the structure was recruited for another use: Memory for simple responses, such as the sequence of pedaling a bicycle, was stored in the same structure. As the cerebellum was recruited for new functions, new structures were added as well. The pons (bridge) developed below the midbrain to relay information from the higher brain structures to the cerebellum.

We've become evolutionary sight-seers. I wanted to go on this excursion to make clear how life's amazing complexity could happen, and how the evolutionary view—that all living beings are the way they are because of their need to adapt—helps us consider the mesh between human beings and the world in which we live, the world of our family, and the world into which we are born.

Based, as Darwin foretold, on the body, the mind has its complexities, continuities, and has enjoyed some surprising "recruits." But first we trace our real history.

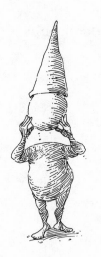

4

Body Building
and Mind Building:
A Very Brief Interlude
in the Long
Human History

The date I've chosen to mark the beginning of human history is about 5 or so million years ago, when the forests of East Africa thinned, and many tree dwellers had to find new homes. Those that had no trouble holding onto their tree homes evolved into chimpanzees. Of those who were forced or attracted out, some did not adapt and became extinct. Others learned to live out of the trees, took up residence in the surrounding grasslands, prospered and survived, and evolved into prehuman beings.

These first beings alloy human and ape characteristics. Tiny *Australopithecus*, who appeared between 3 and 4 million years ago, measured in with a cranial capacity of 450 cubic centimeters. They began to walk upright and probably used their upright position to establish a kind of cooperative life, a sharing of child rearing and food until then unknown.

This was certainly true of "Handy human," *Homo habilis*, who descended from the australopithecines and prospered between 2.3 and 1.3 million years ago. These handy persons were at the boundary of the early humans: They had a progressively upright stance, increased use of tools, greater growth of the brain, and they seemed to live more cooperatively. This set of adaptations, food and tool sharing, communal life, seems to be the theme of early homonid development.

Although their tools were rudimentary, they were a boon to greater efficiency and would have aided in the construction of primitive shelters and settlements. Perhaps more important, *Homo habilis* hunted in groups. Feeding a group on fruits and berries is difficult; most of the day must be spent foraging for food. But a group of hunters can bring home enough meat for several families for days. Food sharing allowed *Homo habilis* to begin to establish a stable home base and a more permanent cooperative society.

Consider the skills hunting requires: speed and accuracy are obvious, but the ability to plan, communicate, and cooperate are even more important. These abilities foretell superior intelligence: to think and reason, speak a language, and create a culture.

And during this time, the brain exploded. The biologist J. B. S. Haldane has noted that the extraordinary increase in the human brain size was the fastest evolutionary transformation known. The transformation from *Australopithecus* to *Homo habilis*, like that from *H. habilis* to *Homo sapiens*, probably happened over a period of about 1 million to 1.25 million years, or about 75,000 to 125,000 generations.

2-6a and b

The heads of *Australopithecus* and modern man.

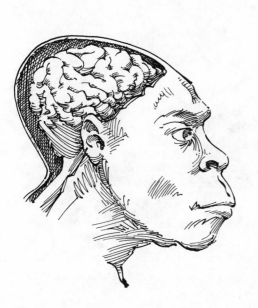
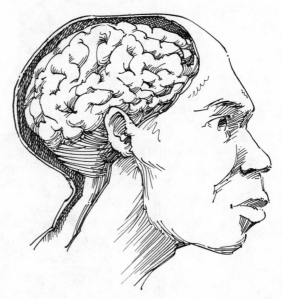

This next version of early man, who walked the earth, made great strides as well in social complexity. *Homo erectus* ("upright human") measured over 5 feet tall and from the neck down the skeleton was similar to modern humans, although the head was more apelike.

H. erectus was the first of our ancestors to migrate outside of Africa, and fossils have been found as far north as Germany, as well as in the Far East. They cooked in pots, handled fairly advanced tools, and worked animal skins—all bespeaking a higher culture. They lived in an ice age and could construct shelters. They invented clothing, used fire, and helped prepare for the characteristic human life: living in groups, being able to survive in new worlds, and adapting those worlds to them. Fire probably extended the day, giving more time for work; and since fire is attractive, it is possible that groups of *H. erectus*, huddled around a fire, were the first to use their larger brains to introduce language.

2-7

The growth of the brain.

Life challenges alone were probably not enough to inspire the astonishing rapidity of brain growth. There must have been another reason. There was great growth in the brain: that of *Homo habilis* ranged from 600 to 750 cubic centimeters; whereas *H. erectus*'s cranial capacity ballooned to between 775 and 1,225 cubic centimeters (the modern range is 1,000 to 1,400 or so). This development occurred well before organized society or language, and long before technology. It is an amazing spurt in growth in the most complicated structure in all biology.

The shape of *H. erectus*'s head was also higher-domed than *H. habilis*'s whose forehead receded rather like an ape's. This is not to say that *H. erectus* in contemporary dress would blend in all that well with a subway crowd, but have you ever been there on a dark night?

H. erectus prospered for more than a million years and about 300,000 to 500,000 years ago began evolving into early *Homo sapiens*. As in all this evolutionary classification, the boundary is imperceptible. Early *H. sapiens* was widespread and variable (as are we now)—some of the varieties were quite different from us, and some *were* us.

H. erectus apparently disappeared when the earliest *Homo sapiens* appeared in Europe, the first of which was the Neanderthal (*Homo sapiens neanderthalensis*), who had a range beyond Europe similar to *Homo erectus*. Although Neanderthals have been classified in the past as members of a side-branch off the evolutionary line to humans, they likely merged with other subspecies of *H. sapiens*. They had an organized society, even ceremonies; one we know of is a ritual burial in an elaborate grave 60,000 years ago. It was found by archaelogists in a cave near what is now Shanidar, in modern Iraq.

This and other evidence of ritual would seem to indicate early expressions of a spiritual life. Neanderthal cranial was as much as 1,500 cubic centimeters, larger than today's average. Culturally, they were far advanced and lived in genuine societies. Having appeared during the Ice Age, Neanderthals adapted to the cold and constructed better clothing, shelters, and more complex tools. As their level of social organization advanced, not surprisingly, archaeology has found that violence and warfare became a distinct element in their lives, just as in ours.

Neanderthals weren't the clumsy and grotesque "lowbrows"

their forehead has made them out to be. This misconception arose because one of the first specimens found was an elderly male with skull thickening from severe arthritis. In truth, there is little or no brain difference between them and modern human beings.

In 1868 railway workers were cutting through a hillside in the south of France when they came upon four human skeletons. The skeletons looked modern, but what was next to them did not: stone tools, seashells, and animal teeth with holes drilled in them, apparently for stringing as an ornament. These skeletons are the earliest remains (from about 50,000 years ago) of *Homo sapiens sapiens* ("intelligent human being").

These people were called Cro-Magnon, after the site of their discovery. There are strategic differences in the skulls of a Cro-Magnon and a Neanderthal. Between their eras the entire shape of the face altered, and the physiological apparatus for producing a great range of sounds expanded. The brain size did not change much, but the brain *elevated* in the skull. The palate enlarged, which allowed greater precision in speech.

With the outburst of language, the pace of evolution stepped up. Everything Neanderthals did, Cro-Magnon did better. Physiological changes, such as the enlarged palate, gave Cro-Magnon greater language ability, enabling them to plan, organize, and

2-8

The brain, through history.

38

cooperate more efficiently. The tools Cro-Magnons used were more elaborate than those of Neanderthal. Shelters and settlements were also more complex.

Art and language are both critical milestones in human evolution because they signify a mind capable of abstraction, symbolism, and invention. Making art is an abstraction of a world not present and often a representation of a worldview or or a spiritual system. The paintings found on the caves of Lascaux show Cro-Magnon's burgeoning mind.

This also provided an impetus to the rate of evolution, both biological and cultural—essentially the modern human—at least 15,000 years ago. There may well have been essentially modern human beings before that, but we have little or no record.

Our recent biological history is important because the same life processes that produced the wing and the eye, the fish and the squirrel, produced the cortex in the fish and, eventually, produced the human mind. Understanding that we are the product of these simple processes working over eons will make some of the mind's moves clear. For the mind, like all else on earth, evolved, and evolved to adapt to the world. We turn next to some of the major puzzles of our nature.

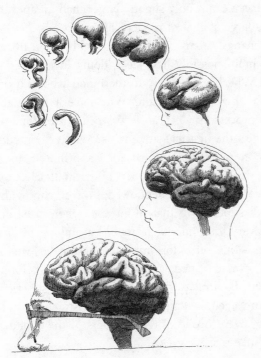

2-9

The brain, through life.

5

The Mind Caesura

"The gap (between us and our nearest living relatives, the ape . . .) is largest, and most difficult to comprehend, in terms of mind.

—RICHARD GOWLETT

The naturalist Alfred Russell Wallace, a contemporary of Darwin who concurrently developed a similar theory of natural selection, believed that the human intellect did not evolve. And, in his defense, there are some striking anomalies. A major mystery in human evolution concerns why there is such a gigantic jump between the brains of *H. habilis* and *H. erectus*. The earlier homonid has a brain only slightly larger than an ape; the later one a cortex as large as that of modern humanity.

The change seems to be almost without justification. What could the brain possibly have been doing in *H. erectus* to require such size? Why be able to fly to the moon when no one has even understood how to make iron? Why have a brain able to work with microprocessors when all it was being used for was the crude hammering of the first few stone tools? Wallace contended that the human brain was overdesigned for its primitive uses and thus could not have been a product of natural selection: "Natural selection could only have endowed savage man with a brain a few degrees superior to that of an ape, whereas he actually possesses one very little inferior to that of a philosopher." If the brain of "savages"—his term for human ancestors as well as modern primitives—was outfitted with higher capacities before they could be exploited, he argued, there must then be a superior force who had a future agenda. Rationality and Aristotelian thought are so compelling, even to one of the founders of the evolutionary view, as to challenge that view.

However, looking either to God or to social forces that gradually developed the brain do not lead to satisfactory conclusions. Let's look the other way. Suppose we regard the mind as just one more shred of the evolving earth, just a bundle of special adaptations and recruits. It isn't completely flattering, I admit, nor is it obvious upon ordinary introspection.

This ego bashing has happened before: It was difficult for most Westerners of the sixteenth century to believe that the sun didn't revolve around the earth. The conception that humanity was the center of the universe first was attacked in 1543. Then the Polish astronomer Nicolaus Copernicus demonstrated that the planets did *not* revolve around the earth, that earth was one of many that revolved around the sun. The Catholic church considered this theory heretical for many years, until the evidence supporting the theory was undeniable and it had to be accepted. Still, Copernicus's discovery did not upset the belief that human beings were unique creatures, especially created to rule earth.

Then came Darwin, whose theory placed human beings under the same rules of life that applied to all creatures. All organisms, he said, have a common ancestor, and adding insult to injury, human beings are directly descended from apes. The Victorian world was appalled. There is a vast distinction between thinking of yourself as created in God's own image and descended from the apes. The famous proper Victorian lady said, on learning of Darwin's theory, "I pray that is not true, but if it is true, I pray that it does not become widely known."

Darwin was the subject of ridicule, lampooned in cartoons and attacked in sermons, debates, and editorials. Smirked the *London Review*: "Look at the educated Englishman and the Australian aboriginal; the one gaining more and more mastery over the laws of this world, the other as almost as helpless a victim of those laws as the brutes around him. Never in nature's kingdom do we see this immense gulf between individuals of the same species, we see it in man alone, because he alone in creation was free to rise or fall."

Darwin's theory has remained controversial to this day. In 1925 an American biology teacher, John Scopes, was fired for teaching the principles of evolution in a Tennessee school, in violation of a state law. The controversy ended in the infamous Scopes monkey trial. Today in the United States, many funda-

We were at the center of the world in pre-Darwinian times.

mentalist Christian groups protest the teaching of the theory of evolution in public schools, at least in the absence of any teaching of creationism, the concept that God created the world, as written in the Bible.

And the mind in all this evolution? Again, it must have a certain purpose and elegance, and while the religious argument about design is not fashionable in the academies, this theological pattern of thought continues, in a belief not in God design but in good design, rational design. But the human mind is not neatly designed and well ordered; it is an aggregate based on what evolved before us and what was advantageous in the world of our ancestors.

It's not as if increased brain size has happened only in the past few millennia. Sixty million years ago, in the Eocene, prosimians (premonkeys) lived in trees, and brain size increased gradually. This was probably due to the need for the improved vision (requiring data analysis in the brain) crucial to moving through space.

In 20 million years, at the end of the Eocene, the prosimian brain enlarged 65 percent. Later, monkeys and apes of the Oligocene and Miocene, epochs roughly 35 to 5 million years ago, continued to develop larger brains that allowed color vision and improved deftness, which bettered tree living.

Unlike most mammals, primates live in groups. Social intelligence is the long-standing legacy. This has its disadvantages, such as competition within groups for food, mating partners, sleeping areas, and so on. But there are boons too—protection from marauders, sharing of care for the young, and organized foraging.

Primate social abilities are surprising; they recognize their kin and form kin associations and friendship alliances; they carry on feuds. Social intelligence, characterized in part by having a good memory for social interactions, is vital to keeping all this straight. Daily events can change the nature of relationships, and the primate's brain must be capable of handling the updates.

This social cognition is not, however, the only striking primate feature. There is the intelligence necessary for deception. Here is one case. A juvenile baboon (observed by Andrew Whiten and Richard W. Byrne from Scotland) came upon a female adult who was partaking of tuberous stems, a gourmet item among baboons. The juvenile sounded a distress call although it was in no danger. Its mother immediately appeared and drove away the falsely accused female adult. The young baboon then finished off the coveted meal.

There is even deception of the "Dynasty" soap-opera caliber: anthropologist Shirley Strum observed as a male baboon with a freshly caught antelope was accosted by a female baboon with a healthy (food) appetite. Aware that he was not the generous type, she groomed him until his guard was down and then raced off with the dead antelope.

Group life is successful life, so hominid and early human social groups produced challenging personal problems. Instead of the hostile forces of nature, our early human's primary opponent was herself. So natural selection, probably, acted upon our ancestors' abilities to devise ways of getting along with their fellows. The social skills and manipulations that were called for in the early human career were unprecedented, adding fuel to the fire.

● ● ●

Our brain is larger than that of any other land mammal relative to body size, but what makes it remarkable is not so much its size as its different structure. The anatomy of our brain is much the same as that of primate brains with the exception of the cerebral cortex, the outer layer of the brain, which is far more developed and complex in man. This area is devoted to the higher mental activities such as learning and planning.

Several characteristics set human beings apart from other animals. I present them here in the rough order in which they evolved, but it is better to think of the process of human adaptation as the simultaneous development of all these characteristics, which each affected the other.

Human beings are bipedal: We walk on two feet instead of four. Chimps and gorillas can stand upright at times, but when they move they typically do so on all fours. Our first ancestor who walked on two legs is thought to be Lucy, an australopithecine discovered by Don Johansen. Although there is controversy about her age, she seems to have lived from about 3.75 million years ago, about 1 million years before the use of tools.

Bipedal walking is efficient; we are the only animals that can climb a tree, swim a mile across a river, and walk twenty miles in a day. Walking enabled our ancestors to travel into new and unexplored territory, which in turn led them into new and often dangerous situations.

2-11

Changes in the pelvis due to bipedalism.

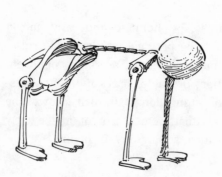
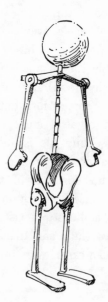

One can't see much very close to the ground, yet a standing animal can spot approaching danger as well as opportunities farther away. A more sophisticated visual system developed along with upright posture. Hands were freed from weight-bearing responsibilities, making tool use possible. Erect posture also led to profound changes in human sexuality and social systems. Although we cannot be sure, this complex of factors girdling bipedalism was of great adaptive advantage.

With the freeing of the front limbs, the hind limbs have to bear the entire weight of the body. The human back was not originally "designed" to support upright posture (which partially explains why back pains are a common complaint). To support the additional weight, the human pelvis grew thicker than that of the great apes, which made the birth canal, the opening through which infants are born, much smaller. This decrease limited infant head—and so brain—size at birth and resulted in a prolonged infant dependency. Human babies require years to develop, through an extremely long period of dependency. Cats, on the other hand, are well on their own within weeks. Try leaving even a two-year-old human on its own.

But humans need this kind of bonding, since during this period of infant brain development a single parent (usually female) could not easily provide it (and herself) with food, protection, and shelter while at the same time guiding it through childhood. Cooperation of others, friends and relatives, was important to allow the time necessary for the large brain to develop over a long period. For those adults who stayed together, the sexual bond enhanced the survival of their offspring.

Because of the long period of infancy, and because of the amazing adaptability of the human brain, with millions of uncommitted cells at birth, the world develops the human brain. And because the environment is grossly different for each person, the specific abilities each of us develops differ considerably, even beginning in the womb. Human beings survive at 12,000 feet, in caves, in hillsides, in deserts, in high-rises, in squatter's shacks, in encampments. We have, it seems, no real ecological niche.

Once our ancestors began to walk, the forelimbs were recruited for hands. Their greater dexterity made possible precise movements needed for fashioning and using specialized tools. Human ancestors began to make tools as early as 3 million years

2-13

Moving through the
trees, our ances-
tors had to act
sequentially.

ago. Specialized tools for chopping, digging, killing, cooking, washing, and skinning led to specialized labor by those who used them.

Although we left the trees, our adaptations for forest life did not leave us. Moving in the trees required sequences of actions and the ability to coordinate series of movements. This "neurological grammar" for the talented arboreal acts of our primate ancestors began in those areas of the brain that later enlarged in early humans and were still later "recruited" for language.

One mark of improved dexterity is the modification in the tools themselves. Those made by *Homo erectus* about 1 million years ago took 35 blows to make. The knives of Cro-Magnon, made about 20,000 years ago, were more delicately fashioned, requiring at least 250 separate blows.

Although the 400-cubic-centimeter brain of australopithecines was the product of hundreds of millions of years of evolution, it took only several million years for the brain to triple in size and become capable of abstract thought—the springboard of further adaptations. No other human organ evolved with such rapidity. It gave us the means to cope with different geographies and climates as we early on migrated out of our native Africa.

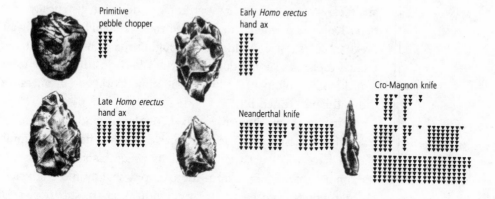

Primitive pebble chopper

Early *Homo erectus* hand ax

Late *Homo erectus* hand ax

Neanderthal knife

Cro-Magnon knife

2-12

The increasing complexity of tool-making. The growing sophistication of human stone implements, and of their manufacture, is illustrated here. Each wedge symbol represents a blow struck in making the tool and the clusters of symbols stand for the different operations during manufacture. (AFTER CAMPBELL, 1979)

The larger cortex gave our ancestors great advantages, from control of delicate muscle movements to the development of speech and, eventually, of written language. This unprecedented sequence has led many scientists to search for the "prime mover" of human evolution: Why did the brain grow so large before such size was needed? Or was it needed by something we know not of? Almost every explanation had been proposed: vision changes, tools use, throwing, painting, social organization, nakedness, clothes, running, walking, stalking, hurling, working, shirking, maybe smirking, and the lot. Almost surely, there was no single "prime mover," but an accidental set of complex factors, all of which combined.

The central bewilderment about the nature of the human mind is this: anyone can see the smooth continuity between most species. In considering our own line, the chimpanzee and the gorilla share many characteristics, and both are similar to the gibbon. These are apes, but there is no chasm between them (they brachiate, or use their forelimbs to swing through the trees) and the monkey.

Then came us.

Superficially, we don't seem very different. In blood-protein analyses, we are only a few percentages different genetically. We don't look too dissimilar to apes, we eat in roughly the same way, breathe, digest, sleep, and see in roughly the same way, but our mental capacities simply don't compare. We're just not in the same world at all—chimpanzees live in the same world as our ancestors did and have created little.

That such an immense gap between us and chimpanzees exists is unquestioned. The real puzzle is why the human mind should have evolved so far beyond its predecessors? Why is not the animal that diverged from the chimp a slightly more adapted, slightly more organized animal, one with, perhaps, superior social organization, planning, and mobility? Why are we so far beyond our "neighbors"? What pushed our ancestors? Was it from within, from society, from without? And we need to consider when it all happened, some time during *H. erectus*'s tenure, more than a million or so years ago, 2 million years after bipedalism and probably well before much organized language.

I believe that this highly unlikely and unexplained leap of cranial capacity helps give rise to our creation myths—that the gods (details differ) fabricated us in their image, they made us out of water, they made us out of clay. We came down from outer space. I don't think such explanations are due only to our ability to make up stories, but are as well a universal and deep response to the seeming impossibility of the emergence of the human mind.

What forces shoved the human mind so far? Most analyses of mind have ignored or shied away from this question or have adopted a version of the *2001* scenario: Invaders from outer space fertilized us and contributed a superior intelligence to the human mind. I'm no expert on the outer space scenarios, those mysterious brobdingnagian paintings on the ground that are visible only from miles up and such so I can't declare firmly that extraterrestrials did not enter the picture. Maybe they did. But this analysis is beyond my capability.

When I grew up (reading science in the late 1950s and early 1960s), the spur for brain growth was thought to have been the manufacture of stone tools. However, early tool production slowed during the million years of *Homo erectus*, just as the brain was exploding at its fastest. It has been discovered since that chimps use tools extensively, which makes the "tool rule" scenario unlikely.

The most charming theory has been the Owen Lovejoy scenario, aptly named for it hypothesizes that the upright posture and the long period of infancy selected for an attachment that allowed love and happiness to develop. This allowed males to hunt and scavenge far from home and to bring back food for sharing with the female who could care for the child over a slower, longer period of maturation. While such a scenario is very attractive, we have no evidence of food sharing during this period. Further, the decade-long period of helplessness, so familiar to any parent and so characteristic of the large brain being wired up in the world, does not seem to appear until later. Holly Smith of Michigan analyzed tooth eruption patterns and found that delayed maturation came millions of years later.

Other scenarios abound. Bipedalism was certainly central, for it freed the hands and thence promoted hunting and the later growth of the brain. Hunting in turn involves selection for cooperation and communication and leads to greatly increased meat consumption (a great source of protein).

Others, including Mary Leakey, believe we evolved upright to scavenge the large herds of game along their long seasonal migrations. The free forelimbs could have allowed the carrying of the young while awaiting natural accidents among the plentiful game. Yet there is no evidence (from tooth fossils) that *Australopithecus* and those hominids that followed closely ate more meat than do modern chimpanzees.

Interesting recent speculation centers on the relevance of the neurobiology of throwing for brain development. Quick, precise throws would have been very important to early human hunters, who were relying on a diet of high-protein meat as opposed to seasonal plant foods.

Evidence that early man was throwing can be found in his tool kit. Acheulean hand axes, dating back 1.5 million years and widely found in *Homo erectus* sites, have no handle and are sharp-edged all around, crafted for throwing rather than hammering. They are flat, which makes them aerodynamic, and fit neatly in the palm of the hand. Thrown vertically overhead, they are suited to hunting birds, their teardrop shape achieving a good spin if thrown in a certain way. And the practice is old—2 million years ago, rocks were transported over distances to be used as early tools.

It may have been our female ancestors who provided the neurological foundation for throwing, not the males. Although the first significant attempt to throw an object purposefully was probably made by a hominid or early human, the basic ability to do so has deeper roots. The evolutionary beginning for throwing skills is most likely the same rapid muscle-sequencing abilities that allow chimpanzees to hammer nuts.

More than 92 percent of this skilled hammering is performed by female chimpanzees. Female chimps are more skilled at hammering, the main purpose of which seems to be cracking nuts. They do not injure themselves in the process, as do males, and take on more difficult nuts than the males do. Early hominids probably employed the same hammering methods on nuts in advance of toolmaking. Though hominid males refined this neurological basis for manual skill, the female chimpanzee and thus our female ancesters are probably responsible for laying the foundation.

Female chimps also devote more time to hunting termites, with sticks that have been stripped of their leaves and are inserted into termite nests, than do males. Although the sticks are prepared by both males and females equally, the females are the more frequent users of these "tools."

Improvements in throwing stones came as a result of neurological changes in the brain or more likely added fuel to the selective fire. Throwing twice as far within a given time requires making decisions nearly eight times as fast. The more neurons devoted to a move, the faster and more regular the timing. Accurate throwing requires more and more synchronized nerve cells. Thus, selection favored brains with parallel circuits for improved temporary synchronizations and extra neurons in important places.

This is a typical scenario. It's well worked out, and it certainly has some import. I am sure that the development of throwing did influence the brain. But the scenarios based on one or another of the behaviors are of limited use in modeling the rapid growth of the brain.

Given that these events took place so long ago, I sometimes become confused with all this story telling. I am sure that I could make just as good a case for throwing stones as important movers in human evolution as I could for stowing thrones. Hiding thrones would force changes in social organization and would indicate a well-developed hierarchy, social organization, and social competition and would select for increased ingenuity, all of which would stimulate the brain to . . .

Although we certainly know more than we did a decade ago and the central event is certainly the ability to stand up, I'm afraid that these scenarios can seem like creationist myths of the paleontological religion. Here is my own dream of a committee of nongod but average bureaucratic designers trying to find the ideal form of humanity, deciding whether to base humanity on the ape or go for a new design.

[a papyrus fragment I somehow found in Lost Altos, California]

. . . if not probable, disaster. The cost savings at this time would seem enormous, more than five hundred water buffalo, but this, I propose, is an illusion:

Within a few hundred thousand years, these savings will be repaid many times over. Remember, gentlemen, we

2-14

One possible design
for the human body.

are sending an unfinished piece of work out, untested. It is quite undeveloped in many ways, yet it can carry food in the forelimbs and can share food with its kin, if only for a few [illegible].

We cannot foresee everything about this new animal, for if it can create its own environment and adapt, then it may be able to form new groups and perhaps begin to make its own alterations in its own living conditions. I must say this: We may well *lose control* of this new hybrid ape. A new design, as Hjurtil has said, will be more expensive (six limbs will require a new support bracing), and it will require extensive internal redesign and development efforts, at a time when there is little money to spend on new designs. We are all aware that the funds spent on the dinosaur were well spent but will be difficult to repay quickly since the budgeted amount has already been surpassed, but we are sure that comparable funds on this new animal will pay off.

However, these new technical developments will reduce the difficulties and compromises that a cheap revision of the orang would cause. If it lives more than twenty-four years, the stresses on the heart from pumping the blood upwards will contribute to heart failure. May I remind you that although inexpensive, this jerking of the forelimbs above the hindlimbs, as the "bipedalistas" would have it, is quite radical: No one has *ever* placed the brain, and an enormously enlarged one at that, so far above the heart—this is too dangerous by far!

If this so-called "Movable Upright Ape" (MUA) can create a new environment for himself, then the old brain structure will not be up to adapting to it—the animal will become confused and . . .

This second fragment seems to be titled "The New Design: QDV-6," although one cannot be completely sure. A portion is illegible, but it seems to be further comment on the inadequacy of using the "bipedalistas' cheapo version," although it seems unlikely that this translation could be completely accurate.

The new and revised design, the quadra-pedal dextral six-limbed version (QDV-6) would obviously avoid such long-term problems, although, admittedly, the short-term cost would be less with MUA. The metabolic savings alone of locating the brain next to the liver, and thus near the heart, would recoup development costs in a few thousand millennia.

Obviously, the radical hindlimbed "jerked-up" design of the "Biped" design group is seriously inadequate. In addition to the heart and lung problems, there will be problems with systems such as the lower bone mass and the limitations on the intelligence and adaptability of this old version. Of course, budget constraints and recent cutbacks make this design a good one for the limited funds, but it may well cost us much more in the long run.

In the completely revised design, although there will be a need for many new parts, the additional organ space made available by locating the four bottom limbs under the central trunk will allow an important development cycle to begin: the lessened internal strain on the legs and skeleton will allow thinner bones and less internal weight and will allow more room for the brain and organs to be developed as one unit and . . .

While this is clearly not a real document, it makes the point that human beings didn't have the benefit of a complete redesign to make us a rationally designed animal. Evolution adapted us on the basis of animals that preceded us. Rapid judgments as well as emotions were here before we were. The separate and distinct adaptations could certainly hold up well in animals that were to live their lives in a fixed habitat, which is the condition of most animals on earth—but not of humans.

6

Cranial Fire

One summer my wife and I went on a short trip to see the caves in which the Modoc Indians lived. These caves are in northeast California, where the landscape seems strangely like that in the Southwest of the United States. And, like the Southwest, it was hot. Simply looking at the scenery and going down into the caves was majestic, but the trip also left me with a different appreciation of how the brain operates in the head.

Coming out of the cool underground caves, one notices how awfully hot it is right at ground level. Then, as one stands up, it becomes cooler above the surface. And it continues getting cooler, the higher one gets. Clearly, a head six feet above the ground is cooler than one at ground level! And a biped would stand tall and stay cool.

Yet, as any mad dog or Englishman knows, it's still hot in out there in savannalike conditions in the sun. So for this trip I ordered a device that claims to keep you cool during the hot summer. It is a cap with a solar cell on top that blows a breeze on the forehead and thus cools the head. It works! The head breeze cools better than a breeze anywhere else on the body, and it got me thinking. The muscles that do the exercise and produce the heat are not in the head. Yet the head sweats a lot. Runners often wear sweatbands across their foreheads to keep the sweat from dripping into the eyes. We're designed to throw off head heat. In fact, human beings have three to four times as many sweat glands per unit of skin on the forehead as elsewhere.

Our ancestors adapted to lose body heat. They lost body hair, to perspire more freely. Body hair also restricts air flow over the skin and makes it impossible to reduce heat by sweating. Even such organs as the ear serve to radiate heat away from the head, at a high point in the elephant.

Why is it necessary to cool the head so much? Because the cortex is at great thermal risk, much more so than the interior of

the brain. The deeper regions of the brain actually are hotter than the cerebral cortex. It seems reasonable to assume that it's very important for us to keep our heads cool. Some important new research, from studies of blood flow during evolution to new analyses of heat-reducing properties of bipedalism, indicates that the need to shed the heat produced in the brain may have been a major factor in brain growth.

A great leap in brain growth would lead to the formation of new cerebral matter which later could well be recruited for novel functions. With all due respect to Blaise Pascal ("the heart has its reasons that reason knows not"), *La cerveau a ses raisons que la raison ne connait pas*—the brain has grown *from* its own reasons, not *for* reason.

Is the Human Mind an Accident?

Although it might seem cynical to think of the intellect as anything but a primary evolutionary goal, it was at best a side benefit of another adaptation. Since early humans did not need a great brain to deal with the hunter life-style, it is unlikely that any cultural adaptation was responsible for this new anatomical complexity. Why build a bigger brain than you need to survive? The question is, what kind of an adaptation might have increased the brain in size, and what does it tell us about our mind now?

We have a brain that is four times as large as our near "neighbors" and capacities beyond their farthest horizon. It is natural to regard ourselves as something special. And we are special in certain ways. We live anywhere, we are preadapted, it seems, to the whole earth, to societies that have not existed. It seems a colossal oversupply of brain, doesn't it?

Obviously, all the suggestions—bipedalism, language, and other hypotheses—contributed to the change. But all these events, though clearly important, don't justify the major leap between the great apes and us. Perhaps one of the major spurs was not social and cultural, but the physiological constraints of the brain, encased in the head.

A group of papers published in 1989 and 1990 makes the surprising suggestion that a spur for the brain's enlargement came from engineering and "packaging" considerations. Then the increase in size combined with other events to produce further changes. While, again, this is certainly speculative, the great increase in the cortex, I believe, must have been fueled by factors other than the social because the brain grew explosively *in advance* of the characteristics we associate with being human.

That the head is hot and needs cooling gives us one clue. Since the brain needs protection from heat, there has to be an appreciable amount of brain cooling. The human brain, as well as its surrounding structure, adapted to shed heat.

2-16

More of our mass is above the (hot) ground than the chimp's. (Adapted from the work of Peter Wheeler)

The brain is especially heat sensitive. It can be damaged by heat stroke very quickly. In our ancestral environment our ability to walk, move, and cover distances also caused an increase in the amount of brain heating.

In other animals this excess of heat in the heart is taken care of. Notice your dog on a summer day, releasing stored heat by panting. The open mouth transfers cool air to the blood through a special blood circuitry. Most carnivores can keep their brains cool enough during exercise because they have an arterial labyrinth known as the *rete mirabile*, "the wonderful net." This net goes through the snout, and when the animal opens the mouth and pants, air circulation cools the blood.

The arterial blood is cooled as it flows through this network (through the evaporation of fluid from the moist lining of the nasal chamber) before it reaches the brain. This enables such animals to keep their brains cool even though they are well exposed to the sun. Unlike our pets and other savanna animals, we have lost our net. Human beings are particularly sensitive to high temperatures because a rise of only of 1 or 2°C in brain temperature above normal is enough to disturb brain functions, and heat stroke can occur with a rise of only 4°C.

When the forests thinned in East Africa, our ancestors found themselves "suddenly," in evolutionary time, with less shade, in higher temperatures. As they needed to cover long distances, the

2-17

The "radiator" in the muzzle. (Adapted from the work of Peter Wheeler)

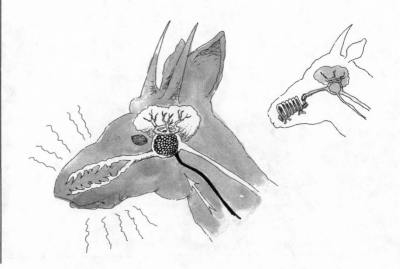

loss of shade made extra cooling a necessity. The requirements of living in a warmer environment made necessary some important body changes that later caused the brain to mushroom. Walking upright was the first adaptation to the increased heat load.

Some unexpected evidence on the origins of the human mind comes from considering the brain as it sits in the head from a building engineer's viewpoint. Upright posture presents less surface for the sun to warm. An upright animal absorbs 60 percent less heat at noon than does one on all fours. And, in thick subtropical vegetation 50 centimeters high, a biped sheds heat one-third faster than one on all fours. The leap of the brain was greatly influenced by the need to stand tall and stay cool.

Hunting was a more reliable means of feeding than exploiting plant life of the African savanna, which was limited, seasonal, and provided less energy than meat. Early hunting was an endurance contest, not so much a violent one. As our ancestors became more mobile, they outlasted and ran down their prey. This meant running and running, chasing and waiting until an antelope fell from heat exhaustion. Stalking game and often chasing it down over many hours under the hot sun as individual hunters (group hunting was a later development) raised body temperature so high that some brain cell death was inevitable.

Our ancestors, it seems, adapted to stand up against long periods of heat, both to shed and to avoid it. And this cooling need may well have influenced the growth of the brain, since early bipedal adaptations were adequate only to a point. When we stood up, the arterial pressure to the head of course lowered, as it would when you direct water upward from a hose. In our case this would, unchanged, cause less blood flow to a hotter head. And since temperatures can vary in different parts of the brain, cells deteriorated randomly. One way to maintain the brain's functions, then, was to produce more neurons.

But the brain didn't have its growth spurt for more than a million years after bipedalism. What was it waiting for? An important physical releaser for brain growth may well have been blood-flow changes occasioned by our upright position. A head farther from the heart needs more blood flow. Gravity, acting to reorient the veins to the skull, may have changed the circulatory system. The giraffe, of course, has a number of valves in its neck to help blood flow. In human ancestors, however, cranial blood flow

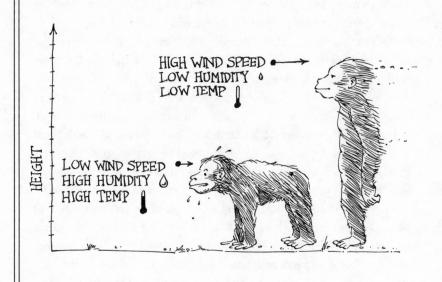

2-18

It is cooler higher up.
(Adapted from
the work of
Peter Wheeler)

2-19

It is cooler standing
up as well.
(Adapted from
the work of
Peter Wheeler)

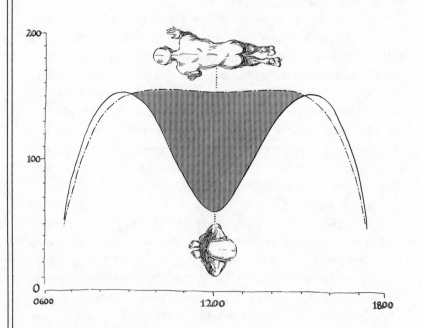

changed its pattern and streamed to the vertical plexus instead of the jugular vein. In the line of our ancestors, there was a radical change in the way blood was distributed in the brain. Our ancestors developed a wide net of emissary veins leading in and out of the brain. In these ancestors brain size increased along with increases in the size of the network but did not increase in those australopithecines who did not develop this wide net. Increased blood flow preceded and probably allowed for a larger brain with a different distribution of cells.

There have been some recent discoveries in brain anatomy and physiology that indicate specific changes in our evolutionary past, adaptations for purely biomechanical means that had the result of spurring the brain forward. Anthropologist Dean Falk points out that one of the most important adaptations leading to the development of a larger brain is a specific cooling mechanism for the human brain based on the emissary veins that we have been discussing. These veins evolved *before* the great brain ballooning of 2 million years ago and did so in the variety of *Australopithecus* that is our ancestor.

The brain heats the blood, and in normal circulation, these veins carry warmed blood from the brain out to the surface of the skull, where it cools. However, when the brain gets overheated, the "radiator" kicks in: the blood flow from these veins reverses. During exercise, blood flows rapidly from the skin *into* the cranial cavity. So under conditions of exercise-induced heat stress, these veins deliver blood that has been cooled into the brain case to protect the cortex. This is probably why, according to Falk, the cortex can survive even when the core temperature goes so high.

The heat hypothesis may provide an insight into why bipedalism preceded the dramatic increase in brain size. It seems that the radiator released a limitation on the growth of the brain and enabled the amazing expansion between *Homo erectus* and *Homo sapiens*.

Polish anthropologist Konrad Fialkowski contributes another insight: The human brain's rapid growth was primarily due to protecting brain cells from heat stress. The blood-flow changes released brain growth, providing extra reliability and protection with more cells, which led to the human brain's parallel organization connected to our capacity for complex thought.

So the bipedal position and the human ability to run selected

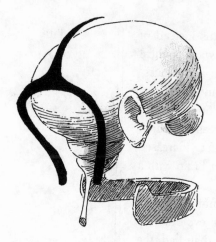 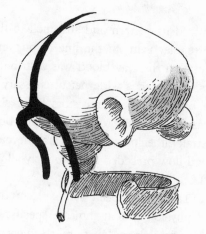

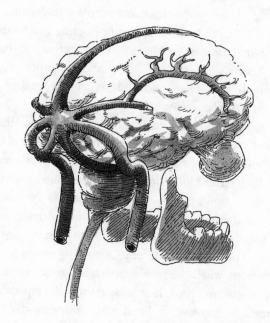

2-20

Two early means of
cortical blood flow
and our current
cooling net.

for increased blood flow and an increased cortical size, to protect
against heat and to cool the brain. This impetus to growth all
worked together to produce first, an animal that could survive
heat, survive long running and extremes. This heat-shedding large
cortex was later recruited for other uses. Lacking a specific
information-processing assignment, brain cells could adapt to different circumstances. We have the thousand forms of mind built
into that design.

The uniformity of the cortex is striking; almost any small piece of the cortex looks like any other piece. And the human brain looks like almost any animal's brain. From mouse to woman, the cortex is made up of the same cells and the same circuits.

The human brain's increase in neurons is due to its greater size, not to greater density, since humans have only about 1.25 as many neurons per cubic centimeter as chimpanzees do. There are approximately 146,000 neurons per square millimeter of cortical surface. The human brain has an area of about 2,200 square centimeters and about 30 billion neurons (more than assumed until quite recently). The chimpanzee and the gorilla have brains of about 500 square centimeters, and with about 6 billion neurons.

The volume of the human brain is so much larger (by up to four times) largely because the neurons in our brain are spread about. Some of the volume enables the increased interconnection among neurons. The greater number of connections offers greater dependability, since one circuit may be able to take over if another fails.

But there are other, often overlooked, consequences of this oversupply of supporting cells (glia). Just as you might surround the inner workings of a machine with an insulator, so the neurons, surrounded by glia and other cells, could make more connections. The growth in size and complexity of the human brain comes from the number of supporting cells. The glia feed the neurons and, because they pack the space, allow more interconnections among the neurons.

Consider an evolutionary change in the human brain: The neurons are more insulated from each other and more insulated from heat production. Extra cells surrounding the neurons provide the "packing space" to enable many more neural interconnections in the human than in the chimpanzee brain. And it is difficult to believe the usual explanations here—those of social complexity, throwing, building a world together, and the like. All these certainly added, as they say, fuel to the fire.

That the human brain has long been known to have an overabundance of structural elements would seem to corroborate the proposal that if you stand to lose brain cells exerting yourself in the heat, it's better to be on the safe side and have cells to spare. This is not that unusual. There is plenty of redundancy in our

The Multiple and Redundant Human Brain

DNA, for example. Every cell of the body contains all the information to generate, at birth at least, all the other cells of the body.

The brain can change its function when damaged. Deaf people use areas of their temporal cortex for processing visual information. Blind people do hear better than the sighted, probably because the visual cortex goes over to hearing. When you learn a second language, the first one can move position in the brain. When the brain is damaged due to stroke, other areas can take over. This plasticity, as this kind of adaptability is called, serves us well when we are under attack.

I'm writing this book on a computer. It is the summer, and it is hot. One of my computers has failed in the heat, but I have another, so I can continue to work. Is it so unreasonable that the brain would have this same kind of backup system, so cells in the cortex can take on different functions? With a couple of backup systems, one can function in difficult circumstances, especially if the circuits are in a parallel arrangement.

So, evolution selected more neurons, insulated them with neural tissue, and thus produced more interconnections. Behold, a bigger brain. The radical expansion of the brain added backup potential with more parallel processes and expanded linkages among neurons. The sophistication of the modern human brain depends on both these factors.

The frontal lobes grew fastest in the early *Homo sapiens* and thus probably contributed significantly to the modern human mind. We owe our high forehead to their development. Our terms "highbrow" and "lowbrow" reflect our attitude about their contribution to intelligence.

This view of bipedalism, brain size, and the leap of the cortex is new, founded on work published only in the late 1980s and early in 1990, by Peter Wheeler in England, Dean Falk in the United States, and Konrad Fialkowski in Poland, so I hardly expect that it will be regarded as anything other than speculative and controversial. Many will have their own say on this unusual scenario, and it may prove inconsistent in time. Yet it offers a new way to look at the brain's amazing adaptations.

To sum up: by reason of heat stresses, organisms adapted by standing up. The blood flow to the prehuman brain changed because of the development of erect posture, which allowed the brain to remain cooler still, which unleashed a larger cortex, with further changes in the "brain-drain" system to keep this highly active set of cells cool. The accident is that the cortex enlarged for purely "engineering" reasons, in some large part to keep the brain reliable during conditions of unprecedented and sudden heat stress. These extra cells could, then, become available to be recruited for other functions, as was the stapes.

The progression is stand up => heat stress on the brain => radiator for cooling => changes in blood flow into the brain => larger brain to provide extra, redundant cells => uncommitted cells in the brain => brain which could be used for other purposes not foreseen, as far along as is opera, science, metal sculpture, microchips, and marketing plans.

It isn't such a satisfying creation myth, this naked, hot, and erect scenario, from any viewpoint. It's not too lofty an explanation of the basis for our achievements. We can't look only to a unique style of life to support any of the paleoanthropological ideas (although many of the food-sharing toolmaking changes would have increased the adaptation). Our intelligence may have just been an accidental benefit of heat packaging.

However, the engineering changes that may have caused a radical increase in the cortex for no redeeming social importance or, in the current jargon, information-processing reason, may underlie the kind of mind we have: diverse, unspecialized, and amazingly plastic, containing many cells that are uncommitted at birth, which can take on many different roles. It is this diverse nature that is at the root of mental operations and humanity's triumph.

That this hypothesis will prove to be a perfect reconstruction of events long ago is, of course, very unlikely. However, it seems to me that we will need to understand that independent forces probably drove much of our evolution, in just such a primeval accident. I believe there will have to be an understanding founded on a separate realm of adaptation, some force that made our brain grow long before it was needed intellectually, providing the raw material for later recruits like language.

Whatever the set of factors, whether they include the need to build a large brain for purely engineering reasons given or not, our evolution has given us a great number of brain cells with little direct responsibility at birth.

These uncommitted cells, then, can be customized to suit very different lives and worlds—the freezing cold of the Himalayas, bedouin life on the desert, growing up poor in New York City, even learning to read upside-down when a book is shared—learning one of the thousands of human languages and cultures. This mind leap, in which our ancestors developed a brain with countless new and uncommitted cells, so far beyond our nearest neighbor, makes us a unique animal, inheriting the ability to go beyond our inheritance.

7

Why Darwin Is the Central Scientist of the Modern Age

DARWIN

Origin of man now proved—Metaphysics must flourish.—
He who understand[s] baboon would do more toward
metaphysics than Locke.
                    —CHARLES DARWIN, August 1838

Darwin's evolutionary view is counter to much of our philosophy and has changed the course of our history. As Darwin well knew, his work would overturn much of the basis of Western philosophy, for it shows that animals and humanity evolved to adapt to the world and thus that many of our reactions were built into the nervous system, and not learned from society. That's why he felt that metaphysics has more to do with what happened to our ancestors than what our philosophers thought, however well-intentioned it may have been.

The problem is always the debate over how much our environment affects us. John Locke tried to develop democratic societies by propounding the idea that all knowledge comes from experience, which would redirect attention to providing increased opportunity for all. Locke and the other British empiricists, David Hume and John Stuart Mill, wrote that the "association of ideas" (a sensation or a thought) is all there is to connect experience. Nothing in us comes into the world knowing anything, in this view. "Ideas" become associated when they occur close to each other in space or in time. Locke wrote in 1670:

A man has suffered pain or sickness in a place; he saw his friend die in such a room, though these have in nature nothing to do with one another, yet when the idea of the place occurs to mind, it brings (the impressions being once made) that of pain and displeasure with it, he confounds them in his mind and can as little bear the one as the other.

The empiricists, who have been quite influential in science's view of the human mind, believed that all knowledge came from experience. They assumed that the mind was "white paper void of all characters, without any ideas—How comes it to be furnished? Whence comes it by that vast store which the busy and boundless fancy of man has painted on it with an almost endless variety? Whence has all the *materials* of reason and knowledge? To this I answer, in one word, from EXPERIENCE."

Consider Locke's first statement. It sounds banal, even obvious. If you've suffered in a hospital, surely you associate that place with suffering. Hay fever sufferers who sneeze watching a film of pollen flowing over a field do the same. But missing is the underlying mechanism: One needs a prepared mind to make the associations.

The idea of mind as blank piece of paper is ridiculous, and it is one of the reasons we've been so slow to understand the innate mesh that evolved as the mind adapted to the world. To give Locke's ideas a test, I went to an office-supply shop and bought a piece of writing paper and let it sit on my desk for a couple of weeks. And I talked and sang to it. I told it to do all sorts of things. I gave it food, I gave it water, I read to it the works of Descartes, I gave it the works of Freud, I tried to get it to talk, I tried to take it for a walk. I put it in my car to see whether it could recognize the ocean as well as the mountain.

The paper was unable to do any of these things. And, anyone, for centuries, could see the silliness of claiming that all there is to the mind is associations. Yet Pavlov wrote as late as 1928, "Any natural phenomenon chosen at will may be converted into a conditional stimulus . . . any visual stimulus, any desired sound, any odor, and the stimulation of any part of the skin." More recent research demonstrates that this isn't true. Babies are clearly prepared to react to sounds coming from one direction or another, to search out the mother, to smile when she does, and the developing sequence of emotions guides actions in infancy through adulthood.

Human evolution selected certain kinds of learning as well. One example of prepared learning is taste aversion. One evening a psychologist went to the opera with his wife. For dinner, he had one of his favorite dishes, a filet mignon with béarnaise sauce. In the middle of the night, he became violently ill. As a result, he developed an aversion to the taste of what had been his favorite sauce, although he knew the cause of his sickness was not food but flu. Moreover, he did not develop an aversion to the opera, his wife, or the friend from whom he caught the flu. Similarly, ocean voyagers may associate food eaten prior to seasickness with nausea, in spite of knowing that the cause of their sickness is the ship's motion, not the food. The tendency to make a connection between nausea and prior food taste is so strongly prepared in us that it defies reason. Even conscious knowledge of why such associations are formed makes little difference.

The tendency for prepared learning can also cause phobias. A little girl sees a snake while playing in the park. Some hours later she accidentally slams a car door on her hand. The result? A fear of snakes! Evidently humans are more highly prepared to fear snakes than cars, all logic aside. Obviously the mind isn't unprepared for the world—it is not a blank slate.

Yet for centuries the Locke view has underpinned much of modern science. Even though I was unable to influence a sheet of paper effectively, there is no question that our thoughts and tendencies are affected by our environment. An extreme example of Locke's legacy in the twentieth century was expressed by behaviorist John Watson, who wrote in 1925,

> Give me a dozen healthy infants, well-formed, and my own specified world to bring them up in and I'll guarantee to take any one at random and train him to become any type of specialist I might select—doctor, lawyer, artist, merchant-chief, and yes, even beggar-man and thief, regardless of his talents, penchants, tendencies, abilities, vocations, and race of his ancestors.

The refutation of the view that the mind is a complete ignoramus is due primarily to Darwin. It was he who inaugurated the modern era in biology, which had great influence on psychology: Sigmund Freud's psychoanalytic theories, Jean Piaget's work on child development and the study of emotions were all consequences of evolutionary theory. Because human beings and other animals descended from a common ancestor, much wisdom could be gained from studying animals. Thus, comparative psychology and ethology owe their debt to Darwin too.

Darwin formed some of his ideas by chance. When he took his young son to the London Zoo, he was surprised at the boy's fear of the large animals, and this probably led Darwin to believe that childhood fears evolved as preparations to avoid certain situations. Freud, in turn, enlisted the support of Darwin in arguing that many childhood fears, especially neurotic phobias, are phylogenetically endowed.

Darwin's theories stimulated others to begin observing children, and thus began child psychology. The emphasis on reproductive success reinforced the importance of sexuality. The understanding that life is basically an adaptive process suggested to all interested that to understand modern humanity, we should look for adaptations from the past as a key to the present.

In addition to providing insight into the evolutionary process (which was to be modified and extended by others), Darwin published the first baby biography, in which he recorded infant development. His *Expression of the Emotions in Man and Animals* was so progressive that, until the last few decades, psychologists added little to his study. Darwin provided the basic insight for modern evolutionary biology, developed in recent decades as "inclusive fitness," but his evolutionary approach lies at the center of Freud's psychology of conflict.

The theory of evolution provoked great interest in variations in human mental abilities. It was thought that if survival depends on adaptation to the environment, then the superior intelligence of human beings must have been important in human evolution. The most intelligent human beings, because of their superior adaptability, would have been selected. These new ideas ignited a great interest in measuring intelligence and stimulated intelligence testing, as well as the work of Piaget.

When Darwin announced to an incredulous Victorian society

that "creation" was not created but evolved by blind mechanisms, he dealt a telling blow to the special position of human beings on the planet. He also probably did more to enable Freud to produce his work than any other person. Freud, in fact, was called "the Darwin of the mind" by Ernest Jones. In his important *Civilization and its Discontents*, Freud sounds just like Darwin when he states,

> The fateful process of civilization would thus have set in with man's adoption of an erect posture. From that point the chain of events would have proceeded through the devaluation of olfactory stimuli and the isolation of the menstrual period to the time when visual stimulus were paramount and the genitals became visible, and thence to the continuity of sexual excitation, the founding of the family and so to the threshold of human civilization.

Freud's genius lay in his breathtaking ability to relate the conflicts of the daily world to their roots in the human ancestral heritage. In a brilliantly crafted, if not exclusively plausible, way, Freud tried to relate traumas to the mismatch between the ancestral specialization of the mind and civilized modern life. But there would have been no basis for such an analysis without *The Descent of Man*. The "Darwin of the mind" is Darwin.

The major message of *The Descent of Man* is that the test of biological success is reproduction, not survival. For if the fittest don't reproduce, then what is the point? Darwin, in his usual studious and exhaustive manner, then provided thousands of examples of how animals evolved different sexual characteristics from one another, such as the giant tail of the peacock. These characteristics evolved along with the brain.

> He who admits the principle of sexual selection will be led to the remarkable conclusion that the nervous system not only regulates most of the existing functions of the body, but has indirectly influenced the progressive development of various bodily structures and of certain mental qualities— courage, pugnacity, perseverance, strength and size of body, weapons of all kinds, musical organs, both vocal and instrumental, bright colors, and ornamental appendages have all been indirectly gained by the one sex or the other

through the exertion of choice, the influence of love and jealousy, and the appreciation of the beautiful in sound, color or form; and these powers of the mind manifestly depend on the development of the brain.

Darwin's writings did much to encourage Freud to study biology and medicine. Evolutionary theory was so pervasive at the time of Freud's schooling that it would be impossible to isolate its influence as it would to imagine modern life without a computer.

Darwin was limited by his era and lacked a full understanding of the nature of genetics. He adopted the then-common assumption that direct reproductive fitness was the only key to evolutionary success—consequently, thoughts of reproduction, conscious and unconscious, would be central to the mind. Freud thus took from Darwin the emphasis of the psyche on sexuality.

Modern developments of evolutionary theory have changed our understanding of survival. It is now thought that much of our social behavior is the outcome of genes ensuring their *own* survival through their temporary hosts, us—"a hen is an egg's way of making another egg." Instead of focusing on the individual, we shift to include the genes' priorities as well.

Thus the important concept of inclusive fitness. "Survival of the fittest" focuses on maximizing offspring. However, many human behaviors lessen our chance to reproduce. Why jump into a cold river to save others? Why do Eskimos commit suicide when they are no longer viable? Why is infanticide common?

Darwin's theory didn't seem able to explain altruism, offering aid to another animal at cost to the helper. If an altruist leaves a safe haven to save another from a predator, the chances for reproductive success decrease because the altruist is exposed to some risk. Why do so, if we are motivated only by reproductive success?

Clues began to accumulate, as well as worthwhile quips. In 1927 the eminent English biologist J. B. S. Haldane quipped, "I would give up my own life for three of my children, or eight cousins." In each case, the number of one's own genes is increased. Similarly, killing one child may (in conditions of poverty) enable others to live.

In 1964 the biologist William Hamilton provided the key suggestion as to how neo-Darwinism could be modified. Relatives other than parents and offspring carry copies of the same ancestral genes: children have half, grandchildren one quarter. So an individual's fitness (the number of copies of his or her genes surviving) is not only reproductive but "inclusive"—the total number of like genes surviving. Therefore, there would be a genetic bias to help relatives. Hamilton found evidence that animals help each other in almost direct proportion to the number of shared genes, thus helping the common genes to survive in later generations. Suicide and other acts that obviously decrease an individual's reproductive success can increase inclusive fitness.

Inclusive fitness widens the early Darwinian description: an individual will act in such a way to maximize not only offspring, but the number of copies of the genetic material. Such a theory would explain actions that benefit his or her family and those closely related. Motives other than the sexual are important in evolution, and their roles in the psyche would have to be evaluated; many of Freud's successors did just that.

Reproductive fitness does not account for all behavior, and the decisions that take place after conception. Sometimes a parent must weigh the benefits of supporting one child well versus supporting many less well or balance the needs of one child against those of another. *Parental investment* is any "provision" (of care, food, support, risk, resources) that enhances the survival potential of an offspring.

2-21

Parental investment.
Inclusive fitness
benefits (curve A) and
costs (curve B) as
functions of par-
ental investment rate
(horizontal axis).

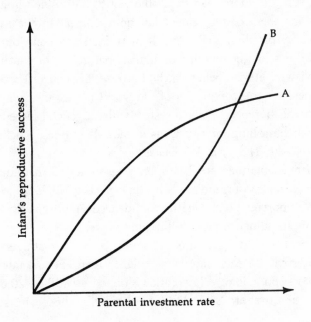

At low levels of parental investment, with little daily care of an infant, the offspring may well die. But at very high levels of investment, when parents devote almost all their resources to one infant, the parent's ability to "invest" in another offspring is limited. Here, such high investment may not be in the parent's genetic interest, for it would be better to produce more survivors.

It is to the child's benefit to increase parental investment as much as possible, for the child acts to maximize survival of *his* or *her* genes. Thus, there is a real biological underpinning for many of the common conflicts between parents and children and for conflicts among children. As a child, the rule would be seek the greatest investment, even at the expense of siblings.

But when one is grown, one's own children will similarly seek more investment than one is willing to give. Individuals act differently at different stages of the life span. Males and females also have different priorities. Darwin's ideas set in motion a completely new view of much of our behavior, one that is slowly gaining credence.

Evolutionary Explanations— Their Uses and Limits

Darwin's work did more than shock the world. It classified human beings as members of the animal kingdom, subject to the same forces that act on all animals. And it more than any contribution launched the scientific inquiry of human nature. It produced a different view of human beings in the universe. Because of Darwin, we now perceive the complexity of the world not as an exemplar of God's works but as an evolved system without general direction. If there is a controlling force, it is, as in the title of one of Richard Dawkins's books, *The Blind Watchmaker*.

Human adaptations are based on past strategies that might have worked for most people all the time in a world long gone. This is an important point, one that influenced Freud greatly and is beginning to influence modern thinking as well.

We spent 99.99+ percent of our history as hunter-gatherers in Pleistocene environments, and we adapted to them. For all intents and purposes, our biological evolution stopped 40,000 to 20,000 years ago, and we are specialized to deal with those ancestral conditions. Thus, we are forever behind ourselves, adapting to keep up with a world that is past. We are like animals rooted in the ground, reaching for the stars. It is no wonder that we are stressed and break in the middle since our rules about how to adapt keep changing.

Every organism has innate capabilities, which are shaped by their environment; of this there is no question. But talk to an orange and you get very little back. Its language is limited to the printed "Sunkist" or "Jaffa" on it.

The problem is trying to specify what an organism does learn and what it doesn't learn. A general-purpose mechanism that blurts out, "Just do what's best," can't adapt to a variety of situations.

"Maximize your fitness so that you survive" sounds good, as does "Do the right thing," but these maxims are just as useful as the advice, "How do you make money? Buy low, sell high." That sounds good, but what do you buy? When do you buy it? How long do you keep it? When do you buy in Asia? What do you buy if you live in Germany? What do you buy if you have $100, what do you buy if you have $10,000? What do you do if the market is going down? When do you sell? What do you sell? Do you buy property? Do you plant trees? Do you make pies? None of these is really answered by the overall strategy "Buy low and sell high."

"Maximize your fitness" is the same kind of general strategy. It is a good summary of how we operate, but it is hardly an operating manual for life. Are stones good to eat? Are peaches good to eat? How do we avoid incest? Should we avoid incest? Should we have sex with every one of our species? How can we tell whether a person is a good mate for us? How can we recognize our kin? What is good to eat? Is it a nice wiggling grub? Is it the dead flesh of swine? Is it beetles? Do we eat vegetables? What sounds signal danger? Are weasels nice? Do men pick up wood, or is that women's work? Should girls be coy? When there is a loud noise in the heavens, do the gods hate us? If an animal is charging, do we smile?

How can we tell what is good for us? Consider incest. It is impossible to write neurological code for "Just don't mate with your brothers and sisters." How do you recognize brother or sister? There is no direct sign on anyone's forehead signifying genetic relatedness. It is not always obvious, especially when living a transient life, to know who your brothers and sisters are. How do individuals decide this?

One answer comes from the Israeli kibbutz, where children are raised communally. In their adolescent and young adult years, children of the kibbutz experience little sexual attraction to those with whom they've worked on the kibbutz.

So this may indicate one way we recognize how to act. In pseudoneurological terms, "Do not mate with anyone with whom you spend extended time between the ages of one to seven" would be how we might inherit this adaptation. For most people for most of the time these instructions would protect quite well from mating with brothers and sisters.

A rule that would cover 99.9?+ percent of the situations is probably all that can be asked. Early environments seem to be able to shape the mind, to awaken the mental organ. Different ones are selected in different early environments. These different activations may well prepare individuals as adults to face different worlds. An infant born in the Yanomamo village will likely be involved in violent conflict and warfare for almost all of his or her life. So would an infant born in certain areas of Northern Ireland today.

Infants seem to sample the world of their mothers and organize their mind around it. And this seems to be a good system for all organisms that live in the same niche as their progenitors. For most of human history, most human babies would live in the same environment as their forebears.

We can't perfectly explain the mind, as we might someday explain the molecule, because we have to deal with the wild individuality of individuals. There will be many exceptions to an individual's ability to adapt to the world and there will be many mistakes, since the mind and other adaptations consist of innately probable strategies. Usually the correct strategy will be followed. But if a strategy has, say, 75 percent success, it will be wrong a quarter of the time.

Adaptation is choosing the best available alternative, not the best possible choice. Thus, the mind attends to the immediate situation and compares the alternatives. Thus, the nervous system organizes itself around these priorities as well as around neural coding. We don't have to be perfect, we don't have to know much, we just have to get along as best we can; over time, these small advantages add up and make the difference.

The woolly mammoth and saber-toothed tiger are now gone.

Because of the great malleability of the brain, human beings are as successful a species as we are because we can occupy a wide range of niches. Other animals have died out because of their lack of adaptability. The saber-toothed tiger was a successful and wide-ranging scavenger who fell victim to an overspecialized adaptation. It evolved colossal canines for biting into the skins of mammoths and mastodons. But when such prey became extinct, there was nothing of such substantial size to sink such stupendous teeth into anymore. These great cats became extinct as well because they were too specialized to readapt.

A compound of Darwin principles and Rumi's perspective forms the beginnings of a complete perspective on the mind. Natural selection begins the unconscious adaptation to the environment. In humans other principles also play a role. Given the cell glut in the brain, we advance to conscious selection and choice. Adaptation, which begins blind, organized around only one environmental niche, turns creative, and human organisms adapt the world to suit themselves. Natural, neural, and conscious selection are the underpinnings of our progress. Evolution, once strictly biological, can become, in us, conscious.

An Evolutionary View of Mind

So, although blind evolution may well have originally selected for adaptability, resistance to heat, and the like, it all comes together in the complex of factors that lead to us: bipedal, capable of graceful movements, needing a large brain to control them as well as speech. And all, or most, of this can well be grasped, if not understood by the processes Darwin described. His contribution to the evolution of our understanding of ourselves is much greater than we'd realized.

In this view we're all a part of the larger world, developing and evolving along with it with our bodies and our minds. Darwin, responding to the criticisms of those stimulated by Paley, wrote: "There is grandeur in this view of life with its several powers having originally been breathed into a few forms or into one, and while this planet has gone cycling on according to the fixed laws of gravity from so simple a beginning endless forms most beautiful and wonderful have been and are being evolved."

8

Feeling Fit

Thou thinkest thyself enthroned, but art outside the door.

Thou hast no sovereignty over thine own passions, How canst thou sway good and evil?

—RUMI

A psychiatrist I know received an emergency telephone call from the San Mateo (California) Police Department: "This is Officer Thomas. Your patient Alfred R. is standing at the edge of a cliff on Skyline Drive and Aronda Road, and he is threatening to jump off. Can you get out here and help?" My friend ran to his car and drove up the hill.

There was Alfred on the ledge, over the canyon. What do you say to someone ready to jump? My friend tried asking Alfred if he knew what this would do to his mother. How hurt would she be? But Alfred knew. Think how this will affect your kids—it will hurt them for their whole lives! But Alfred knew. What about his robotics company, just about to make a breakthrough? He knew. And didn't Alfred feel he was at last coming to grips with some of his problems, that in a few more weeks he could reestablish his relationship with his wife? Nothing my friend said seemed to have any effect.

Finally, my friend walked away, desolate, hoping that a police expert, more trained in these matters than himself, could say something or do something or promise something, anything, to prevent the suicide. He didn't have much hope for Alfred, though.

But the expert never arrived, and Alfred didn't jump.

What happened was this: Another police officer, on patrol, pulled his car up to the site, unaware of the drama. He took out his power bullhorn and blared sharply to the bunch of people on

The Physical Emotional Brain

the cliff: "Who's the ass (he went on a little in this word, actually) who left that Pontiac station wagon double-parked out there in the middle of the road? I almost hit it. Move it *now*, whoever you are." Alfred R. heard the message, and he got down at once from his perch, dutifully shuffled out to his car, parked it precisely on the side of the road and then went off, without a word, in the policeman's car, to Stanford Hospital.

It's easier than we might imagine to make radical shifts in our mental state, especially when our emotions are involved. Our mental state and status change radically; even our memories and ideas change without our knowledge. These kinds of shifts can happen because our minds incorporate different reactions and different selves. Alfred R. had worked out, in his rehearsal and his consideration of his suicide, all the reasons and all the answers with respect to the momentous step he was taking to end his life. He understood why killing himself was for the best and why, while suicide would surely taint and hurt his family, he should still do it.

But he had rehearsed within one mind only, the one concerned with his life and future. He didn't realize that his other minds have their own priorities, and some don't care too much about life crises. So his suicidal resolution was not worked through. It was simply overcome, moved out of place by the automatic shifting of his mind, which replaced the suicidal fanatic with a simple reflexive law-abiding citizen. This kind of sudden shift of mind can occur because emotions don't have the same routing inside the nervous system as does more ordinary information. These minds were laid down in separate eras.

While this was one dramatic and unusual happening, most of the time, our emotions seem to have minds of their own. Why did I run away? Why did I move from my resolve not to get angry? Why did I act seductively? The biological reason is now clear and simple: Emotional reactions have a different neural network than conscious, reasoned responses.

Emotional information fed to the brain enters via a different neural network than other, perhaps more ordinary, information. Most of our brain science has until recently assumed that all signals to the cortex travel over the same routes, but this seems not to be so. New research shows that emotions have a separate system of nerve pathways, through the limbic system to the cortex, allowing emotional signals to avoid conscious control.

This signal separation is beneficial in emergencies—we don't have to think before we run. But it can make us act in ways "we" don't want—we can't control fears of loud noises or heights, even though we know they're not dangerous. We may also get angry at a friend's manner of speaking, even though "we" know we shouldn't. Emotions contradict conscious impulses.

This set of findings is but one instance of how modern scientific analyses of the nature of the mind have become sharper and more focused as research accumulates. Most early theories of the brain supposed it to be undifferentiated, with many areas having equal potential for any kind of learning and accomplishment —an equal brain for all. Much recent analysis about the brain and emotions, however, concerns differences in the two cerebral hemi-spheres. They seem to be as specialized for emotions as they are for thought. The left hemisphere responds to the verbal content of emotional expression and the right to tone and gesture.

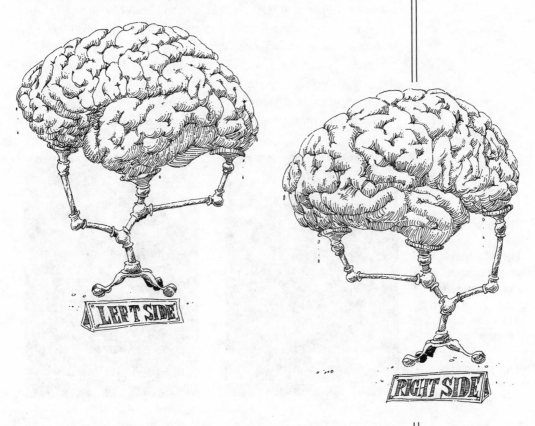

One study recorded frontal-area brain waves while stimulating and encouraging different kinds of feelings. People were asked to recall the saddest or happiest episodes of their lives while looking at two faces in different visual fields to judge which had stronger feeling. When happy, the left hemisphere was most active; when sad, the right. One face was neutral; the other, either happy or sad. When one of the two faces was happy, people more quickly recognized it when it was projected visually to the left hemisphere; when sad, people more quickly distinguished it when it projected to the right hemisphere.

Anger and sadness involve the right hemisphere more than the left, while emotions such as happiness involve the left hemisphere. Even week-old babies respond to different emotions differently within their two frontal lobes.

Since the right hemisphere controls the left side of the body and the left hemisphere the right side, are there differences in the expression of emotions on each side of the body? Look at Leonardo da Vinci's *Mona Lisa* below. She has a smile described as enigmatic, puzzling, ambiguous. Why? Look carefully at each side of her face, then at the reversed image. Only the left side is smiling, the side controlled by the right hemisphere. Perhaps this is why the expression is considered so ambiguous. And notice the two line drawings on page 83*: Which do you perceive as happy?

2-24

The *Mona Lisa*'s smile. The celebrated ambiguity of the smile of Leonardo da Vinci's *Mona Lisa* might be attributable to the fact that she is smiling only on the left side, the side controlled by the right hemisphere of the brain.

*From *The Origin of Consciousness in the Breakdown of the Bicameral Mind* by Julian Jaynes. Copyright © 1976 by Julian Jaynes. Reprinted by permission of Houghton Mifflin Co.

"These faces are mirror images of each other. Stare at the nose of each. Which face is happier?"
(Julian Jaynes, 1976)

Look at the three faces below. Which seems to express disgust most strongly? These three photographs were specially created: The one on the left is a normal photograph of a man expressing disgust. The middle photograph is a double image, a composite of two *right* sides of the man's face. The one on the far right is a double image of the *left* side of the face. Most people feel that the right-most photograph, which expresses the right cerebral hemisphere, shows the emotions strongest. The results are the same with eye movements and with interpreting facial expression. We seem to express emotion on the left side more than the right (at least in deliberate expressions), and we interpret emotions better on the left than the right.

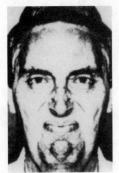

2-26

Expressing emotion: The two sides of the face and the brain. The far left photo shows a man expressing disgust. The middle photo is a composite of two right sides of the man's face, and the one on the right is a composite of two left sides of his face. Do you agree with most people that the photograph on the right—a double image of the side of the face controlled by the right side of the brain— shows disgust most strongly?

Why do we have such separated emotions; why are they divided in the brain? It may relate to the way different emotions mobilize the body. The two hemispheres oversee different forms of muscle control. The right seems to have more control of the large motor functions, which move the great muscles of the limbs, while the left seems to be involved in the smaller muscle movements, such as those of the fingers. If running were controlled by one specific neural system, it would make more sense to put the emotions that are associated with running and moving the arms, fighting or fleeing, in the same area of the brain.

The right hemisphere's control over the large muscle systems allows us to move quickly and to avoid trouble, while the left hemisphere's control over the small muscle system allows us to approach things that make us happy. Think about how your muscles would respond to a threat or to the sight of a loved one. The feelings and the motor control are perhaps lined up in the brain. We may have different positive and negative self-emotion systems, which divide control of many behaviors.

The brain's control of the facial muscles is exquisite. There is more area devoted to the control of the face than to any other surface of the body. This very detailed control serves a purpose: to express feelings. Feelings can be "read" as patterns on the face. We send emotional messages by our facial expression: a raising of the eyebrows here, a downward turn of the mouth there. Since emotional expressions are universal, it is possible to learn how to identify the emotions in various facial expressions.

Surprise is a response to a sudden experience:

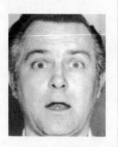

- The brows are raised and curved.

- Horizontal wrinkles mark the forehead.

- The eyelids open, and the white of the eye is more prominent, particularly above the iris.

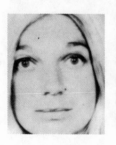

- The jaw drops open, but there is no tension in the mouth.

Each one of these clues may express part of the feeling. And since our perception fills in the gaps, the rest of the face may seem to convey the emotion as well. A face may seem to express mild surprise, as only the raised brows convey that emotion (left).

Fear is a generalized preparation to flee or defend ourselves:

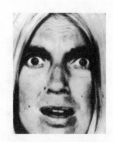

- The brows are raised and draw together.

- The forehead wrinkles in the center, not the sides.

- The eyes open wider.

- The mouth opens and the lips tense.

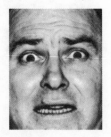

Fear may be accompanied by other emotions. For example, expressions of fear and surprise merge when someone is surprised and afraid, but not as afraid as in terror.

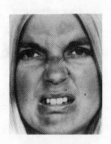

Disgust usually involves a response of repugnance or aversion caused by something offensive. It is expressed largely in the lower face and eyelid:

- The upper lip is raised and the lower lip protrudes slightly.

- The nose wrinkles.

- The cheeks lift.

- The brow lowers.

A mixture of digust and surprise produces a new expression that seems to convey disbelief or skepticism.

The expression of **anger** is strong and direct, conveying strong displeasure. It is easy to read. There is much redundancy in the anger message, making it clear to all.

- The brows lower and draw together, causing vertical lines to appear between them.

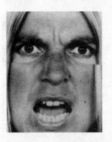

- The eyes may have a hard stare and may bulge.

- The lips may press together or open into a squarish shape, as in shouting.

Anger often blends with disgust. Here, the wrinkled nose blends with the angry eyes and brows—"How dare you do this to me?"

Happiness is welcome after all these difficult emotions. It shows in the lower face and eyelids:

- The corners of the lips draw back and up.

- The mouth is upturned in a smile, either open or not.

- The cheeks lift, causing a wrinkle from the outer edges of the mouth to the nose.

- Laugh lines or crow's feet wrinkle outward from the outer corners of the eyes.

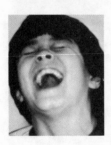

Anger can blend with happiness into a gleeful "gotcha" expression.

The link between our face and our feelings is strong in our culture. We "put on a happy face" in times of adversity. Recent research shows, surprisingly, that the position of our facial muscles influences our feelings. Test the results: Pronounce "cheese," and hold it for a few moments. Then purse your lips in a pout, and hold the word "few" on your lips. Doing so changes your feelings. Saying "cheese" (a smilelike pose), produced pleasant feelings, while "few" produced unhappiness.

We *can* control emotions using only facial expressions, somewhat like method acting. In a pioneering study, Paul Ekman and colleagues asked people to assume facial expressions, such as raising the eyebrows and lowering the lips. When they did, they felt the emotions they were expressing, such as anger and happiness.

Though we may be able to control emotions consciously, their innate guidance is far greater than reason can comprehend. The infant wouldn't survive without crying or manipulating her parents with feelings. The infants responding to the mother, bonding at critical times, and in adult life surprise, panic, fear, and disgust all nonconscious mind programs that serve us and have served our ancestors very well indeed.

Over the course of the summer I go to the Berkeley Shakespeare Festival, for productions that are sometimes wild, weird, or well done. However woolly the production, it is always rewarding to be reminded of what a good precognitive psychologist Will Shakespeare was.

One summer there was a particularly goofy production of *Othello*. I almost left but as usual stayed and gained insights through Shakespeare's characterizations of Iago and Othello. The manner in which these characters operate gives us, if we transpose the actions inside ourselves, a way of looking at the relationship between emotions and decision-making processes inside the mind.

Othello comes to believe that his wife, Desdemona, is unfaithful. She isn't, but the courtier Iago proceeds to rouse Othello's jealousy. Iago never *says* that she is adulterous nor really implies it. But he directs Othello's attention to suggest problems concerning Desdemona and Othello's lieutenant, Cassio.

In Act 3, Scene 3, "Did Michael Cassio, when you wooed my lady/Know of your love?" (lines 94–95). He insinuates that there are conclusions to be drawn but refuses to draw them. Othello eventually responds, "By heaven, thou echoest me,/As if there were some monster in thy thought/Too hideous to be shown" (lines 106–8). And, so prepared, Othello's mind follows the path Iago laid out. He grows suspicious and, through further misinterpretation of succeeding discussions along the lines Iago provides, comes to a horrible conclusion.

What I want to focus on here is the way the characters illustrate the role of the emotions in the mind. Psychology is split on the subject: feelings do not figure much in most psychological analyses of the mind, except the psychoanalytic, as they're the essence of irrationality.

*The Iago
and the
Sappho of
the Mind*

Many individuals also distrust emotions, seeing them as disruptive, against "our" interest. They disorganize us, confuse us, lead us astray, or make us irrational: "If you thought about it, you'd see that you shouldn't: marry him or her; move to India; run away from home; panic and bolt." Or should you?

Emotions rarely disorganize thought to the person's detriment, And disorganization isn't always a plight. When an organized situation such as a job or a marriage isn't working, the surrendering organization is adaptive. The worry that emotions are disorganizing is wrong, anyway. Indeed, they are the chief *organizing* system of the mind.

Outside consciousness, emotions, like Iago, direct the mind toward particular conclusions. They are mind systems adapted to short-circuit deliberation, to making the correct response in life-and-death situations, when fitness is paramount.

Immediate feelings highlight events, sending the rest of the mind a message that something important is happening. An animal that becomes fearful and excited about an approaching attacker is readier to respond and to defend itself. A human who experiences sexual love is more likely to reproduce than one who does not. An enraged organism is prepared to attack; a fearful one is prepared, immediately, to flee. They, like all our reactions, aren't always correct in all situations, but on the average emotions mesh us with the world.

Emotions come to the fore when rationality is maladaptive. You don't have time to decide whether some food you're eating is slightly spoiled or in fact is poisonous. You could test it yourself or feed it to ten other people in a nice little rational investigation. But then you might be dead. So you make a face and throw it out or throw it up. Sometimes, of course, your reaction might be incorrect—the food might be fine, but how could you know in time? And would it be worth the risk? We remember, think, and feel every day because of the way our mental processes were organized. When dramatic, life-altering or life-threatening events occur, people are likely to recall an unusual amount of detail about their circumstances at the time the event occurs. These vivid memories are called "flashbulb memories," because it seems as if, at these tense moments, the mind takes a picture of the scene. People who are old enough to remember President John F. Kennedy's assassination also remember exactly where they were and what they were doing when they heard the news.

The heightened charge at the time of the event increases the strength of memory, as if our emotions are telling us what is important. Feeling affects recall in many laboratory demonstrations, as well. Two psychologists asked people to listen to lists of words, some of which had emotional associations (breast, corpse, rapist). They remembered the emotion-associated words better than the neutral words. More important, they remembered more of what was going on when hearing emotional words—in this case, which voice had spoken the word.

Emotions are like the connections across cells—active links in the mind. Freud noted that individuals can't recall a past experience sundered from its emotional setting. The experience, he wrote, "remains as though isolated and is not reproduced in the ordinary process of thought. The effect of this isolation is the same as the effect of repression with amnesia." Deprived of emotion, according to Freud, recollections are unrecognizable. Emotional moments mark the mind. They organize the mind. For many purposes, they are the mind.

We remember times of robust feeling. The arousal seems to be our own internal marker, a marker to the rest of the mind that something important is happening. It is as if the strong emotion of a public event such as an assassination or a private shock fixes our memories of those moments. We all experience similar moments that we will always remember—an announcement of marriage, the death of a loved one, an unexpected shock. We remember trival details of the moment that our mind focuses on such an event, for example, what the room looked like when receiving the news that a parent has died.

We remember these exciting events as turning points and rehearse them over and over. Emotional points are points of change for us: when we got asked to be married, when a loved one dies, when we almost drowned, and the like. They're marked "for us" as signals to remember, by the emotional mind. It doesn't always correctly choose the events to be marked, however. Sometimes we become aroused when we should, sometimes not: "When I see you my voice fails. My tongue is paralyzed. A fiery fever runs through my whole body. My eyes are swimming, and can see nothing. My ears are feared with the throbbing din. I'm shivering all over." This is not a description from a physiological study of emotion but from the poet Sappho, written 2,500 years ago. Emotion marks events through activation of the body's emergency reaction, allowing us to prepare for immediate action, such as the "fight-or-flight" response. Most of the reactions involved in emotions activate mechanisms of the sympathetic nervous system. They underlie most strong feelings, such as anger, fear, and joy. Strong feelings are most often negative, since it is probably more important to send a message that something is very wrong and needs change than that something is okay.

The process works in several steps. An increase in the secretion of norepinephrine in the bloodstream by the adrenals activates the internal organs. Then heart rate, blood pressure, and blood volume increase. This allows more blood to flow to the muscles and the face (the origin of the flush that often accompanies excitement). Skin resistance decreases; respiration, perspiration, salivation, and gastric motility all increase; pupil size increases. There seems to be nothing in the physical arousal system *alone* that defines what the emotion is.

Our own explanation of the physiological state leads to different emotional experiences. Interpretation of the reasons for the physiological response can be difficult when the circumstance is ambiguous. In one study students saw a film of a ceremony an aboriginal tribe used to mark manhood. The rituals included the subincision of the penis with a knife. Psychologists measured autonomic nervous system arousal during the viewing. The measure of arousal used was a standard measure of skin resistance called the *galvanic skin response (GSR)*. One group saw the film without a voice track. A second group heard narration that emphasized the cruelty of the ritual. Two other groups heard narrations that minimized the cruelty by denying or intellectualizing it. GSR measures of arousal increased for the narration that emphasized the cruelty and decreased for the narrations that minimized it.

Negative emotions have a different information value because the number of threats is much greater than the number of pleasures. Positive feelings read in the mind as a signal to continue to do what we are doing, while negative feelings are more urgent, and signal that something should be taken care of.

Consider the happiness we derive from sweets. Enjoying sweets encourages us to search for more sweet things to eat, using fine motor movements activated by the left hemisphere, which is more involved in happy feelings than the right. Our sweet tooth had adaptive value in our evolutionary history because sweet fruits were more nutritious and more likely to be digestible.

You run longer and faster when afraid than bored, an adaptation that is useful in avoiding danger. Coaches capitalize on this response, giving pregame pep talks to get the team emotionally involved. The description athletes use is "pumped up," one case in which slang is quite accurate.

Fear is an immediate and specific emotional reaction to a specific threatening stimulus. Young birds show fear if the shadow of a hawk—even a wooden one—passes over them. However, as we ascend the phylogenetic scale, fear may become highly symbolic and/or more future oriented than immediate—anxiety rather than fear.

Anxiety is broader and may develop in response to the anticipation that something harmful may occur in the future. This harm may not be physical but psychological, as in a threat to a person's self-esteem.

2-28

A pattern produces response, no matter what it really is.

Fear is an innate shortcut to action. In the long course of evolution, emotions probably evolved to match well the needs of most organisms. Fear of snakes probably saved many lives. For human beings, emotional roles are different: The dangers of the modern world are unprecedented. The fear of nuclear war is not as palpable as fear of snakes. Radiation provides no identifiable stimulus, no obvious and immediate course of action.

The stress emotions, while unpleasant and disorganizing, alert a person that something is or may become wrong. A copywriter anxious about a deadline is more likely to work harder than another who is unconcerned. Healthy fear may keep someone from walking alone at night in dangerous sections of town.

It seems that the positive/negative emotional system is the most primary. Most of our questions about events center on whether they are good or bad. And such evaluations seem built in below consciousness as well. People who see strangers subliminally start to like those they've seen more often than those seen less. Most likely the repeated exposure deconditioned anxiety and fear: Repeated exposure to a stranger who caused no harm reduces normal apprehension.

As the poet e. e. cummings wrote, "Feeling is first." Feeling is first in two senses: Emotions appeared first in the mind's evolution, to operate as special-purpose organizers. Second, they are at the front line of our experiences. Since they evolved to short-circuit deliberations, they spring quickly into action, before rational deliberation has the time to function. So the common experience of not knowing why we are attracted to someone may have a basis that is unavailable to our normal understanding.

Some experiments bear on the question of how some emotions are communicated, far below reason. Shocked rats release a stress odor. If one group of rats is exposed to odors produced by other stressed rats, they react as if they too had been exposed directly to stress. Just one whiff on the stress odor sends the unstressed rats scurrying: They become more active, ready to fight or flee. The scent also triggers the release of endorphins, the brain's natural painkillers, making the rats less sensitive to pain. This pain relief allows the animal to ignore injury long enough to either fight or flee the immediate threat. Many animals communicate via gland odors, feces, and urine. Cats mark territory by depositing scent from their facial and rump glands. Dogs mark the boundaries of their space with urine.

Ready for the tiger—or the lion or the bear or the crocodile.

How often are our moods so influenced by others? Sex is strongly linked with smell. Pheromones, special aromatic chemicals secreted by one party to affect the physiology of another, kick off sexual interchange and intercourse. Around ovulation the female monkey secretes copulins, which signal male monkeys that she is available. It is the scent, not the female's amorous calls and inviting postures, that attracts the male. If experimenters block the male monkey's nostrils, the smell-less males are more interested in bananas than receptive females. Human beings also respond to sexual fragrance. Somerset Maugham once asked one of H. G. Well's mistresses why such a fat, unattractive writer had success with women. "He smells of honey," she said. And we respond to other factors as well. The number of human pregnancies peaks seasonally, as do those of other animals. The effect isn't that pronounced, remaining something of which we are unaware.

When we meet someone attractive, how much of the attraction is due to scent signals? In experiments, hidden signals affected attraction. Women are more attracted to men whose clothing was treated with the dusky scent androstenol. Women's reactions to photographs of male strangers become more positive when small amounts of androstenol are secretly sprayed into the air or when wearing masks containing it.

Consider the adaptive nature of falling, perhaps irrationally, in love: One component seems to be an attraction via smell. Smell, according to the biologist Peter Medawar, may signal different tissue rejection groups—an indication of who may be a good mate. There is the wrenching experience of feeling deeply that someone is right for us even though, rationally, they don't meet the criteria for wealth, height, looks, social class. Maybe smell signals Ms. or Mr. Right.

Most animals evolved effective display signals, such as odors, postures, facial expressions, and gestures, that communicate information about probable behavior to other animals. These signals and gestures are social releasers. A dog cannot say "please go away," and so it snarls. The message is conveyed. Such emotional signals as facial expression, tone of voice, and body posture convey meaning between the lines. A person may verbally express interest in what you are saying, but blank stares, yawns, and passivity signify boredom.

That emotions are adaptive doesn't imply that they will always, in everyone, at all times, be perfect. Like other general laws, they work well enough for the greatest number of people most often. Like much that is given in evolution, the prompts we receive aren't general, such as "Pass offspring on to the next generation," but directions on how—with whom to mate. They are strategies that usually work in the average environment.

We all suffer from too much emotion at times, or too little, and individuals may chronically feel these effects. Recall that it is impossible for all individuals to adjust at all times to all circumstances, but, like the law, we evolved to do the best, on average, over all animals.

So, when emotional reactions become too great, they interfere

Facial expressions chimpanzees use to communicate emotions. These diagrammatic drawings, done from photographs and descriptions, illustrate "glare," anger (A); "scream calls," fear–anger (B); infant's "cry face," frustration–sadness (C); "play face," playfulness (D); "hoot face," excitement–affection (E). (AFTER EKMAN, 1973)

as well as disrupt. A student may be too anxious to study for a test, or a person may become too afraid to leave the house even during the day. That many emotions activate us alike—joy often looks like pain—caused scientists to think all brain and bodily emotion signs are alike. But emotions are not binary computers, merely off/on, good/bad, stop/go systems.

I grew up, intellectually, in the cognitive tradition and began work on information-processing studies of the mind. I chose time as the subject and later on studied consciousness. But, like most of my colleagues, I tended to overlook how basic emotions were to the mind, because I didn't look at mind in an evolutionary perspective. Mental processes, I have come to believe, are not organized around thought or reason but around emotional ideals: how we feel we want something to be. These may center on getting rich, getting married, getting angry, getting even, getting ahead. These inner goads drive us. They suggest to the person where he's going, what she should do, what should happen.

The relationship between emotional drives and reason is like the relationship between an entrepreneur and her lawyers. The entrepreneur knows what she wants to do and employs the lawyers to tell her how. Engineers and architects may be called upon to carry out the plan, provide the proper procedures, and supply other "rational" parts of the design, but the direction springs not from the lawyers or the architects but from the entrepreneur.

Being there first, emotions act as the driver—the entrepreneur—of the system. Their role in our life is much greater than we'd like to think. A scientist may be committed to the scientific worldview, but it is in large part because he may, in fact, be so emotionally committed to this level of explanation that he decides that rationality is important. Other people may be passionately committed to the arts, music, their emotional lives, or to ignoring their emotional lives.

2-31

Two identical
monsters, yet we
don't see them as
such, because
of their apparent
sizes and positions.

The subject of the passion doesn't seem to matter. What matters is that emotions, like Iago, set our agenda. And they do so largely without our being aware of them. Far from being disorganizing, they are the focal point of the mental system's activity: They govern our choices, they determine our goals, and they guide our lives. We are, for the most part, in most of life their servants, and we are usually not conscious of them.

As our rational selves try to act properly, or think properly, the autonomous emotions seem to be a problem. We become angry when we don't want to be, and we seem to "fall" in love almost by accident.

I am not saying that, because feeling is first, feeling is correct—if it feels good, it is good—but that unnoticed influences on our lives are more often emotional, working through the rational, than most of us want to admit.

Emotions are a standard part of the human program. Darwin observed that all people, from an Oxford don to an aborigine, express grief by contracting their facial muscles in the same way. In rage, the lips retract and teeth clench. There are similarities in the snarl and in disgust. All over the world, flirting signals are the same: a lowering of the eyelids or the head, followed by direct eye contact. Embarrassed people close their eyes, turn their heads away, or cover their faces. And anger is easily recognizable in all cultures. Such universality indicates that emotions are part of the innate set of adaptations we possess.

Emotional expression develops in a sequence that meshes the infant's needs with its mother and its world. At first infants respond to everything with general excitement: increased muscle tension, quickened breathing, and increased movement. This general arousal gradually becomes distress (at three weeks) and anger (three months). Later come reactions of disgust (three to six months), fear of strangers (seven to eight months), and jealousy and envy (fifteen to eighteen months). The predictable, reliable sequence of these changes indicates an innate maturational component to emotions. Crying occurs earlier than smiling, perhaps because crying serves immediate survival needs.

The German ethologist Iraneus Eibl-Eibesfeldt filmed children born deaf and blind. He found that basic facial expressions— smiling, laughing, pouting, crying, surprise, anger—occurred in appropriate situations. Blind children show the same pattern of development of smiling as do sighted children. The difference is that, around six months of age, social smiling becomes increasingly associated with the mother's voice and touch instead of with her face.

Newborns have many important abilities, emotional and not, that seem to be the seeds from which adult capacities grow. They identify with other human beings almost immediately—they imitate, coo, and smile at the sight of other people. Babies are born with a number of reflexes that help them face new experiences, such as sounds, hot and cold temperatures, movements, and pain. Babies are ready for these changes; they turn toward interesting noises and away from unpleasant ones, and they know how to signal distress: They cry. A baby's cry gets the attention of the caregiver, usually the mother, who provides comfort.

Only two hours after birth, newborns can follow a slowly

moving light in front of their eyes. If a nipple or a finger is put into their mouths, they begin to suck on it, a reflex that helps get food. If you gently stroke their cheeks or the corner of their mouths, they turn their heads in that direction in an attempt to find the mother's nipple. Many of these inborn movements are the building blocks of sophisticated motor skills, such as walking and speech.

What does an infant know? William James wrote that the experience of the newborn is a "blooming, buzzing confusion." Jean Piaget characterized it as a transitory world: "There are no permanent objects, only perceptual pictures which appear, dissolve and sometimes reappear."

These portrayals are somewhat accurate. The world to the infant probably appears to be more disorganized than to the adult and most likely seems highly unstable. Because the sensory systems are relatively well developed at birth, the newborn's world probably consists of a sequence of sounds, sights, and other sensations with less stability than adult perception.

The infant world is not so much confused as it is simpler and more selective than the adult world. Newborns are obviously unprepared to function in the adult world, on their own, but they are prepared to function in their tiny world. Their extreme egocentrism is adaptive: An extremely narrow persepective is important for survival.

They seem designed to recognize the mother by smell. Newborns notice objects that are very close to them, things that are a part of their very small world. Later the newborn's world expands, as does its thought and perspective. It becomes less egocentric. At birth newborns can focus up to only 10 inches away, about the distance from the breast to the mother's face. By six months, their range of vision has expanded so that they can focus on objects at any distance. Newborns can distinguish between figure and ground, have some depth perception, and can respond to different smells.

From birth, babies are more interested in faces than other forms. Robert Fantz showed newborns a set of six discs. Babies looked longer at patterned discs than at single-color discs and longest at the pictures of a face. At first babies look primarily at the edges of objects. By six weeks they look at peoples' mouths, especially at the mother's mouth when she is talking. This inborn preference most likely exists because being attracted to human being is important to survival.

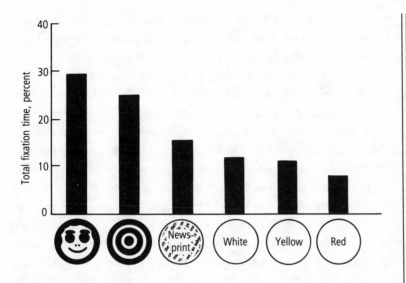

Babies seem to be born with a set of rules for seeing the world: (1) if awake and alert, open your eyes; (2) if you find darkness, search the environment; (3) if you find light, but not edges, begin a broad, uncontrolled search of the environment; and (4) if you find an edge, look near the edge and try to cross the edge. It seems likely that the infant comes into the world with a predisposition to search out new features of the environment.

2-32

Visual preferences of newborns. In experiments exposing infants to various visual stimuli, newborns as young as ten hours old to five days old looked longer at the disc with the black-and-white face than at simpler discs showing a bull's-eye, newsprint, or solid colors. (AFTER FANTZ, 1961)

2-33

Innate form preferences. By turning their heads to look at the "face" with the features in the right places, rather than at the other "faces," babies less than one day old showed an innate preference that could indicate they were born with a "face" schema.

There are several types of dispositions—perceptual, cognitive, motivational—that direct the course of our lives, and these dispositions seems to appear very quickly. The child shows striking preference for viewing the face as opposed to many other stimuli and has an attentiveness to the sound of the human voice. A baby is apparently able to distinguish the sound of its mother's voice from that of other women; most likely this occurs because of its constant exposure to this voice during gestation. Infants begin to produce the phonemes of all languages, and they do so *long before* they are exposed to the sounds that they are producing.

Early in life infants can distinguish facial expression, and they can remember facial expressions following brief exposure. As the infant matures, she becomes sensitive to faces, words, and gestures by caregivers. Babies become attuned to the people who will help them. There is an almost amazing mesh between the individual's development and his or her world. Children can recognize emotions without having seen them before.

As the child matures, his or her social world expands from the small world of child and parents to friends, religion, nationality, and thus emotional experiences also expand. But due to the special way the nervous system operates in the first years, the relationships formed in the first few years have a special and enduring quality. It's not irrational for the child to show distress when his or her caregiver leaves, for it indicates successful bonding, so necessary in the long period of human helplessness and infancy.

In a very important work, the British psychiatrist John Bowlby made clear that attachment is innate and that strong emotional attachments in infancy help the child adapt and aid survival. Because an infant relies for protection on his primary caregiver, it is safer for the infant to spend most of his time clinging to or close by the mother. Babies do not necessarily become attached only to their primary caregivers but to people who interact with them socially. The connection to others is stimulated early.

Even a young infant can tell the difference between the mother and other people: The baby's eyes follow her more than anyone else, and it smiles more enthusiastically at her. By eight months most infants have a strong attachment to their mothers. They smile, coo, and attempt to stay close to her. When frightened, they go to her and try to cling to her leg or demand to be picked up. As long as she is near, an infant feels free to explore.

At about eight months, the infant often shows extreme distress when the mother leaves. When the mother returns, the child will often cling desperately. The child cannot be comforted by just anyone—only the primary caregiver brings relief. This bonding and early attachment serves to keep the helpless infant close to the mother where it can be protected. Early in our evolutionary history, infants who wandered too far probably did not survive to reproduce.

And this mesh between our development and the world continues. Before infants develop separation anxiety, they become afraid of strangers, a fear called *stranger anxiety*. At four or five months, infants smile at almost anyone. By the last quarter of the first year, however, they are likely to scream and cry if a stranger approaches, especially if they are in a strange place or if their mothers are not around.

A breaking of the mother-child bond produces a three-stage response: (1) anxiety, disbelief, and searching for the lost one; (2) depression, withdrawal, and despair; and (3) acceptance and recovery. The first two stages are flight-or-fight responses. Animals experience the same response. When infant monkeys were separated from their mothers, on the first day, there was agitation and increased heart rate. A day later the infants settled into depression, marked by decreased heart rate and low body temperature. After four days, the physiological signs returned to normal. Similar attachments occur in adult human beings, although the response is not under such strict genetic control. But the same agitation, the same arousal, and the same feelings of grief occur. There are also dire health consequences of losing a loved one—breaking attachments can affect the immune system and the heart.

Generally, human infants become more attached to people who interact with them socially, whether or not they provide any caregiving functions. Many researchers believe that communication is the primary ingredient in the development of attachment. This argument is supported by observations of father attachment. Infants whose fathers are around often and relate closely to them show strong attachments to their fathers as well as their mothers. So, the emotions, along with the rest of the infant's mind, develop in the same way all over the world, and adapt the infant to those most important to her.

III

The Inner Workings of the Mind

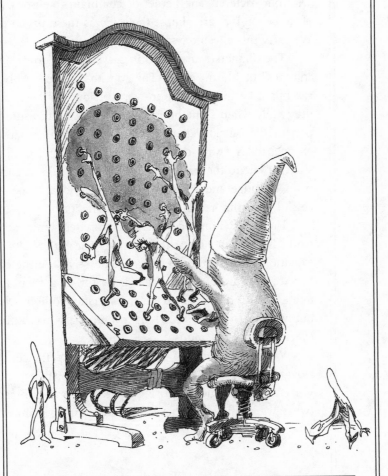

Making connections

We must remember that all our provisional ideas on
psychology will one day be explained on the basis of
organic substrates.

—SIGMUND FREUD, "On Narcissism"

In the beginning, before the first animal, before the first emotion, there was a nerve cell, which in turn developed directly
from bacteria. The kernel of our brain's neurons, the millions
of mitochondria, are almost the same as these primordial bacteria.
We carry this ancient system in each of our cells.

The human mind's routines were laid down by the basic
"physics" of life on earth. The way the neuron evolved (*Neu-ron
run* might be the modern do-wop version of Freud's statement) to
fire wildly when something new happens, to measure the proportion of the outside energy, and to stop firing when there is no
change, today sways daily thinking everywhere, from judging the
size of a line to the size of the federal deficit. We use that same old
brain to judge and to select. If an evolutionary operation is successful, it can be recruited for other functions.

How that immense and uncommitted brain adjusts to the
world is another part of this section. The hit-or-miss workings of
evolution seem also to go on inside ourselves during each lifetime.
For we are, as Rumi said, the inheritor of a thousand forms of
mind. Not all get "selected" in the specific locale in which we live,
but we are, whether it be by evolutionary recruitment or not,
oversupplied with minds.

We are a blend of cells, neurons, experiences, and selves.
How these relate to our lives is what these next chapters are about.
We end with some surprising work on how our conscious self
(what we think of as "us") is a constant spectator to our own
actions.

9

That SOB Within Us (Same Old Brain)

Enter a neuron, and you will see scores of chemicals being released, flowing from cell to cell and back again. In these explosions lie our thoughts and our brain's control of our body. Since the fundamental unit of the mind is the neuron, we consider how it operates. We are much more primitive in our basic patterns of judgment than we, or even Freud, might believe.

Each nerve cell and the brain itself is like an internal pharmacy. It dispenses a stream of powerful drugs to influence and control moods, thoughts, and bodily functions. The brain superintends the body through this continuous flow of chemical messages.

As the mind evolved, it recruited its higher routines on the characteristics of neurons. Neurons fire when something different happens and don't respond significantly when they are continuously stimulated. They adapt to constant sounds, weight, or pressure and respond to changes in the world. The mind built up higher levels of judgment on the basic routines that originally developed to handle sensory information.

Hence the same old brain: We are limited all the way up by the way we're limited all the way down. Many of the mind's works are based on biological adaptations of more than a billion years ago. If we are aware of how these basic neural processes show us the world, we may be able see through them as well.

Since organisms' needs are usually immediate, the mind adapted to focus on current events and to compute changes in the world immediately, or in computer terms, "on-line." Specialized to operate instantaneously, the mind has its own news evaluation system. The neurons respond to the first occurrence of an event, less to later changes. The first star to appear on a dark night makes an impression. Later the same night, that star is just one of many. The

Neurotransmission. The presynaptic neuron and the postsynaptic neuron meet at a tiny gap called the synapse, across which the transmitter chemicals "jump" to transmit their signals.

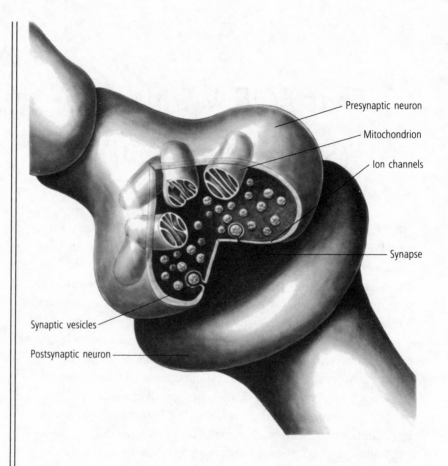

Presynaptic neuron

Mitochondrion

Ion channels

Synapse

Synaptic vesicles

Postsynaptic neuron

first cry, the first noise arouses us, then the excitement recedes. The on-line reckoning actions of the mind make first impressions of other people important, make us strongly remember our first dollar earned, our first love, and our first home.

And this characterizes operations in social and policy situations. Most mental operations focus upon news, a sudden appearance of something unknown. Unexpected or extraordinary events seem to have fast access to consciousness, while an unchanging background noise or a constant weight or a chronic problem soon is shunted into the background. It is easy to raise money for emergencies, such as the few victims of a well-publicized disaster, but it is much more difficult to raise money for the many victims of continuous famine. We quickly respond to scarcity and danger. We are streamlined to respond to the onset of an event, and then the offset.

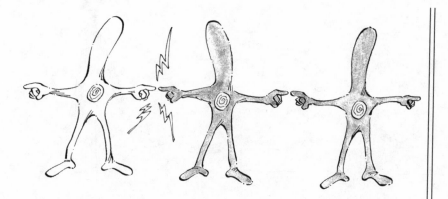

Neuron-run-run.

Thus recent events distort judgment. I asked thirty educated people which foreign country has invested the most in America. Twenty-six said Japan. But Japan is news, and Holland (first) isn't. The Dutch have held much of the United States for so long that their massive presence isn't noticed. And Japanese purchases have received much more publicity.

The neuron and the mind both share strong reaction to new information. The news in the mind is determined in the same way as it is by the media: selection of those stories that signal change, signal beginnings and endings, signal new circumstances. Responding immediately was certainly adaptive for the mind as it evolved long ago. It rains; we move. Hordes approach; we grab sticks or run. A comrade breaks a leg; we rush to fix it.

3-4

We respond to the beginning and the ending of a stimulus—not in between.

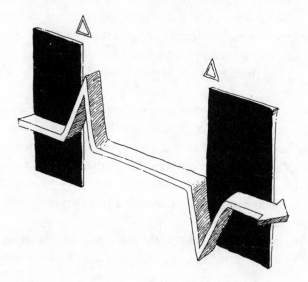

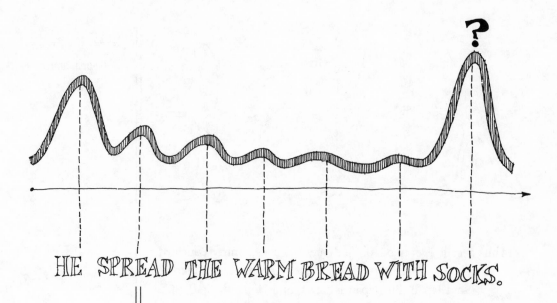

HE SPREAD THE WARM BREAD WITH SOCKS.

Gaining access to new information, even accidentally, changes the mind; this is one reason small changes can make large differences in the way we operate. The immediate access to information shifts our ability to recall and our judgment. One study asked people to name any fruit that begins with the letter *a;* next, those that begin with *p.* The second question was answered faster. The first question summoned up the storehouse of information about fruits, making the names of fruits more readily accessible for the second question.

You can see how changes in the mind's access work in your service. When you go to a city you've visited, you suddenly may remember the streets and directions, even a restaurant or park you liked. You had no access to this when you were in your home city, since it was hidden under other, more immediately important ideas.

It would make sense to have the most useful information most accessible. An analogy is a storehouse: Often-ordered items are at the front, where they are easy to reach, and items that are rarely called for are tucked away in corners, less accessible. Most living beings, including us, have their priorities for acting prominent in mind. So when we access any information—no matter how—it influences us.

The mind also tunes out the familiar—the background noise of the heater, joint pain, or the dog next door howling every night.

When an event continues, we stop noticing it. The air conditioner in the room, the noise of the street, our breathing—all seem to "disappear." This happens because our senses don't respond to unchanging stimulation. This decline in response is called sensory adaptation. It reduces the number of irrelevant sensations, allowing us to focus on new events in the environment.

And this system is recruited for more advanced judgment: we adapt to continual pain, we adapt to continual noise, pollution, to the kindness or roughness of others. Only when it stops do we observe what we have lost: a loving spouse, a great actor, a chronic ache. Why do we have a system like this?

Our nervous system has to cope with billions of events and did so using routines that were available. To act economically, we simply cancel responses to things that don't change. This leaves neural room for responses to things that do change. You don't always need to hear your heart beating or your breathing or see your nose (note, close one eye and you can see that it's still there).

If something is present all the time, it seems adaptive for the nerves not to bother about it. This system worked well in responding to sudden danger, which is probably why living beings developed it. A loud boom is perceived, and we're ready, ready to run or fight. For immediate survival in a primitive environment, it was good.

3-6

When a noise repeats, we stop listening.

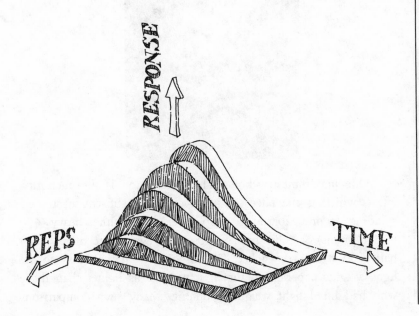

Since most emergencies are sudden changes, the mind is set to respond to those changes, not to what is really occurring. Response begins at the receptor level. During your next shower, run water as hot as you can take on your hand, and keep it running. Then cool down the water, while you step away. Run this cool water on your torso and quickly on your hand. The water feels warm in one place, cool in another. The change signaled to the brain was based on a comparison of two events. Adaptation is doing the best thing, so the mind compares options at each moment.

3-7

Whiskers are so important to a mouse that its brain has a section whose structure almost exactly reflects the external layout of the rat's snout. For each row of whiskers in the bottom photograph, there is a row of patches of cells, each corresponding to a whisker, in the rat's cortex. (AFTER WOOLSEY AND VAN DER LOOS, 1950)

One important psychological phenomenon is the anchoring effect, which is the effect of information on subsequent understanding. In one experiment people were given either heavy (400 to 600 grams) or light (100 to 300 grams) weights to judge. Then half of each group switched. Those going from the heavy to the light weights experienced the light weights as lighter than those who had lifted light weights all along. Many such comparisons affect judgment: An envelope that weighs the same as a suitcase is likely to be perceived as weighing more, because we have set an adaptation level based on the smallness of the envelope, to which we compare its weight.

The same kinds of anchoring effects occur in everyday life. A spell of cool weather in summer is refreshing, so 75°F feels great after a series of 90°F days, but 75°F in London in the summer sends conservative bankers out with their shirts off.

From a biological point of view, it is obvious what an advantage our response to change is. Neurophysiologists talk of the grandmother cell, a unique brain cell that fires when your grandmother is near; yet we cannot have a cell for everybody. What happens when we see them from the back, wearing a new dress, older, with a new haircut?

To adapt means doing the best job we can. Sensory adaptation serves this end: It makes instant comparisons, to pick the stronger, louder, riper, more delicious, less frightening alternative. This is an important part of how we are built: Since we never experience the exact same situation twice, it would be uneconomical to have a system that responded in a different way to each new stimulus.

The mind evolved extreme sensitivity to recent information. Emotional upsets such as a breakup of a romance last for a while, then fade out of consciousness. Terrible disasters such as an air crash force attention on airline safety problems, and all sorts of reforms start. But then the spotlight fades.

3-8

The same price looks very different, depending on what we expect.

"Forgive and forget," "Time heals all wounds"—these maxims are really descriptions of how the mental system operates: We let go of dangers as they move into the past. The dangers may, however, continue, like the continuous dangers of smoking cigarettes, but constancy or slow changes are not what the mind works to detect.

The mind's moves adapt us to the world in more than 99 percent of situations, to respond to the important changes in the world. It is more useful to react too strongly to a threat, for instance, and flee needlessly, than it would be to react statistically. A bias such as "Oh, it seems that the average base rate indicates that tigers only maul 0.0344 percent of their prey at any meeting, so I'll continue with my knitting" presumably wouldn't be inherited by many offspring.

But now our lives are filled with long-term problems, not immediate dangers. And now our collective survival depends on judgments that cannot be recruited from the primitive base of the mind. For now, however, it is best to at least know who that SOB is.

10

The Mind of the Individual and the Individual Mind

To each person I have allotted peculiar forms,
To each have I given particular usages.
What is praiseworthy in thee is blameable in him,
What is poison for thee is honey for him.
What is good in him is bad in thee,
What is fair in him is repulsive in thee.

—RUMI

The first thing we notice about the individual mind is that minds *are* individual. How did and how do they get that way? Different people have discrete abilities. An anecdote reported by Idries Shah, which is usually told about the British, applies to each of us as individuals:

> Three men are about to be hanged, a Frenchman, a German, and an Englishman. The Frenchman steps up, is put in the noose, but when the signal is given, the trap doesn't open. By custom, if the execution fails, he is freed. The German steps up, sees what happened, looks down at the trap, and understands what was wrong. He laughs and hurries to get hanged. The trap doesn't open.
>
> The Englishman is put forward. On his way up, he says: "I think that hinge needs oiling and de-rusting." It did.

113

Different men and women don't have the same set of minds, and those with particular abilities don't always use them in the proper circumstances. Some, like the Englishman in the story, can't prevent their mind from acting on their ability.

Some have good memories for faces, and others are good with names but not faces; there are people who are good at finding their way in new surroundings but can't hear music or reason; there are those who can reason but can't find their way around.

And individuals differ on the ways in which they use their talents—some people seem able to keep six "wheels" spinning at once, while others focus more closely on one thing at a time. Memories differ too, and the way we search out the world differs. Some worry about threat, some seek pleasure. Ronald Reagan, it is said, saw his drink glass half full; Nancy Reagan looked at the same glass and wondered how to give hell to the bastard who stole half of Ronnie's rum and Coke.

The world is different to different people because of the way their brains become organized. Why do different individuals have different kinds of minds? Or different kinds of anything? You would think that evolution would strive to make us all alike. In an influential paper, John Tooby and Irvin De Vore analyzed the biological reasons for individual variations. They concluded that variation results from the different world each individual confronts and the different situations throughout one's life. Often the interests of individuals are in conflict. Parents have different interests compared to their offspring. Offspring have different interests at different times of their lives. Saving oneself versus saving relatives is also a different interest.

And individuals are adapted to their individual situation, not only to their local habitat. An individual's best strategy for survival may differ according to circumstance; it may depend on hundreds of different factors, including family size, position in the family, diet, height, sex, ability to attract parental attention and support. And many of these seem to have an effect on a person. Firstborns are more conservative, for instance, than those born later; tall people have a different path through life than those less gifted in the altitude department.

Evolution cannot provide a system that enables every individual to adapt perfectly. Instead, animals evolve to supply the *average* individual with the average number and level of abilities for the average environment in which the species evolved, in order to survive best.

You are your parents' bequest to human evolution. You can probably see much of them in your looks and bearing. But the common human heritage is manifold: all of us develop a large brain, erect posture, color vision. Nevertheless, each human being is also one of a kind—at once like all others and like no other person who has ever lived.

Generations differ in two ways: through the sexual recombination that occurs as each parent donates half of the child's chromosomes and through mutations. A mutation is a spontaneous change in the structure of one or more genes. Mutations, then, are accidents in the normal functioning of genetic replication.

Mutations happen by random generation, a mistake when the chromosomes from the mother and the father are combined at conception, caused by mistakes in DNA replication or physical damage to DNA molecules, which can be caused by environmental events, such as radiation.

Sexual reproduction introduces variation. Thus, sex is at the root of our individuality, in ways far more subtle than Freud thought, and in ways much more profound. Of course, it is a very important topic of both ordinary life (most people spend much of the time deciding about, choosing, switching, but mostly complaining about their partners) and in evolutionary biological thought.

Let's think of it this way. Consider any successful, that is, living, reproducing organism, be it a bacterium, plant, or animal. If it is adapted to its circumstances, why not clone it? The organism, by thriving and surviving, is by definition fit and survives well in the world. Why fix something that ain't broke? Why don't animals just produce carbon copies of themselves and not change things around? Why should evolution have selected the very complicated and risky process of sexual reproduction? Why take such a costly gamble to introduce genetic mixtures that might not be as good as the original plant or animal?

The very complicated evolution of sexual reproduction has, as would any development involving such difficulty, many justifications. One relevant incentive may well be that sexual recombination evolved in part to protect our ancestors from pathogenic forces—disease-producing effects of the environment.

Microorganisms, which carry the diseases, seem to be less able to attack sexually reproducing animals. Large, long-lived animals are great hosts for the multitudes of short-lived, rapidly evolving parasites. Large animals have large, warm, wet areas that are very delightful to the pathogens around them. And these pathogens have plenty of time to breed as well, for during an animal's lifetime an assaulting microorganism may have millions of generations to evolve to attack the host's physiology and immune system. This is one reason why there is always a constant risk from evolving viruses, the most lethal of which currently is the HIV virus. Once a microbe has solved the problem of attacking a host's immune system or other defenses, it can attack successfully all genetically identical individuals, such as a set of identical plants. Large living beings that reproduce as carbon copies would be ideal targets, and would all be wiped out.

So there might be one great advantage in evolving, at very great cost, the mechanics of sexual reproduction, as it would greatly reduce the risk of getting extinguished. Once done, this method of reproduction produces great variety, as we all know—in hair color, faces, weight, temperament; it produces variety in brains and minds too.

By mixing genes with those of another individual (and even one pair of human parents, at one mating, can produce 64 trillion genetically different offspring), an organism can protect its offspring from many, if not all, of the disease forces that have adapted to its own physiology during its life. But this means that any individual human population will do better if most of its members are genetically diverse.

Analyses of the differences within and among human populations lead to surprises; different ethnic groups do not differ substantially in the type of genes found among them, but individuals within each group do. The usual genetic difference between two average Italians is twelve times greater than the genetic difference between Italians and Malays.

Striking in human evolution is the small differences among regional groups and the large genetic variation among individuals. This is consistent with the view of sexual reproduction: In the world in which our ancestors evolved, an individual wouldn't be likely to catch diseases from organisms living across the world, but from neighbors. Individuals would need to evolve defenses against the illnesses of their neighbors. So we would expect each human population to comprise a large number of extremely different individuals, each with different kinds of resistance.*

One way that individuals differ is in temperament. It seems that some basic dimensions of the personality differ among people. And these differences are inherited. Some of us seem to do everything quickly and tackle several projects at a time, while others slowly, slowly labor, again and again, at each point. This difference in tempo makes some biologically destined to be accountants or stock traders, but not both.

3-9

Squadron of
simpletons.

*I am indebted to John Tooby and Leda Cosmides, as well as their collaborators, for this analysis.

People misjudge others greatly because they interpret temper-amental differences—speed of action, cleanliness, messiness, as reflections of the conscious mind. But these characteristics seem rather to be components of the personality over which we have little or no control. If this is true, we will all have to learn, in getting along with others, that there is much about our friends and spouses that we and they will never change. Consciousness can make some changes, some quite important ones, but it cannot, it seems alter some of the mind's individual and most fundamental routines.

Important here is the awareness that educational systems and family environments may need to differ greatly to be effective for different people. A sociable child may not mind the sting of rebuke if it is followed by a loving interlude, but a more introverted child may be affected far more seriously. We have much to do in the future to alter schools, to take into account the differences in students' minds. The way the world develops these "thousand forms of mind" is more striking than we had thought. It sets us on a course that determines our lives. The things of our youth—important attributes such as language and accent, unimportant ones such as food preferences—seem to influence us like nothing else in our lives. They play a major role in the way we adapt to our local world.

11

How the World Develops the Mind

The growth and flourishing of an individual being, like the process of evolution itself, is a contest. Where biological evolution is a sluggish struggle, one whose outcome is not perceptible for millennia, which does not change an individual's nature within a lifetime, our own development is a vicious struggle inside our brains and bodies early in life.

To trace how the world selects the mind, we will not be able to consider the complexity of the billions of brain interactions at once. To get a better idea of the principles involved, consider a simpler system than the nervous system—the immune system. Here too the world develops individuals differently. We adapt to the pathogens in our immediate world, and when we move we are subject to disease. And until the sixteenth century, the different adaptations were isolated. But when world travel began, so much later in the body's history, unprecedented illness resulted.

In 1969 Gerald Edelman worked out how the antibody molecule operates, providing an important clue as to which structures within the body are needed to produce the millions of different kinds of antibodies to defend us against disease. The immune system is not a set of visible organs and structures, as is the nervous or the pulmonary. It comprises many different cells and

Neural Darwinism.

molecules throughout most of the body. And, as Jonas Salk pointed out in a seminal paper, the immune system has similarities to the nervous system. Both respond to a great variety of stimuli; receive and transmit signals, which are either excitatory or inhibitory; and show learning and memory.

The system has to recognize what is foreign—not of the body—and what is not. When a foreign body is recognized, the whole system springs into action. At the same time, the immune system must not attack the cellular and molecular constituents of the body itself. And this restraint is difficult, because diseases differ throughout the world.

But babies can be born anywhere. So how could evolution have prepared us to develop specific immunity to the individual diseases in the many different locales in which human beings develop? The immune cells differentiate wildly in embryonic life. And, like the thousand forms of mind, this process produces a vast range of cells, each one with different specific surface receptors. Specialized cells in the blood produce one of the many kinds of antibodies that become attached to the cell surface. An antibody molecule that fits into an antigen—a virus or bacterium—binds to the virus or bacterium.

The connection of antigen and antibody sets off cell division, producing thousands of copies of the same antibodies, which then bind to the foreign agent. The body then is easily able to rid itself of a virus or any foreign body if the cells in the bloodstream are able to multiply. Usually many different cells do this. After early development, the immune system doesn't have to learn; it is already preadapted to the pathogens the organism is likely to encounter.

Thus, the invading virus, by its molecular shape, selects its defender and selects its own demise. When a specific disease entity appears, it has already been selected for by events in the organism's development. And during development, other systems, the digestive and the nervous among others, learn to identify what is us, what we do, and what we don't.

The World Health Organization was recently surprised to find women in Ghana carrying infants to term with a daily caloric intake far below that needed in the West. Were they cheating, or were they adapted to a different set of circumstances, so that they could operate differently on the same but less food, somehow incorporating more nutrients than do Western women accustomed to more abundance? The brain and mind, too, learn what is us and what isn't during this time of development.

Edelman considered whether the brain, too, may function as this kind of selective system. His theory is called *Neural Darwinism*. It assumes that natural selection of a different sort happens to neurons; like the immune system, neurons select themselves and connect together during development as a function of their stimulation. The world wires up the mind.

The most dazzling biological achievement in nature begins when a male's sperm unites with a female's ovum. During the next nine months, the fertilized cell divides again and again, forming the brain, internal organs, muscles, skin, and bones. Only about fifty divisions of that first cell beget a baby! No one knows why some cells become brain; others tongue.

What we do know is that a speck starting so small that it is barely detectable under a microscope bursts upon the scene in forty weeks in the form of a 7-pound baby. Although babies are helpless and immature at birth, the seeds of adult abilities are present from the beginning. But they have to develop in a specific world.

Neural selection must happen because genes don't specify exact structure, only potential. As the embryo develops, the original cells divide, move, and become specialized. There is no particular specialization of the kinds of cells during embryonic and fetal development. A cell in a particular site in the embryo may become brain because of *where* it is, not *what* it is, and in another place may become the heart for the same reason. The myriad brain cells in the human brain can thus assume many identities.

This is because the cells' ultimate destination is not commanded by their individual nature, but by their place in the scheme of things. A cell in one area becomes skin, another, part of the liver. If their locations were reversed during development, so would be their final nature.

The process is similar to how the components of any structure are refined to form the structure. The same molecule of ink can have different meanings, dependent on place. It may become a letter *n* in *now*, or it may become the letter *z* in *zoo*; without having to change its own structure, its higher-level organization and its meaning changes. Thus it is that cells are formed into neuronal

groups, which are like the letters of the brain, the basic operating units, each capable of working in various "stories."

Because the environment is so different for different human beings, different circumstances develop the brain in different ways. Through neuronal selection in infancy, the cells in the brain that strike a match with the environment thrive; those that do not, fall into disuse. These are the thousand potential forms of mind. Maybe there are many more, but each of us has only a few of them. Again, we need to be a little technical about our inheritance.

During development, different stimulation causes the brain to be wired up differently. Enshroud the eye of an animal, even for a few days, during critical periods of development, and examine brain structures from which the eyes feed. There are remarkable differences. In the eye with normal development, you see a normal functioning of the visual cortex. In an organism that has had its eye covered even for a few days during development, however, you see an almost atrophied set of cells in the cortex. This is because during development there is the same kind of competition within the brain of every organism as there is among individuals in society.

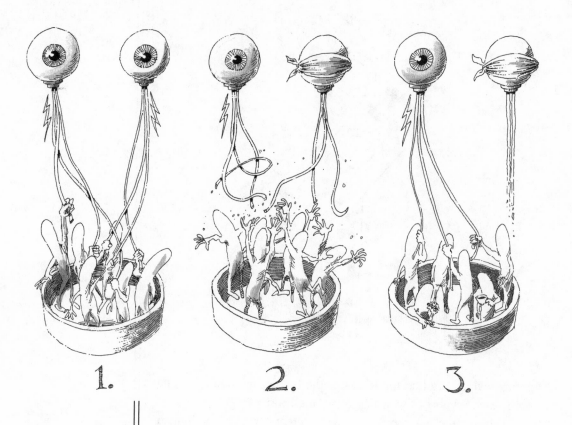

1.   2.   3.

3-12

(1) Early on, all cells have an equal chance. (2) During the period of "exuberant" growth, they connect. Here, with one eye covered, cells connect only to the sighted eye. (3) Only one eye gets wired up.

In the embryo, each individual develops a specific pattern of neural connections inside the brain. After birth, at different fixed periods in different organisms, new patterns of neural connections develop. The selection of these patterns occurs in groups of cells that relay messages to each other in response to environmental stimuli—horizons, sunrises, the sounds of a language. This is a way of understanding how different kinds of adaptive behavior arise in the strikingly different environments that animals and human beings inhabit.

Each individual center of action seems to be doing the same thing. When we read a book, we don't read letters but words or sentences. Sometimes we read ideas. And most often, usually when we are unaware, we simply understand something without knowing how or why.

I TOOK THE CAT OUT.

Different means, same message.

I took the cat out can be conveyed in hundreds of different ways, if not thousands. It can be printed as it is in this book, it can be written in capitals, it can be written in lower-case, it can be printed in any one of a number of different typefaces. The letters can be written in any form of shorthand. It can be said over the telephone, it can be relayed via telegraph, it can be in a random dot message on a screen. An infinite variety of signals can convey the thought *I took the cat out.* They can be produced or grasped in many different ways, part of the second system of thought we have, producing a semblance of the world.

Producing a semblance is a way around the zillions of possible combinations of things we would otherwise have to learn. For the brain works in layers, storing signals from one layer and eventually creating more abstract representations. Otherwise we couldn't even recognize a cup from different angles.

Since we are equipped for action, not comprehensive understanding, our brain seeks significance, not specific bits of information. We learn general semblances of the world, just enough to get by. That's why we don't, can't, store the zillion ways we could write or communicate *I took the cat out* not to mention the billion other sentences we could think of immediately.

During early development nerve cells compete with one another to survive, to connect into working groups, so that they persevere. If cells are given a certain kind of stimulation, some connect to others and form neural groups; if not, they conjoin with others. Because of experiences early on in the world, the nervous system gets wired up in a different ways.

Consequently, individuals have different brains because of their early experiences. Of course, later development can also have an effect. Early experiences, especially those of deprivation, can be overcome, and later experiences, such as the shock of battle, can dramatically and permanently change the nature of the brain. But it is in the first years that most of the world's selection of the mind takes place. Here I do not refer to those events close to us that we remember—a loving father or a distant one, fights or cooperation with one's brothers and sisters—but much more basic parts of the psyche.

Consider language. Like immunity, it "picks up" the surround, and it isn't, for the most part, taught. During development the mother coos, talks, and makes the sounds of almost every word in the language of the area in which, of course, the child is going to be speaking. At the same time, the child babbles and produces the sounds of almost every known language. Those sounds that relate to the language that's being spoken (say, English) get wired up in the person; those phonemes and sounds, expressions, and gestures that are not used in the language group do not link up. At this point in life, specific features of speech such as accent become fixed, based on the kinds of intonations a child hears during this period. And accent is difficult to change, though it isn't taught. The world just does it, as the brain seems to wire up around the sounds and sights it hears, in a process similar to the way the immune system is organized.

Again, our amazingly redundant brain oversupplies us with possibilities for living all over the earth (or, rather, has made this diversity possible). It is as if we are given the ability to speak hundreds of thousands of languages, make thousands of gesture and sign organizations, be able to live in thousands of different areas, and that evolution, working to adapt to the world and working to protect our physiology, has provided us with a brain with "a thousand forms of mind."

Even what the baby hears in the womb affects the blossoming brain. One recent investigation began with a group of women in their thirty-second week of pregnancy. The women, as part of a research study, recited a paragraph of a children's story three times in a row each day until birth. Each mother voiced one of three different passages.

The newborns then heard all three passages. Two days after birth the babies were given a special nipple and earphones. (In babies the sucking reflex is probably the only reflex that can be conditioned; by changing their rate of sucking, they could choose to hear one of the three passages.) The babies chose the familiar passage. So before birth, fetuses apparently can learn something about the world they will inhabit. This selection moves the child's development along one track or another, selecting some information, rejecting some. The sounds an infant hears in the womb probably predispose it to respond to the language group into which it is born. Even during development in the womb, the outside world selects neuronal groups.

In another study twenty-four newborns listened to the sound

of a heartbeat or a woman speaking. They were able to indicate which ear should hear the sound by varying the frequency with which they sucked a pacifier. Babies chose to hear speech in the right ear and heartbeat in the left. So the brain seems to be already specialized, if rudimentarily, at birth for hearing language. The two hemispheres of the brain seem to be to some extent acting in a lateralized way at birth.

When we enter into the world, we live in one certain area with one family in one culture eating one style of food at one elevation at one distance from the ocean in one style of house in one natural ecology. No brain could be prepared for that, so it comes into the world incompletely organized. During the long period of infancy, our early environment "selects" the specific minds to survive.

While human beings, unlike almost any other animal, are preadapted to live all over the earth, no single human being lives everywhere. Most don't need the high-altitude adaptations of the ancient Inca Indian near Machu Picchu or the development of the !Xosa click sounds. I don't need to speak Sanskrit. A peasant in the Philippines doesn't need to speak English. I don't need to be adapted to eat hot food; the Japanese aren't adapted to cheese.

Adaptation takes place when we try to learn a language. Most of us find no problem learning a first language. We imbibe it, as it is, with our mother's milk. As we imbibe her immune molecules, we also imbibe her phonemes. We learn how to speak, we hear certain tones that signify English speakers or certain tonal groups that signify Chinese or other speakers. Those neurons that produce tones that are not used in our language group wither. Consider the difficulty that most Westerners have when trying to learn Japanese when they are middle-aged or that Japanese people have trying to learn English when they are middle-aged.

Kittens raised so that they see only horizontal lines can never develop the capacity to detect vertical lines to the same degree as horizontal lines. They can learn to see vertical lines but not very well. Such is also the case with binocular vision when kittens are raised in the dark. Without the opportunity to use the eyes together in the critical developmental period, the kittens can never develop the capacity to overlap the visual fields of the two eyes.

Early restrictions also affect humans. One study compared students from Western cities, which contain many horizontal and vertical outlines but few oblique ones, to a group of Cree Indians, whose homes contained lines in all orientations. The students had less acuity for oblique lines than the Indians did.

The nervous system begins with a great number of possibilities and elects them during our early years. An infant born in Milwaukee or Nîmes or a Pygmy tribe can expect a peaceful, monogamous situation. Most likely mechanisms in the brain monitor cues that are reliable over evolutionary time in predicting the kind of world in which the child will be raised. If you were treated violently as a child, chances are probably good you were born into a social milieu in which violence is important.

Abused children are much more aggressive when they become adults, which would seem to indicate that such abused children learn that abuse is a way of life. The average child witnesses

15,000 murders before adolescence; one wonders how this affects how their minds are constructed. Different events in our young world may activate different kinds of strategies.

So the human brain, coming into the world with a vast oversupply of nerve circuits, wires up differently with different early experiences. It is a contest among the neurons like that of evolution itself; hence the name, neural Darwinism. Selection here is offered by the local environment, so to specialize our very general mind. The great brain gets developed differently so that each individual has a better chance to match her or his specific small world.

IV

Pieces of the Puzzle: Brain Processes and Organization

Each of us has talents that never develop.

The brain evolved primarily to control different body reactions. It is more like the liver than it is like a computer. It isn't organized for thought. Those operations that seem most human—language, perception, intelligence—make up only a small fraction of the brain's functions. If you were to ramble through the brain at random, checking cells here and there as you moved, you might at most find 1 or 2 percent working on thoughtful acts. Thus, the idea that we aren't using 95 percent (or some percentage) of the brain can't be true for a living being, since most of it is completely engaged.

The brain "minds" the body, as its neurons control temperature, blood flow, and digestion. It monitors every sensation, each breath and heartbeat, every movement, every blink and swallow. It directs movement: walk this way, take the hand off the stove, lift the arm to catch the ball, smile. If you weren't an educated human being, you might think of the brain as just the body controller, not the seat of rationality.

Yet the cortex does contain something rather new: Recruited in less than a million years, nestling separate from the rest of the brain, is a complex of new talents involving language, symbol making.

You might call it the modern communication center, for the emergence of modern humanity was in part based upon cooperative efforts. Organized groups can accomplish what no individual could, so cities were built, land was farmed, and industry and technology were created out of nothing. An important part of the specialization of the human brain is to communicate complex information that connects individuals into a larger group, a society, one in which their own chances to survive are improved, as are their chances to pass on their genes.

12

The Divided Brain
and Its Divided Minds

The cerebral cortex is only about one-eighth of an inch thick. Of all mammals, human beings have the most enfolded cortex, perhaps because such a large cortex had to fit into a head small enough to survive birth. The cortex is layered with specialized cells arranged in columns. The columns each have specific functions, such as the visual detection of corners and edges. They act as data-processing centers in the cortex, serving as "modules" for the interpretation of information.

These columns of cells do the basic analysis work of the mind. They interpret a pattern of sounds and translate it into language. They analyze millions of bits of visual information to determine size, shape, and position. They decode a set of squiggles, such as 2 + 2 = 4, into meaningful mathematical symbols. They track the position of the limbs to allow you to turn and avoid an oncoming car. They interpret the sounds of music and much, much more. There are probably modules for specific reactions and patterns of activity too.

Inside the cortex are centers of talents. Talent is an unusual word to use but describes brain operation. Most people probably have more of one talent than another. These abilities, moving gracefully or speaking fluently, exist as mental, behavioral, as well as anatomical, units. Each has a rich concentration of certain abilities. If you imagine each of these areas as a patch, the cortex would look much like a folded patchwork quilt.

The cortex is divided into two hemispheres, connected by a large structure of 300 million neurons called the corpus callosum. The division of functions into two separated hemispheres is what makes us distinctively human, distinctly creative, and distinctly isolated from our mental processes. It is the most recent development in human evolution, less than 4 million years old.

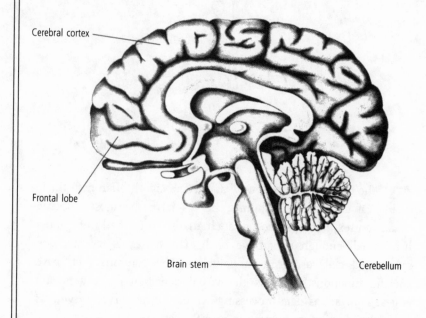

Cerebral cortex

Frontal lobe

Brain stem

Cerebellum

The cerebral cortex. The visible part of the brain is the surface of the cortex, which is thin and enfolded compactly to fit inside the skull. Fifty percent of the cortex is enfolded. The cortex is shown here in relation to the brain stem and cerebellum and to the limbic system, to which it is linked and which it surrounds.

The left hemisphere controls the right side of the body. It also controls language and logical activities—things that happen in a specific order. The right hemisphere controls the left side of the body. It directs spatial, simultaneous things—which happen all at once—and artistic activities. These differences probably appeared when our ancestors began to make and use symbols (both language and art).

In the 1960s Roger Sperry and Joseph Bogen of Cal Tech invented a radical treatment for severe epilepsy in human beings. They cut the callosum, producing a split brain. After the surgery, if patients held an object, such as a pencil, hidden from sight, in the right hand, they could describe it verbally. However, if the object was in the left hand, they could not describe it at all. Recall that the left hand informs the right hemisphere, which has a limited capability for speech. With the corpus callosum severed, the verbal (left) hemisphere is no longer connected to the right hemisphere, which communicates largely with the left hand. Here the verbal apparatus literally does not know what is in the left hand.

Sometimes the patients were presented with keys, books, pencils, and the like, all out of sight. They were asked to select the previously given object with the left hand. The patients chose correctly, although they still could not verbalize what object they were taking. It was as if they were asked to perform an action and someone else was discussing it.

The surgery revealed two systems at the "top" of the human brain. They govern our abilities to create, in language and in art, and to discover new connections in the world. To do this, we evolved such mental regional authorities, which can work efficiently while not knowing what is going on in the rest of the head. In part this works because the sequences of information underlying language are a different adaptation than the all-at-once ideation that underlies art and movement in space. How well could you dance if you thought about each foot and arm movement? And how well could you read if you did not read every word in the correct order?

As startling as the split-brain studies are, an important question remains: How do the hemispheres operate in normal people doing normal things? In 1969 I began a research program that was to examine the rapport between brain and mental state. One way we have of finding out what a normal brain is doing is by measur-

4-3

Major structures of the human brain.

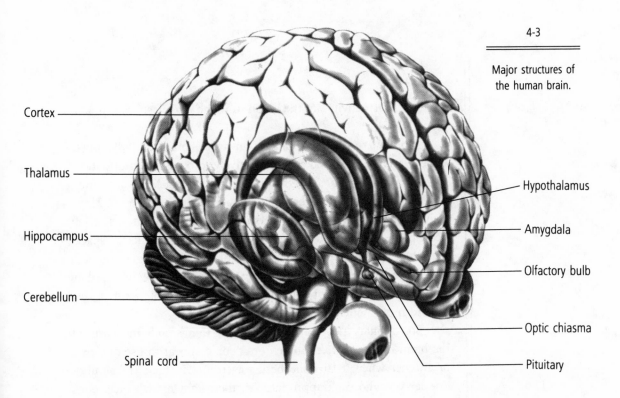

Cortex

Thalamus

Hippocampus

Cerebellum

Spinal cord

Hypothalamus

Amygdala

Olfactory bulb

Optic chiasma

Pituitary

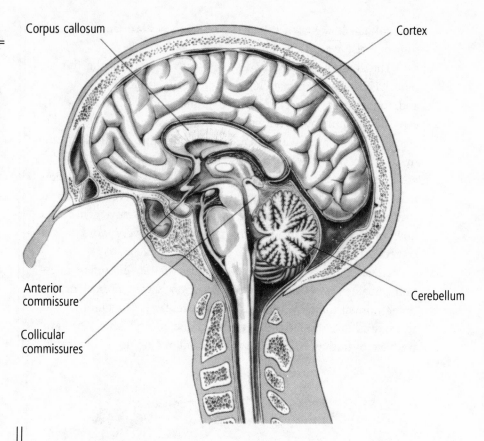

Corpus callosum

Cortex

Anterior commissure

Collicular commissures

Cerebellum

ing electrical activity in the brain through an electroencephalograph (EEG).

Alpha-wave activity indicates an awake brain on "idle"; beta waves indicate an awake brain actively processing information. David Galin and I, at the University of California Medical Center, were able to show that the right hemisphere showed more alpha activity than the left while a person was writing a letter; the left hemisphere showed more beta. While arranging blocks in space, the left hemisphere produced more alpha than the right, and the right hemisphere showed beta waves. When people write, they turn off the right side of the brain; while arranging blocks in space, they turn off the left hemisphere.

So, ordinary people doing everyday things shift the parts of the brain that are active. Sometimes people appear to use one part or another when it isn't the best: they're not in their right mind. The lawyer who can't appreciate art, the ceramicist who has poor

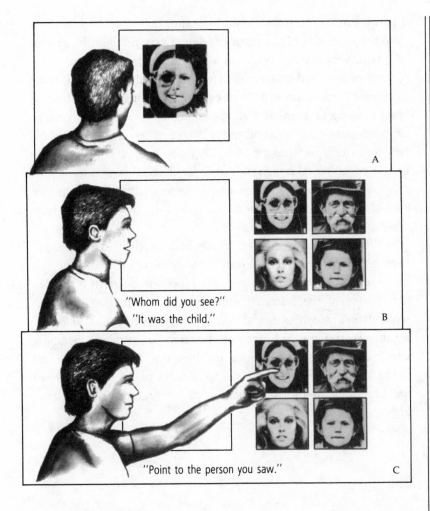

"Whom did you see?"
"It was the child."

"Point to the person you saw."

Hemisphere specialization and visual input. A composite photograph of two different faces is flashed before a split-brain subject (A). When shown a group of photographs and asked to pick out the person he saw in the composite, he will *say* it is the face from the *right* half of the composite (B). But if asked to *point out* which one he originally saw, he will indicate the picture from the *left* side of the composite (C). Such experiments suggest the two hemispheres are independent to some degree, each performing different functions in different ways. (AFTER SPERRY, 1982)

verbal skills—both are obvious examples of people who are stuck in one mode or another of brain function.

However, in a later experiment, Charles Swencionis and I found that people can change their patterns of brain activation. We recorded brain activity while people mentally rotated objects. This operation normally involved the right hemisphere. When asked to do the task analytically, by counting the boxes, subjects by and large "switched over" to their left hemisphere. People can use their hemispheres differently in problem solving at will.

These two hemispheres appeared in our ancestors as specialized systems some time during the long period of human evolution. Of course, they weren't recruited without a preliminary basis, since New World monkeys have specializations in their hemispheres. But in humanity, some time after that great brain expansion, the two sides of the brain developed very different functions.

Size, which we've been discussing at length, isn't everything. A stack of hundred-dollar bills, after all, would take up the same space as a stack of dollar bills or even of wrapping paper. After the brain fired up to its modern mass millions of years ago, the cells so supplied developed specializations. There is evidence of this (so far) ultimate specialization 40,000 years ago, and it probably happened earlier, although no earlier fossils exhibiting it have been found. These specialized faculties are the most distinctively human part of the brain, that portion that makes us most different from other animals.

While the major division in the brain is that of the cerebral hemispheres, more recent research makes clear invisible divisions in the way the brain handles separate functions. Sections of the left hemisphere of the human cortex seem well suited to operating sequentially, which is useful for deciding speech and following arguments and the like; the rest function for parallel operation, which underlies spatial abilities and intuition. But the work I did in the 1970s following Sperry's seminal work of the 1960s was just the beginning of the turn away from the "rational" single-brain idea.

13

How the Brain Knows What You're Doing Before You Do

He who sees not the hand which effects the writing
Fancies the effect proceeds from the
motion of the pen.

—RUMI

One sees the components of the mental system in extremities of action, some extraordinary. A famous event occurred in 1988, famous to those interested in Formula 1 automobile racing, anyway. What is interesting about this story is what it tells us about the way consciousness works and sometimes doesn't work. It took place in Monaco, the most picturesque "race track," actually not a track at all but a route that winds through the streets of the coastal city. The race is a slow one by Formula 1 standards, because it is a very engaging one that requires much concentration. The driver is constantly shifting, braking, accelerating, and watching for others on the track.

A recent world driving champion, Ayrton Senna, found himself driving in an extraordinary way during the race at Monaco. He felt as if someone else, not him, was doing the driving. And it was during his most impressive effort, as he describes it to a British journalist:

139

I remember starting: going quicker and quicker, I was on pole [the fastest in qualifying]. I was on pole by a few tenths of a second and then by half a second and then over a second. I was just *going*. More and more—there was a stage when I was over two seconds quicker than anybody else [which is unheard of], including my teammate with the same equipment.

I realized at that moment, suddenly! (Senna snaps his fingers) that I was well over something conscious. Monaco is small and narrow, and at that moment, I had the feeling that I was in a tunnel—the circuit was just a tunnel for me. It was going-going-going and within the physical limit of the circuit, it was like I was on rails. Of course, I wasn't on rails. Then, suddenly, I realised it was too much: I slowed down. I drove myself slowly back to the pits and said to myself that I shouldn't go out any more that day.

Because for that moment I was vulnerable for extending my own limits, and the car's limits: limits that I never touch[ed] before. I was not aware, exactly, of what was going on—not that I was not in control—I was just going-going-going. An amazing experience.

Ayrton Senna is not only one of the greatest drivers today, one who is noted for performances that seem to go beyond himself. But perhaps some of his greatness, as in other great athletes, comes from allowing one of his "minds" to operate independently, outside voluntary control. In this case a mind deep inside gained control and ran the show, driving in an unsupervised and uninhibited manner until the conscious Senna, the one who could give this interview to Britain's *Car* magazine, became alarmed at what this nonconscious mind was doing as it took over. (Incidentally, Senna must have loosened the usual conscious controls in his mind, for he went over the edge the next day for the single time in his career and had a rare unprovoked crash.)

Virtuosos in all arenas, women and men who produce at the edge of their ability, such as concert maestros, make hand movements much faster than can be controlled consciously. And not only virtuosos can accomplish such feats, for typists do the same. Another mind takes over and doesn't ask questions, doesn't require any conscious direction.

My concern here is not about sports, virtuosos, or grand prix racing but some very important research on the brain's functions during voluntary action. There exist different centers of mind in the brain, and "we" often don't know what we're doing until we see what we do. However, one has to look for it carefully.

Usually the transition between the controlling forces of the mind is smooth, and we never notice shifts in control (although it is easier seen in children). In some adults, such as those with multiple personalities, the mind switches function more crudely. But in all of us, minds shift in and out of place, minds analyze the world for distinctive signals that tell us what to do, minds act as dedicated world processors so seductively that we never know what is happening.

Senna's insight while functioning at and just above the limit demonstrates that different parts of the mind can control it without our awareness. We do not know who is in charge. Such nonconscious control can happen to us while performing in sport, making music, creating a painting, or just cooking or thinking. Some times, rare times, we experience ourselves as more selves than one. Obviously evolution built self on self, specific reaction on top of specific reaction. But what are they, and where are they?

New technology and research have turned up evidence on how different centers of the brain operate, which may form the foundation of a scientific analysis of this split-mindedness. Before plunging into this material, let's go back and see how we use brain electronics to help us understand the mind.

That the brain is electric has been understood since 1875, when the English scientist Richard Catton wrote that "in every brain hitherto examined, the galvanometer has indicated the existence of electric currents. . . . The electric currents of the brain matter appear to have a relation to its function."

Fifty years later, Hans Berger developed the first system for recording brain electricity that did not require opening the skull. Berger's experiments became possible thanks to advances in electronics allowing undistorted amplification of minute quantities of the energy current in brain waves. (A typical alpha wave has an amplitude of about 50 microvolts, 50-millionths of a volt. And an alpha wave is a big one in the brain.) With his technique, brain waves could be recorded with small metal plates, called electrodes, applied to the skin of the scalp.

Although the electroencephalogram has made it possible to study the brain function of intact, healthy humans and animals, it is not a very precise measure. It is crudely analogous to assessing the activity levels of large populations, in this case groups of neurons. Studying brain function with the EEG is like trying to understand what is happening in New York by recording the overall noise from different areas of the city from a satellite 250 miles above the surface of the earth. Although the measures would be very faint, we'd find that the satellite's recordings bear relationship to activities in the city. In the central business area, the records would show a lot more noise at noon than they would at midnight. The activity would disperse at the end of a workday, fanning out to a low-level hum more evenly distributed among several areas.

We know that this aggregated noise might involve any number of individuals traveling to and from work, working in a central area, and then leaving for the evening. We also know that people would be doing all different kinds of things, making deals, making drinks, making plans, making trysts, that stock prices would be going through the ceiling or the floor, and that all of these activities would be happening in different places.

However, the relation between the total sound level produced by all the people together and an individual's action would account for almost nothing. There is no way to tell how the stock market is doing from the noise of the city in the suburbs on a quiet Sunday night. There is no way to tell about the quality of an ad campaign from the noise of the city in the center at 2:30 in the afternoon. And, likewise it is impossible to know much about the particulars of neuronal function from the EEG.

So, measures of the brain activity, while they might seem very impressive to nonscientists, because they are recorded in millionths of volts, are really very poor tools. Moreover, individuals have different kinds of brain structures, so that some areas of the brain may be enfolded away from the skull in certain people but not in others. All these make trying to understand the brain much more difficult, in fact, than trying to understand the works of Picasso being displayed at the Museum of Modern Art with but three sensors on a satellite 250 miles above New York City. It's not even close.

One lucky event for brain science is that the areas of the brain that most interest us, the "new" areas that ballooned up 2 million years ago, which now play a role in human creativity, thought, and action, sit by chance (perhaps for heat dissipation) on the outside of the cortex. The activity of the cortex is the area best represented in the EEG.

Although our methods are still barely adequate, there has been progress in studying the mind within the brain. In 1942 Wilder Penfield, a neurosurgeon, made a startling discovery while working on a patient with a brain tumor. To study which parts of the brain were active, he stimulated the brain at different locations with electrical current. Penfield probed once and received no response; again, and the subject's fingers twitched. And then:

> 11-"I heard something, I do not know what it was."
>
> 11-(Probe repeated without warning the patient) "Yes, Sir, I think I heard a mother calling her little boy somewhere. It seemed to be something that happened years ago." When asked to explain, she said, "It was somebody in the neighborhood where I live." Then she added that she herself "was somewhere close enough to hear."
>
> 12-"Yes, I heard voices down along the river somewhere— a man's voice and a woman's voice calling . . . I think I saw the river."
>
> 15-"Just a tiny flash of a feeling of familiarity and a feeling that I knew everything that was going to happen in the near future."
>
> 17c-"Oh! I had the same very, very familiar memory, in an office somewhere. I could see the desks. I was there, and someone was calling to me, a man leaning on a desk with a pencil in his hand." I warned her I was going to stimulate, but I did not do so: "Nothing."
>
> 18a-(Stimulation without warning) "I had a little memory—a scene in a play—they were talking and I could see it—I was just seeing it in my memory."

Each time Penfield's electrode was inserted into a particular spot, a similar experience was stimulated. Penfield writes: "I was more astonished each time my electrode brought forth such a response. How could it be? This had to do with the mind. I called such responses 'experiential'."

The nature of the experiences evoked depended on where on the cortex he applied the current. Penfield had discovered a clue to the relationship between mental experience and the architecture of the brain. If nothing else, he showed that the electricity of the brain was important to mental experience. Neuroscience was now off and running, trying to localize which parts of the brain were responsible for which functions of mind and body.

These days, few educated minds would be boggled by the notion that minds have, in general, something to do with the brain. However, as technology advances, so does our ability to measure and examine the functions of our brains, and some of the results are boggling indeed. Recent findings in neurophysiology and neuropsychology raise deep questions about who is responsible for our actions—even our deliberately, consciously willed ones. Suppose I asked you to move your right index finger sometime in the next minute without planning to do it at any specific time. Just move it spontaneously. Now what would you say if I told you that, working as a neuropsychologist, with my recording equipment and computers, I could predict when you were about to move your finger *before* you could? This flies in the face of our normal belief that we, our conscious selves, are in immediate control of our behavior. Nevertheless, it seems that all of our movements are planned and initiated outside of our awareness, by one of the many simpletons within the brain.

Twenty-five years ago, German neurophysiologists discovered that prior to physical movements gradual shifts in the electrical potentials appeared in the brain. This "contingent negative variation" shows up when a person is warned that at some time soon she will have to do something such as press a button as quickly as possible when a red light flashes.

It is not too surprising to find that, when we are waiting and preparing to do something, our brains reflect this state of preparedness. However, another gradual shift in the electrical output from the cortex has surprising properties. This brain wave, called the "readiness potential," happens before voluntary, self-willed action. It begins to appear from about a half second to up to three seconds before the beginning of a movement.

These waves occur only before consciously willed movements, that is, not before reflexive actions such a pulling away from a painful stimulus or scratching an itch. One whole second or more

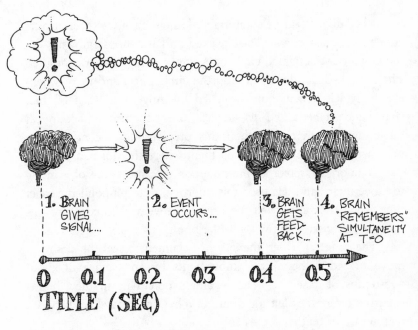

1. BRAIN GIVES SIGNAL...

2. EVENT OCCURS...

3. BRAIN GETS FEEDBACK...

4. BRAIN "REMEMBERS" SIMULTANEITY AT T=0

0   0.1   0.2   0.3   0.4   0.5

TIME (SEC)

before you move, your brain is already preparing to move even when the action is "spontaneous." Now, we certainly don't feel as if there is a one-second lag between our commands to our muscles and their obedience. So what is going on here? Are automatic mechanisms, unavailable to consciousness, running the show, allowing us but the illusion that we are in control? Maybe, and for those who still doubt, Benjamin Libet and his colleagues set up an experiment that spelled out plainly the temporal relationship between the conscious will to act and the events in the brain.

Their work demonstrates the existence of independent centers of neural control in the mind. These individual control centers produce a crowd of cerebral actors, each clamoring to get on stage. The result is that internal conflict is endemic to the nervous system. This is not a flaw. It makes sense for survival, because it is simpler to have a squadron of simpletons acting for us, rather than one all-knowing system, just as it is more efficient to have an office of specialized assistants than to do everything yourself.

Libet asked his experimental subjects to tell him when they were going to do something. He looked for the appearance of the readiness potential and compared the time of its onset with the timing of the subject's report of the onset of the feeling of "wanting" to act. He found something startling: The brain begins the process of moving before the person even knows about it.

The subjects sat in comfortable lounge chairs with electrodes attached to their heads. They relaxed and watched a glowing dot moving around a lighted circle on a screen attached to a computer. They watched the dot go around the circle once, and then, whenever they felt like it, quickly flexed the fingers or wrist of their right hands. Libet asked his subjects to "let the urge to act appear on its own at any time without any preplanning or concentration on when to act." Then he asked them where the dot had been on the circle on the screen at the time they became aware of wanting to move their hand. He used this information to pinpoint the exact time when the subject felt the urge to move and to compare this time to the onset of activities in the brain.

The times at which the subjects claimed to feel the desire to move preceded their actual movements by an average of about two-tenths of a second. The readiness potentials in their brains occurred *before* they felt the desire to move by somewhere between one- and four-tenths of a second.

You might think that the readiness potential could be a general preparation for a movement and that consciousness would monitor the timing of the exact movement. However, there is evidence that movements are not just preceded by general unconscious preparatory processes, but that the brain activity preceding a movement predicts what part of the body will be moved and how, well before the moment of conscious realization.

The type of movement to be made is reflected in the length and size of the readiness potential in the brain. Foot movements show a pattern distinct from that of finger movements. Pianists show preparatory brain activity longer before playing a melody than before playing a single note. Smoothness, effort, and the intention behind an action all affect the timing and size of the readiness potential, and all this happens before you are aware that you have begun to act! The scientists who pioneered this work, the Germans Pfurtscheller and Berghold wrote, "As early as 2 seconds prior to movement one has already decided which side of the body will later be moved."

Think about this. It takes about two seconds to say quickly, "I am going to pick up this pencil now." That is about how much time your pencil-moving simpleton spends preparing the action. How is it then that I can respond in less than two seconds, when, for example, the car ahead of me stops suddenly? The answer is that of course you can react more quickly than in two seconds, depending on who you think *you* are. Decisions about quick reactions are necessarily delegated to the simpletons below consciousness.

A "spontaneous" act therefore begins before we are aware we have "decided" to act. The decision, then, is often not up to "us," our conscious selves. Rather, we watch a part of our minds begin actions, "on their own authority," and can sometimes veto the orders before they make it out to the muscles. Our Englishman on the way to be hanged in chapter 10 would have been well advised to veto consciously his automatic advice-giving mind. Thus, we see the role and value of the conscious self in monitoring our behavior.

These studies of the origins of decisions to act show how two different components of mind can act independently or in concert. An unconscious decision center may decide to initiate an action, then there is a period of time during which the conscious self can choose to stop the action. Consciousness, the center of the mind/ brain system, may well have "negative options" on our actions, vetoing the proposals of the separated minds. However, it does not control or even know about the birth of these action-ideas and may be, in the same way that the left hemisphere is ignorant of the doings of the right, unable to "tell" why one of the minds has done something.

This is why, I believe, people will say, "How do I know what I think until I hear what I say?" And why much human creativity— painting, writing, dancing—comes forth without the conscious intervention of the artist. Once the idea for the artistic work is revealed by the unconscious creator, the artist can consciously manipulate and refine it. We do not possess one great teeming unconscious, but instead have a system of many small unconscious minds, each with its own program. We are each somewhat like a mutiple personality, organized and controlled to a limited extent by the conscious self.

Our ignorance goes even further than unawareness of the origins of our own behavior. We naturally assume that when we become aware of something around us, we see it as it happens. However, Libet has produced evidence suggesting that consciousness doesn't become aware until other centers are.

Libet's study of the minds above and below consciousness began more than ten years before his voluntary-action studies. At that time, he had the opportunity to work with patients who, for medical purposes, had electrodes implanted in the surface of the cortex and the interior of the brain through a small hole drilled in the front part of the skull. The brain contains no pain-detecting organs, so no anesthesia was required during the experiments and the patients were fully conscious and interested in assisting.

Libet and his colleagues set out, following in Penfield's footsteps, to determine the nature of conscious experiences evoked by electrical stimulation of various parts of the brain. He discovered that by applying a series of electrical pulses to a certain area of the cortex in a particular pattern he could cause the patient to feel a nearly natural sensation of being touched on the arm.

These sets of electrical impulses had to last for about half a second before the patient would feel a sensation. Therefore, Libet hypothesized that the cortical neurons he was stimulating needed to be active for at least half a second before the person would become aware of a tactile stimulus. He called this minimum length of activity required for the perception of a conscious sensation "neuronal adequacy."

He then gave an electrical stimulus to the patient's wrist two-tenths of a second after starting a cortical stimulus lasting a half a second. He expected that in both cases there would be a half-second delay from the start of stimulation before the patient felt a sensation, and that since the cortical stimulation started first, it would be felt first. However, the patients felt the sensation from the skin stimulus *before* the one resulting from cortical stimulation. These same people had reported no sensations arising from electrical stimulation of the cortex that lasted less than half a second, so the skin stimulus must have been processed in an unexpected way. Libet then applied the electrical stimulus to neuronal pathways in the brain before they reached the cortex. This time he found that the subjects perceived the sensation caused by the brain stimulation at the same time as the sensation from the skin stimulation.

What difference does it make to the brain if the stimulus begins at the skin, before the cortex, or at the cortex? Both skin and subcortical stimulation produce an "evoked response"—a spike of neuronal activity—in the part of the cortex responsible for processing touch sensation. However, stimulation directed at the cortex does not produce this response. If the neurons of the cortex have to be active for a half second before a stimulus can reach neuronal adequacy and be felt consciously, how can we feel an electrical pulse at the wrist almost instantly?

Apparently the mind assembles experience like this: Something happens in the world, and it is perceived by our sense organs. This initial detection produces a spike of neuronal activity, the evoked potential, in the cortex. A half second later, if the stimulus was big or important enough to keep the neurons in the cortex that process it active, the stimulus reaches neuronal adequacy and the conscious mind becomes aware of it. However, and this is the tricky part, the conscious mind sees, hears, or feels the event as beginning at the time of the evoked potential, just a few milliseconds after it actually occurred. It is as if the brain, below our awareness, spends a half second deciding whether we should be allowed to know about what just happened. If it decides that it is best that we know, then it also informs us of when the event happened. However, note that, although we become conscious of the sensory stimulus, we cannot use our conscious will to respond to it in less than a half a second. This leaves our unconscious minds responsible for initiating any rapid reactions to the world.

So, we aren't consciously aware of events at the time they happen, but we think we are. A concrete example of this process in action is the experience of the runner at the starting block. He is off in a tenth of a second or less after the starting gun fires, long before the sound could reach neuronal adequacy in his brain. Nevertheless, he claims he heard the gun before taking off. Unconscious processes triggered his running, yet he has the impression that he consciously directed the action, because his brain refers his experience of the gunshot back to the time it occurred and triggered an evoked response.

This kind of delay between a stimulus and the attainment of neuronal adequacy for experiencing it may allow the mind some lag time to clean up inconsistencies or may act as a mechanism for "repressing" unwanted perceptions, something like the tape loop used in the public media to catch and delete "undesirable" speech or events. The requirement for neuronal adequacy could serve as a filter to prevent too much trivial information from entering consciousness. And the referral back in time would allow this brain "tape delay" to occur without putting us a half second out of synchrony with the world. The delay between events in the world and the brain's decision to let us know about them may mean that any fast (quicker than half a second) responses to events in the environment that are processed in this way must happen before the stimulus reaches conscious levels. Thus, we react to many things of which we are not even conscious.

Our experience of the world assembles in a fleeting instant, with no time for thinking but just enough for producing a best guess of the world. Later chapters will show that this process is much like a dream. Our waking world is as dreamt up as those we inhabit when we are asleep. Most, if not all, the time, our waking "dream" is accurate enough for us to get on just fine in the world. But you can feel for yourself one way that we fabricate the world in this simple, everyday example: Close your eyes and slide the point of a pencil or pen along a slightly rough surface, such as a carpet or tablecloth. Where do you feel the texture? You feel the bumps and ridges at the point of the pencil. This is an ordinary experience. But with what sense organ are you feeling this? Do you have receptors out there at the point of your pencil? Of course not, but the brain automatically refers the sensation of the pencil traveling over the rough surface to the spot in its map of the world where it locates the pencil point. Such perception occurs all the time, but we don't notice it, or rather, we don't need to notice it. This fabrication of reality happens from moment to moment, underlying all of our experiences, from the most simple to the most complex.

Ayrton Senna saw how the unconscious mind is in control, for he was operating at the limit, where fractions of a second are essential to performance. Consciousness can reach its limits in a world driving champion moving at breakneck speed or in a concert pianist moving her fingers at a breathtaking rate or in anyone else whose skill requires finesse in timing measured in tenths of a second. When we are operating at the limit, we may become aware that we cannot consciously control our actions and still function at peak. Nonetheless, our every action is initiated unconsciously, with the later permission or veto of consciousness, but we usually have no "need" to be aware of this.

Although it may seem like a complicated mess in there, multiple brain organization maximizes our ability to respond to a few essential dimensions of the outside world. We have many different kinds of minds within, some of which are specific to different situations, such as avoiding injury or seeking a mate.

Some are separate biological centers with specific abilities, such as smelling or recognizing faces. Some of the brain's specializations reflect the orgaization of the brain (left and right hemispheres) and some are tendencies of the mind—the need to respond to new events, to notice changes, to compare information and process it to produce a consistent and simple whole.

These "talents" range widely, because all organisms, especially human beings, have to do many different things at once. Some talents are standard features, such as the memory for odors; some are higher level and require training, such as calculating the trajectory of a comet. The most basic of the talents concern immediate survival; the more complex concern adapting to the world as it changes; and the most elaborate concern the ability to reason and the sense of the self. There are independent centers for memory, for movement, for mathematical ability, for decoding and producing speech, for sensory analysis, and much more. All of these centers seem to have independent minds, often acting without the awareness of the weak conscious self.

14

The Self Itself

Why don't we act the way "we" want ourselves to? Because "we" are not the same person from moment to moment, not the same "self" at all. Libet documented how the different centers of mind act, but such diversity can be witnessed all the time outside the lab; for example, when we don't know whether to trust our first intuitive response or to follow our more deliberated plan of action. What we might call intuition or subliminal perception may be the receipt of information by a center inaccessible to consciousness.

Not only scientists and thinkers misunderstand the nature of the mental system; all of us do so, every day. We assume that we are more consistent, more unified, than we are. We do so because the self itself is just another one of the many simpletons inside the brain, with its own limited role and insight. The idea most people have that they are consistent in the diverse situations of their lives is an illusion. The consistency in which we believe so much is not "us" any more than our panic reaction is us; both are just small, secluded, and separate sections of the mind, with no special access to the rest of mental processes.

Isolated, usually uncoordinated and alone, each section has restricted knowledge. The restriction on information underlies why, although we act wildly differently in special situations, we maintain a constant illusion of our personal unity and stability. But our personal judgment is wrong. We are not consistent, not stable; it is only our little self who believes so.

It is a constant hope that we're rational and that a judicious component of the human brain controls and orchestrates this parade of talents. Unfortunately for those who hold such a view, but fortunately for the biological survival of the organism, the commanding, controlling mental operating system (which might be called the self) is much more closely linked with emotions and the system of automatic bodyguards than with conscious thought and reason.

The frontal lobes intersect the pathways that convey information about people and events in the world and information about one's own state. They also contribute to the control of basic systems such as heart rate. Certainly there are different forms of emotions represented within each of the lobes, as well as some control of the expression of emotions.

The pivot of the internal self is emotion. This dominant "self-ish" brain lies in frontal lobe and limbic system linkages that appraise threats in the environment and organize quick actions. Human beings can override this usual mode of operation: Actions can be reconsidered, we can learn and grow from experiences, conscious control can modify ineffective tendencies. But most often and most reliably, especially in eras long gone, feeling our way through worked best.

The central readout within ourselves is an emotional appraisal of a change in the outside environment: Is it harmful? Should I move toward it or not? Should I stop or change what I am doing? Is it surprising? Should I attack? To ensure a rapid response to these appraisals, the self is linked with certain automatic response patterns, emotions, which prepare us for action.

While there is much more to emotions than a simple positive/negative, stop/start, approach/avoid program, more of our life is determined by these primitive appraisals than we, the conscious thinkers, might believe. Emotional response affects so much because it has been around so long a time and we must work through it in almost all normal activities.

Damage to the frontal area results in a loss of self—knowing identity, what we're doing. If these lobes are disturbed, we become incapable of planning, carrying out, or comprehending a complex action or idea and can't remember which clothes to wear when or even how to dress, or tragically, who friends are.

People seem to lose "themselves" in a most terrifying and disheartening way when something in the frontal lobes is destroyed. They seem able to deal well with situations in which they have experience but have difficulty knowing what to do in new circumstances. They lose the ability to monitor how they are behaving and how their actions relate to their intention. They often don't know why they are doing something. Their direction, their self, is largely gone.

But also important is that the evidence from such disorders reveals that the "self" is separate from other mental faculties, which are governed by another component of the brain. In Oliver Sacks's *The Man Who Mistook His Wife for a Hat,* one patient was describing the possible names for staff around her and felt that anything at all could be possible:

> "Of course," she said, with a chemist's precision. "You could call them *enantiomorphs* of each other. But they mean nothing to *me*. They're no different from *me*. Hands . . . Doctors . . . Sisters . . ." she added, seeing my puzzlement. "Don't you understand? They mean nothing to me. *Nothing means anything* . . . at least to me." Nothing any longer felt "real" (or "unreal").
>
> Everything was now "equivalent" or "equal," the world reduced to a facetious insignificance. When this woman lost her frontal lobes, she somehow lost the sense of who she was as a person.

Chimps with frontal lesions don't seem to mind if they make mistakes, probably because there is no self there to "mind" the matter. The vogue, now thankfully deceased, for frontal lobe lesions in the 1940s and 1950s was spurred in part by the placidity that such surgery evoked in people. (The originator of the operation, Walter Freeman, a neighbor of mine in Los Altos, produced a brochure on the technique saying that the operation had helped many State Department officials!) Again, they were desouled or deselfed, and there was nothing left to oversee the sources of voluntary action. The squadron of simpletons had lost even their weak leader.

We see ourselves through a selective filter, the conscious self. But, like shining a spotlight in a dark area, everything we see is illuminated by our own spotlight. We can't see where we have no illumination. Thus, we assume that our mind is more stable, more complete than it is. Individuals think they are rational, and philosophers think they are consistent.

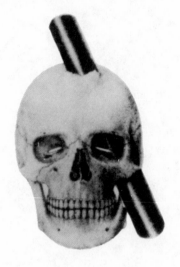 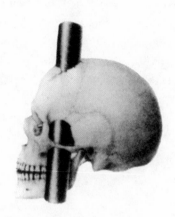

Phineas Gage, a railroad worker, suffered severe damage to the left frontal lobe of his brain when a device to set tamping irons accidently exploded, lodging a spike in his skull. He survived, but his personality was drastically altered.

We are blinded to our own nature by our evolved nature, by the very system that makes it possible for us to survive. Yet unconscious decisions for action go on constantly inside the head, for they form the evolved basis of our adaptation to the world. The broad but shallow processes of the mind are all we have to transmit the outside world to us.

V

The Dream
of
the World

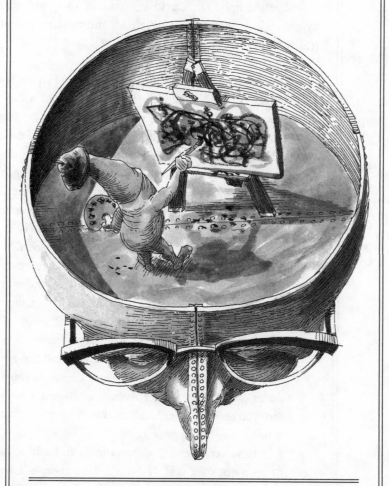

Dreaming up the world.

Imagination and memory are but one thing, which for divers considerations have divers names.

—THOMAS HOBBES, *Leviathan* (1651)

At a symposium in September 1990 on health that the Institute for the Study of Human Knowledge organized, one of the speakers, cognitive therapist Dr. David Burns, told this story about the big psychological difference between an individual's realities and the reality in the world:

> Coming home from the airport one day, when his taxi was crossing a set of railroad tracks, he noticed a car being driven very slowly on the railroad tracks, not across them, but bumpety-bump, right along the tracks. So he had the cab stop, being an altruistic sort, and he looked at the guy, waiting a couple of minutes to see if he was going to turn off at the next crossing or what was going to happen. In that next couple of minutes, two things happened. One, the guy continued to drive at about 2 miles per hour along the railroad tracks, and two, Burns could see down the other side the light of an approaching freight train. Most people would believe that getting out of the way of a freight train is cause for great hysteria, if not immediate cardiac activation.
>
> Dr. Burns came up and ran across and said, "Hey, you are driving on the railroad tracks." And the guy said, "Well, can you tell me how to get to Center Avenue?" And Burns said, "Well, Center Avenue is 10 miles from here. But you're on the railroad tracks. And there is a train coming. You better get off."
>
> However, the man drove ahead, and Burns, running to keep up, then said, "Now, right up there is a way you can turn, turn off, and then I will tell you how to get to

Center Avenue, but get off the tracks." And Burns, a cognitive therapist, was getting quite hysterical about the situation. The man began to make the turn and then stopped. Burns came up and said, "You've gotta get moving, you gotta get off. The train is coming."

Now Burns could see that, even though there were three tracks, the train is actually coming on the track where this guy's car is. He starts screaming, tries to grab the wheel. The guy rolls up his window and just sits there. So Burns has to ditch it. And he has to run as far away as he can. A freight train has so much momentum that once a driver can see something in its path, it is already gone, because one cannot stop a freight train in time. The train drivers put on their brakes, but the train plows into the car, rips it in half. Half of the car went off to the right and exploded, and half was on the other side of the tracks. The man was parked just past the tracks.

Burns, shaken, went up to the guy and said, "Uh, are you all right?" And the guy said, "Sure, I'm fine; which way do I go to Center Avenue?" Burns said, "What are you talking about? You've just been hit by a freight train!" The guy turned around to him and said, "I have not been hit."

Being a cognitive therapist, Burns could handle it; he said, "Why is your windshield destroyed?" And the man said, "Well, yeah, it is." And Burns said, "Well, turn around; there is no back half of your car. There is an explosion over there." The guy said, "You might be right."

So Burns called an ambulance and went to the hospital. The next day he went back to the scene of the accident. He sees a younger man walking around, picking up pieces from the car, and the man says to Burns, "My father was here yesterday. He has some organic brain loss and doesn't ever really know what is happening to him, and every once in a while, he takes the car out and never knows where he is or where he is going. And someone helped save his life. But he seems quite calm now. He is back out of the hospital."

Even though he had preached for several years that what really counts is the way you understand what is happening to you, it was very difficult for Burns to realize

the extremes to which such a concept could be taken.
Here a man's car has been sundered by a freight train, and
though he was in it all the time, he didn't notice it.

The world we experience, all the horses, the leaves, the coffee,
the sunrises, the remembrance of things past, is all a dream of the
mind. And more, for the mind is filled with different dreamers,
some of whom don't know about each other. They contradict each
other, as dreamers do.

We have to make quick life-and-death decisions based on few
signals. Is the sharp thunder dangerous? Is this culvert a secure
spot on which to stand? Is she trustworthy? The mind's systems,
emotions, comparison processes, select new information to make a
quick judgment of the world.

Remember, the mind based its organization on the most
important of the ancestral adaptations; those specialized for life-
and-death decisions. Since these circuits were in place early,
and have enormous consequences for life and death, these same
quick processes were recruited for commonplace percepts. This
works well in life-and-death conditions, but it also sways all the
mind's routines, even into perceiving what we read, how we link
forms together, and what we hear.

We live in a dream of our own making. Some try to get
around the dream. Some succeed. Our experiences, percepts, memories are not of the world directly but are our own creation, a
dream of the world, one that evolved to produce just enough
information for us to adapt to local circumstances. Here we trace
some of the heritage of our extracting signals from the chaos, then
linking them into semblances. Then we see how this underlies our
conscious experience, memories, and dreams.

15

The Mind Is a World-processing System

Evolutionary and neurological analyses have, obviously, transformed our self-understanding. But it was not, for most of human intellectual history, so natural to look to the workings of the nervous system and bodily structure to discern the nature of the mind. Our understanding of ourselves evolved. And the modern progression of thought followed from the work of René Descartes, although he wasn't necessarily the first to make the necessary connections.

By "modern," I mean the attempt to find in our anatomy and physiology some answers to, or at least information on, many long-standing philosophical questions. In 1637, René Descartes set the modern study of mind-brain relationships in motion. After a great deal of deliberation, Descartes came to believe that human knowledge did not depend on the church's postulation of a disembodied spiritual soul but on the brain and nervous system. He then proposed the existence of an intrinsic set of abilities through which the "mind" directs the automaton of a body. He even proposed a physical location for this interaction, in the pineal of the brain, for it is one appendage of the brain whose structure is single rather than dual.

In so doing Descartes transported medieval thought into the modern world. He questioned the authority of the medieval church to define human knowledge. Descartes sought the kind of secure knowledge that an individual would be able to have about his own mind. Could the church dictate our ideas about ourselves?

Descartes also felt that science would be the basis on which

Of Descartes, the "Animal Spirits," Anschauung, and the Modern Mind

161

The world-processing
system.

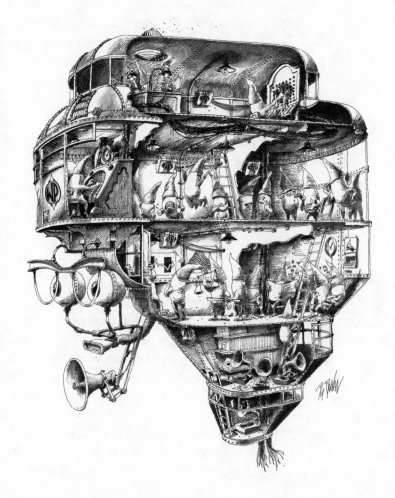

one could view and develop an understanding of man. So he took
his famous sojourn in a Dutch farmhouse to escape authority and
contemplate humanity's innate nature. He said that his first rule
was:

> Never to accept anything as true unless I recognized it to
> be evidently such: that is carefully to avoid precipitation
> and prejudgment, and to include nothing in my conclu-
> sions unless it presented itself clearly and distinctly to my
> mind that there was no reason to doubt it. The second was
> to divide each of the difficulties which I encountered into
> as many parts as possible and as might be required for an
> easier solution. The third was to think in an orderly fashion.

His *Discourse on Method* analyzes the nature of the "animal spirits," the living forces in animals. Medieval philosophy taught that these enlivening forces originated outside our physical nature, in God. After discussing how the heart works, how the blood leaves the left ventricle and tends toward the brain, Descartes then makes the leap to modernity in the relationship between the body and the mind:

> And I continued by showing what the nature of the network of nerves and muscles of the human body must be, to enable the animal spirits to move its members as one sees when freshly severed heads still move and bite the earth although they are no longer alive. I showed what changes must take place in the brain to cause wakefulness, sleep and dreams; how light, sounds, odors, tastes, heat and all the other qualities of external objects can implant various ideas through the medium of the sense and how hunger, thirst and the other internal passions are communicated. I explained what must be understood by the animal sense which receives these ideas, by memory which retains them, and by imagination which can change them in various ways and build new ones from them, and thus, distributing the animal spirits in the muscles, move the parts in the body in response to the objects, which are presented to the senses and the passions which are in the body.

Not considered here is how Descartes made some other, more questionable judgments about separating the source of the soul from the "animal spirits," but I wonder how much was Descartes halted in his writings by the consequences of a possible heresy.

The real question for most of us is how the nervous system responds to the outside world. Here modern thought is beginning to side more with Immanuel Kant than with John Locke, as Darwin prophesied. Kant emphasized that innate ideas "are the determining factor in mental life," and in his book *Prologomena to Future Metaphysics* set up the discussion vis-à-vis Locke about how much of our knowledge is governed by association and how much is given:

163

But it would be well to consider that the human understanding is not to be blamed for its inability to know the
substance of things, that is, to determine it by itself, but
rather for requiring to cognise it, which is a mere idea
definitely as though it were a given object. Pure reason
required us to seek for every predicate of a thing its
proper subject, and for this subject which is itself necessarily nothing but a predicate, its subject and so on indefi-
nitely (or so far as we can reach). And hence it follows that
we must not hold anything, which we can arrive to be an
ultimate subject, that substance itself can never be thought
by our own understanding, however deep we may pene-
trate even if our nature were unveiled to us.

If Descartes released philosophy from the medieval depen-
dence on authority, Kant, in trying to seek the principles that
determined all thought, began the latest step. To Kant, knowing an
object in the world is *Anschauung,* a word for which we have no
real equivalent in English. Perhaps one equivalent would be as a
comparison to the term *insight,* which means understanding something within. Think of *Anschauung* as comparable to "outsight"
—understanding the nature of something outside of ourselves. To
Kant sense perceptions in the outside world key off a mechanism
inside ourselves which produces, in modern terms, a representation of an object. Insofar as the object and the subsequent action
coincide, *Anschauung* works fine.

Signals and Semblances

Kant's analysis, the *Anschauung*—knowing an object—is the genesis of the modern understanding of how outside objects are represented in the mind. Through a set of nonconscious intuitions, the
mind forms, or as we shall say, "dreams," semblances of the
world, so as to operate in it. A guess about reality, a semblance of
it, is made, and it is checked against known information. The
mind uses the very faint signals from the sense organs as its raw
material and its check system. This is the same kind of double-
entry processing found in neural Darwinism.

Continuing our army-mind analogy, the signals might be

thought of as the flashing lights in the fictional (maybe they are real) military situation rooms shown in the movies, lights that can stand for troops massing on a border or for suspicious movements. These lights *signal* that something is happening. They don't have any relationship to the action. The light, by its location and by the common understanding of those interpreting it, comes to *mean* troop movement or carrier deployment.

The outside world contains signals about temperature, about ripeness of fruit, about edges, about threats, about needs, about emotional moods. This means of simplifying selections evolved to afford the mind sufficient information to resolve what's there without the information being in any way close to complete. There is no time to perceive everything that goes on outside of us. We dream it up "on-line"—in a trice—to adapt to the changes in the world.

But how did the mind evolve to help its carriers survive, stay healthy, and reproduce, and look after relatives? Like the ear, the mind developed a few distinctive ways of extracting from the world the information it needs.

All animals' "world-processing systems" highlight events that inspire action. For human beings, such an event might be a sudden noise heard over the normal clamor of traffic; one person in a crowd of faces with a gun; a few coughs interspersed among the hundreds of thousands of breaths you take. Our evolved system simplifies everything that happens, to make sense out of an enormous amount of shifting and chaotic external and internal information and to adapt to the world *sufficiently well* to survive. There are only a few features of the millions of possible features in the world that we need notice. We simply discard the rest.

Everything outside goes inside into the world processor; what comes out are a few features of the world, features that usually kick off our reactions and our percepts. And the system usually works. When was the last time you bit into a nice hard rock? When was the last time you decided to run straight into a wall? Have you started reading things that look like fssooijo sapw8iklsj?

The neural underpinnings of the mind evolved in part to select only that which is of use to survival. Consequently, the mind tends not to care too much about frills that modern, well-educated human beings are trained to think important, such as self-understanding and accurate perception.

What evolved is not complete understanding but a strategy for doing the right thing. And doing the right thing, in considering incest, in considering emotions, in considering the attachment of baby to mother, doesn't require much rationality or deliberation. The mind needs quick action to help avoid poisons, avoid dangers, and prepare to fight. There is no time for self-understanding, no way—no need.

So, we have sets of simpletons who select their bit of the outside world, fight for control, and act in a way that helps us get along, and this system has served living beings in good stead for a long time. If the mental system is now at a breaking point it is because our "world to be processed" is so different than the world for which the mind evolved. We'd better have a good idea of the possible change points of the mind, to know how we take information from the world, in which bits, what is hard-wired, and what can be changed.

Like a word-processing system, the mental system evolved in two basic routines, feature identification and concepts. Alone, the letter *e* has no meaning, yet it is a consistent feature of *feature, sex, ellipses, some, bone,* and the rest. Individual letters, like cells in the nervous system, have no meaning in themselves. Letters combine into higher-order concepts, like words. *Es, As, Ts,* and the like can combine themselves into specific concepts, such as *eat, ate, tea,* or *ETA* (estimated time of arrival), depending only on arrangement. Our vision and our hearing and thinking work in the same way.

We select pieces of the environment based on eons of natural selection. We can't see patterns of ultraviolet light, which is visible to butterflies. You can't hear a dog whistle or smell the scent of an escaping prisoner. There is a system designed to perceive the features and an intuitive system designed to link the features quickly into small concepts and larger ones. It is a system much like emotion, in which distinctive features of the world—a frown, a loud noise—instantly push the mind into action.

Unlike a connect-the-dots game, the mind doesn't carefully and rationally link features together, nor do we do so even when speaking or reading. Just as we don't read every word letter by letter, so the mind does not interpret the world piece by piece. Rather, it receives sensory signals and interprets them as a whole, quickly making an assumption about the environment. In short, we dream up our conclusions about the world. And most times we dream correctly and we use the correct dreamer inside of ourselves.

In many philosophical and spiritual systems, the "world" is to be shunned as an illusion. It is portrayed as being seen on the wall of a cave, reflected through distorting lenses. Modern research confirms it; we experience the world the same way we remember it and dream about it. The mind works through a few simple combining processes, using the evidence available to it to make the best guess possible, illusion or not.

The way it does so is simple but inexorable, a logic we see sometimes in children when they are clearly dealing with information beyond their ken. Monsters appear in the night, and even in the day, as information is incorrectly analyzed and a conclusion is formed. Logical processes parallel perceptual ones. A three-year-old of my acquaintance, when complimented on his crayon set, instructed me with an echo of a parental shopper's avid advice: "You get this from the Easter bunny, and you have to ask early."

We can observe this system at work within ourselves, when looking over a lake in the mist. Is that a tree? Is that a hunter? Is it a rock? When signals are ambiguous, we can see the semblances shifting around in the mind. Sometimes we see the hunter, sometimes the tree. If fearful, we may see an attacker. In ambiguous situations, we are like children, unable to connect the most adaptive likeness.

The same image of the world is present in blind people. They have another kind of "sight." Indeed, they can draw! What do blind people think the world looks like? Are their mental images of people and things very different from those of sighted people?

Three drawings by
blind people.
Note perspective!

John Kennedy asked people blind since birth to draw pictures. At first you might think that was a ridiculous request; most of the blind people thought so. Since the blind use touch, Kennedy gave each subject a plastic sheet that makes a raised line when a ballpoint pen is moved across it.

5-4

Focus on the dot within the circle. Then move the book until the X within the circle disappears (about a foot away or so). Note that you see the checkered pattern fill in the space.

He first asked them to draw simple objects—a cup, a hand, a table—and later, more complicated scenes. The blind realized almost immediately that some aspects of reality must be sacrificed in a drawing: We can have only one view of a pen, not all sides at once; a point of view must be selected.

The blind artists communicated meaning in ways understood by sighted people. Surprisingly, the blind artists understood perspective. There is more to seeing than meets the eye and more to visual perception than sight. These people somehow created the same kind of semblance (corrected, of course, for their lack of experience) in their drawings as do sighted people. The same signals aren't transmitted, but something else has sparked the semblance, perhaps touch, perhaps movement, perhaps something else.

16

The Eye's Mind: How We Discern the World

There is great evolutionary advantage to perceiving the world—at least those parts of it that are useful for remaining alive and bearing viable offspring. Our ignorance of the world may be a concept difficult for us to grasp, given the great richness of experience.

Consider the eye again, which evolved its great complexity from humble origins. It receives but one-trillionth of the information that reaches it. This limitation is the result of the physical makeup of our sense organs and neural connections. Our nerves are wired in a certain way to ensure that we catch specific features of the environment, from which our brains dream up our entire experience of the world.

If we were bombarded with all the sensations in the world, experience would be chaotic. The air in the room you are in is filled with various forms of energy: an entire spectrum of light, sound and radio waves, and more. Yet you are aware of only a small portion of it. Light is a lilliputian portion of the band of radiant electromagnetic energy. Each living being's world-processing system experiences only what it needs. The cat sees in the dark; insects see infrared radiation, which we feel as warmth; and a frog sees only things that move.

The contemporary analysis of the visual system was set in motion by Jerome Lettvin's famous study "What the Frog's Eye Tells the Frog's Brain." Lettvin and his group presented an assortment of objects, colors, and patterns to a frog while monitoring the activity of its optic nerve. For all the information wiggled, flashed, shoved in front of the immobilized animal, only four messages were transmitted to the frog's brain. These messages first furnish frogs with a general outline of their environment; second, detect moving edges; third, perceive small dark objects (very useful for bug detection if you find bugs luscious); and fourth, alert the frog to sudden decreases in light (a boon to enemy detection, such as a bird approaching from above).

Human beings perceive a world of far greater complexity than the frog's. We can marvel at the shades of a sunset, goggle mesmerized by intricate Oriental carpets, become merry or morose in response to the expression on a lover's face, and understand abstract concepts by reading words on a page. But, because our eyes and brains evolved and were not designed, there is much to reality that we cannot see.

Human brains, like frog brains, have built-in wiring for detecting particular features of the world. This has been discovered by painstaking work, measuring the output of even single neurons in the visual cortex. The rate of firing in a single axon can be measured and recorded by a hairlike electrical probe. By flashing a light at an animal's eye and recording the response to individual nerve cells, we can find out which cells respond to the stimulus. The area of stimulation (often circular) to which a cell responds is its receptive field. The function of the cortical cells is different from that of cells in the optic tract—they respond best to specific signals in the environment and are called feature analyzers.

There are over 100 million neurons in the human visual cortex, and it is difficult to know their specialization. It appears that each species of animal evolved feature analyzers that pick out the signals—objects and events—that are important for it.

In the early 1960s, David Hubel and Torsten Wiesel made a startling discovery: Neurons in the cortex of cats fire rapidly when a certain kind of object appears. Moreover, these cells do not fire if the object is absent. The cat's brain detects edges, angles, and objects moving in different directions.

These studies give us knowledge of the "hard points" of the mind's works—the innate and relatively unmodifiable parts of the mental system, our points of contact with reality to which evolution has given great attention. Some of the most important hard points connect the light-detecting organs of the eye to cells in the cerebral cortex.

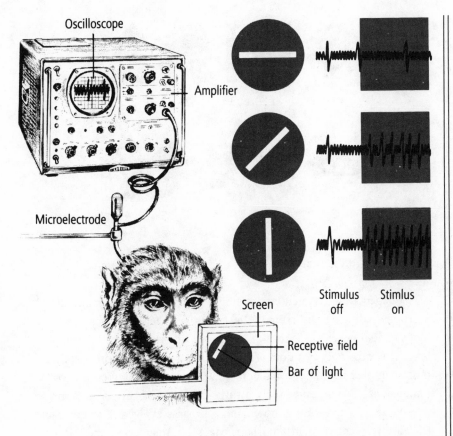

Oscilloscope

Amplifier

Microelectrode

Screen

Stimulus off

Stimulus on

Receptive field

Bar of light

Feature analyzers' responses to different receptive fields. The response of single cortical cells to various stimuli can be measured by an oscilloscope. When bars of light (left) are flashed in the subject's eye, the most vigorous neural response is to the vertical bar. This suggests that this particular cell is a feature analyzer intended to detect and react to visual stimuli that have a vertical orientation.

Monkeys also have cortical cells that respond to specific features of the environment. One group was quite astonished to find a monkey's neuron that, after they had tried and tried in vain to excite it with object after object, suddenly "lit up" when one of the experimenters waved good-bye to the monkey! They happened upon a monkey's "monkey hand" detector cell.

Originally, it was thought that these cells were detecting identifiable parts of the world, such as edges or blobs, and transmitting information about their presence straight to the cortex. However, after the initial exciting discoveries of feature-detector cells in the cortex, the pace dwindled. No new feature detectors were found. David Marr then devised a radically different approach for explaining how the mind evolved to compute semblances of the world from sparse signals.

Marr's idea was that the brain, instead of directly "reading" signals from the retina, computes the layout of the environment from the shadings of the light available, which look like bands.

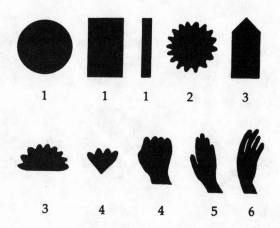

The monkey paw detector. These shapes are arranged in order of their ability to make a single cell in a monkey's brain respond to the sight of them. Some shapes (1) produced no response; some made a neuron react a little (2 and 3). Those shapes somewhat like a monkey's paw (4 and 5) produced a greater response, and the maximum neural response was to the shape most closely resembling a monkey's paw (6). Clearly, there are brain cells intended to detect and react to very complex, highly specific features. (AFTER GROSS, 1973)

Many different alternations of light and dark combine to create the scene before us.

First there is a sketch comprising primitive forms that make up a crude outline of the scene. The primitives include edges, bars, blobs, and line ends, with the attributes of orientation, contrast, length, width, and position. They are filled in with more detail, more complex features, to make a "full primal sketch," then a two-dimensional sketch, and finally a three-dimensional representation.

What is interesting is how such a process evolved: The circular on/off receptive fields, perhaps via recruitment, became ideal tuned spatial frequency detectors. Only light and dark bands that exactly fit the "on" and "off" centers and surrounds can cause the relevant cells to fire. Instead of a simple assemblage of specific parts, like a child's Lego structure, we began to move closer to the idea that the world is dreamt. And as is the case with many of the mind's processes, very little is needed to make much: For instance, only six tuned spatial frequency channels would be required to explain the amazing acuity of the human eye, which can resolve details finer than a photoreceptor cell.

The discovery of these cells in the visual cortex has greatly affected our knowledge of how the mind evolved in separate, modular systems. The cells are arranged in columns, each column corresponding to one kind of analysis, such as edges and corners. The word *module* denotes a fixed plan or unit, signifying that the components are standard. There are many different modules in the brain; they are encapsulated, that is, they do not communicate with other modules. They are domain specific—the analysis rou-

Preferred orientation and direction

Preferred orientation and nonpreferred direction

5-7

Some cortical cells respond best to bars and edges at certain angles and particularly to those moving in specific directions. (AFTER HUBEL AND WIESEL, 1962)

tine for smell, for instance, may be very different from the analysis for shape or for language. Just how complex and how "hard-wired" these modules are is the subject of much current research.

It is the hard points of the mind that enable us to perceive color as well. There is no color in nature. What is seen as color is wavelengths of light reflected from different surfaces. These wavelengths stimulate the three kinds of cones in the retina, which in turn send their coded information to the brain. The experience of color is a product of the coding in sensory systems. That we see red, green, blue, and yellow as "pure" is the result of the way the wavelengths of light are processed by the nervous system and not because of any intrinsic property of the light being processed.

Once the brain receives signals of lights and darks and color, it apparently must perform a few more wired-in routines before it produces semblances. Rather than passing straight from retina to cortex, visual information travels along separate pathways, which process form, color, movement, and depth. The functioning of these systems determines experiences. For instance, the color system is slow, with poor resolution, while the form system is quick and sensitive to detail. This is why the colors blend together in an impressionist painting, creating the illusion of a unified scene. If you look closely enough to see the individual blobs of paint, the illusion is lost. This would explain why such great artists as Matisse seem surprisingly casual or even "sloppy" with colors, putting them only near the image they are supposed to portray. In many watercolors the colors don't not conform precisely to the contours of the form; the lack of acuity of the color system allows the image to appear adequate anyway.

Psychologist Anne Treisman has also been teasing out the primary aspects of vision. Recall the primal sketch composed of signals from which a scene can be constructed. Treisman has identified a set of basic features that may operate as the "building blocks" of vision. They include color, size, contrast, tilt, curvature, and line ends. These signals are perceived *before* one comprehends the objects they compose. Treisman briefly showed people collections of figures and asked if a certain figure that can be made by combining other figures is present—for instance, if an arrow were present in a composition of angles and diagonal lines. And, because we dream up or assemble the world from specific components, people frequently see arrows where there are none.

Treisman also found that objects are more quickly identified in a group if they differ in basic features. Basic features seem to be analyzed in parallel by the brain, so that the difference of one feature is seen instantaneously. However, if objects share the same features that are organized differently, more time is needed to distinguish them, because the observer has to process the location of each component, one at a time (serially). Thus, a diagonal line can be linked with an angle to make an illusory arrow: In the short time allowed, the observer is unable to attend to the features sufficiently to assign them roles. The idea is similar to commonsense practices that we use every day. In labeling possessions that you need to select quickly, for instance, labels with different basic features are more efficiently recognized than those with the same features combined in different ways. A red suitcase tag is easy to differentiate from a blue one, but tags of the same color with different words are not so quickly distinguished.

Evolution wires the visual system to select those parts of the world of interest. Retinal cells respond to wavelengths of light and alternations of light and dark. Three visual pathways process this information to give us knowledge about motion, form, depth, and color. We can instantly perceive differences in basic features such as color, size, contrast, tilt, curvature, and the presence of line ends. And such perceptual systems exist everywhere in the mind. Selection and analysis take place in the auditory cortex; 60 percent of the cortical cells there respond to specific tones. There are even cells in the auditory system of the squirrel monkey that respond most strongly to the sounds of other squirrel monkeys. There are probably many more such systems, especially organizations of cells that respond to territorial intrusion via smell.

So the mind puts a few feelers out to the world and uses these highly evolved sensors to check what's going on. From the information output, we link events. Then we render an environment in which we can thrive, find food, safety, and the like. We don't see colors but make them up; evolution selected a set of colors that give us the information we need. And the mental links to dream up the rest.

17

Making Up Your Mind: The Process of Unconscious Interpretation

Children confuse dreams with reality, as well as memories. As we grow older, we learn that dreams are not real, and later we learn that memories aren't real either, but a reconstruction, like an anthropological fabrication of an entire beast from a bone or two.

So how does our mind get made up? Neural networks merely gather and transform various forms of energy. Here is a simplified and abbreviated example of sensory information as it is transmitted to the brain: "Increasing 700 nanometer waves to the right, accompanied by increasing pressure of sound waves of 60 to 80 Hertz at 40 to the left." Information in this form does not mean much to us. However, the message "A bear is coming, and fast, from the left" certainly does.

The mind's job is, somehow, to imagine semblances of what is outside from the sensory signals. Our world processing must accurately reflect the world around us; to see people approaching if we are to avoid bumping into them, to identify food before it can be eaten.

Op art, popular in the 1960s, played with this disposition to make sense, semblances, from signals. Op art is at once intriguing and unsettling because we try continually to organize certain figures that are designed by the artist to have no organization.

The second step in "assemblage" is interpretation. Consider the approaching bear: First the raw info is organized into "bear." But what is the meaning of "a bear" in your presence? What action do you take? Suppose the "bear" suddenly says "Trick or treat!"

5-8

Resistance to stable
organization. Op
art such as this
can present many
different and
changing meaningful
patterns of
organization. This
runs counter to
our perceptual
preference for stable,
invariant patterns
of organization.
(AFTER CARRAHER
AND THURSTON,
1968)

Now you remember that it is Halloween, and the significance of "bear" becomes quite different than if you had been camping in the woods and heard a growl.

When something is organized, it is simplified. The experience of many different "dots" on a page is quite complex, but a dalmatian near a tree is organized and simple. Because of the vast amount of information in the world, it is important that we simplify it so that we can act quickly.

Both drawings below are of a cube, seen from different angles. The simplest interpretation of the one on the left is as a two-dimensional hexagon rather than a cube viewed from one of its corners. We see the drawing on the right as a cube in three dimensions because that interpretation is simpler than seeing it as a group of rectangles.

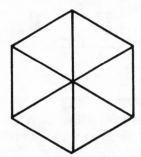

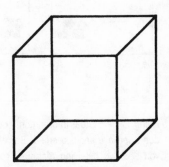

5-9

It is easy to see the
left drawing as
two-dimensional and
the right as three,
although both can
also be views
of a cube. (AFTER
HOCHBERG AND
MCALISTER,
KOPFERMANN, 1930)

Cleaning up
perceptual
information. After
looking at these
figures for a
few seconds, cover
them and draw
what you saw.
What does your
drawing indicate
about how you
interpret what you
perceive?

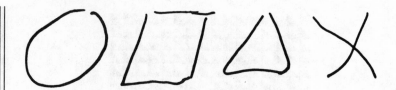

Because we unconsciously dream a semblance of the world, our experience "cleans up" information and "straightens it out." Look at the figure above for a moment; now cover up the figure and draw the shapes. You probably drew the slanted ellipse as a circle, made the "square" with straight sides, completed and connected the sides of the "triangle," and drew the "X" with two straight lines. You cleaned up, corrected, and connected the figures to match your interpretation of them.

The diagram below is composed of three acute angles spaced equidistantly between three squares, each square with a small piece missing at the corner. You probably "saw" three squares, however, with two overlapping triangles. The "white" triangle is something you "filled in" by the process of interpretation. We fit our experience to the best form available to us.

Because we experience our semblance of the world, it is stable, even though the signals reaching us change. A building may appear as a small dot on the horizon, or it may completely fill our field of view. Yet we assemble a vision of a building to the same size and shape regardless of vantage point. The main purpose of the reception, organization, and interpretation by the perceptual processes is to perceive a constant world.

   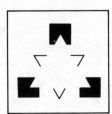

5-11

Filling in perceptual information. Look at the first three figures in the sequence: You don't see a triangle overlaid. But when you see the figure as a whole (lower right), you see two overlying triangles. You are interpreting or subjectively "filling in" the white central one, which does not actually exist. (AFTER COREN, 1972)

The pear and the triangle don't exist, except in the mind.

The world can be distorted, inverted, darkened, lightened, and we learn to handle it. Ivo Kohler investigated adapting to distortion. His observers wore various kinds of distorting lenses for weeks. At first they all had great difficulty seeing the world. But in a few weeks they had adapted; indeed, one of Kohler's subjects was able to ski while wearing the distorting lenses. People can also adapt to color distortions. In another of Kohler's demonstrations, his subjects wore glasses in which one lens was green and one red. Within a few hours they sensed no difference in color between the lenses, having created an acceptable semblance.

When we listen and read, we fill in the gaps. As we read text, we are able to predict the words we expect see. These predictions were probably good enough to allow you to fill in the missing word *to* (before *see*) in the preceding sentence.

"I went to the new display last night" can produce a shocked reaction in someone who heard "I went to the nudist play," because the sounds are the same. When I was very young, my father told me that the "prince of whales" was coming to the United States. I asked him for weeks if we could go to the aquarium to see this majestic marine mammal. When sounds are ambiguous or difficult to hear, we fill in the gaps. Two psychologists did an interesting study on this process. People heard the following: "It was found that the __eel was on the _____." Different subjects were given four different words with which to end the sentence: *axle, orange, shoe, table*. They were then asked to repeat what they had heard. Those who had been given *axle* recalled the sentence as "It was found that the *wheel* was on the axle." Those who had heard *orange* inserted *peel;* those who had heard *shoe* inserted *heel,* and those who had heard *table* inserted

A jazzy woman
indeed, yet we
can see only
one at a time.

meal. The subjects did not think that they were guessing the word, but that they had *actually heard* the sentence. They filled in the sentence with the most likely element.

Like a caricature of a president's face, only a few aspects of reality are emphasized. Why should that matter? It matters because for billions of years of evolution, our ancestors were in situations in which extreme caricatures sufficed for survival. In order to understand our present limitations, we have to understand their origins. Evolution would never favor organisms that invested in sensory frills energy that could be used to enhance reproduction.

Close your eyes, then open them. What you just saw is a result of all the processes discussed here. Light enters, passes through the retina, and is transduced to the brain. Orientation analyzers and color analyzers do their jobs.

The quick and rough analysis system of the mind thus evolved to select signals from the world. On-line we assemble and reassemble a dream of what is happening. During every moment of life, the nervous system samples the world and checks the facsimile it has made. We update our dream moment by moment, so the beautiful world we see is something more beautiful, our own dream. This is why real dreams are so malleable and memories do not exist but are made up on-line, as is the rest of life.

18

Why Memories
Are an Illusion

Our psychic mechanism has come into being by a
process of stratification; the material present in the
form of memory traces being subjected from time to
time to a *rearrangement* . . . — to a *retranscription* . . .
memory is present not once but several times over.

—SIGMUND FREUD, letter to Fliess, 1896

Remembering is not the re-excitation of innumerable
fixed, lifeless and fragmentary traces. It is an imagina-
tive reconstruction, or construction, built out of the
relation of our attitude towards a whole active mass of
organized past reactions or experience, into a little
outstanding detail which commonly appears in image
or in language form. It is, thus, hardly ever really exact,
even in the most rudimentary cases of recapitulation,
and it is not all important that it should be so."

—FREDERICK BARTLETT, 1932

I once worked in a mental hospital. One day I was taking care of
Michael S., a patient who suffered from amnesia, due in this
case to a blow to the head. He told me a story I will never
forget. "This morning a woman came to see me in my room. I felt
attracted to her. She was very pretty, and I liked talking to her. I
asked her for her name. 'Ellen,' she said. I asked why she had
come to visit me, as I thought she was a hospital volunteer. She
slumped and burst into tears. She said, 'Michael, I'm your wife.

We've been married for twenty years!' I just didn't know what to say. I don't remember her at all."

How can someone forget a spouse of twenty years? How can someone remember a performance from long ago, yet not his last spoken sentence? No one really knows, but the answers must lie in the nature of our system of memory.

To adapt to the world, we have to remember our friends, our house, how to drive, how to walk, and even who we are. We don't, however, have any real memory as an image of the past. Instead we remember the world in the same way we do everything, by picking a few signals and then composing an image on-line.

This memory underlies the mind's workings because it allows us to fill in the gaps when we receive new information and to assume "facts" on the basis of partial information. But memories aren't consistent; even simple concepts, such as "robin," are remembered and classified differently on different days. Indeed, the common wisdom about memory seems to hold that it is a permanent storage of everything we have ever encountered.

Wilder Penfield's patients, whose stimulation with electricity produced a flashback of the past in their mind, were also fooling themselves. Their memories can be influenced just as much by current events and priming as any other memory.

Memory for events depends on the situation; it isn't fixed, recorded knowledge like a camera's. When the brain is stimulated during surgery (I did some of this myself), experiences arise. But are these experiences real memories? No, they aren't. They have as much to do with current thoughts as any daydream, but the person, of course, can't tell the difference, as we usually cannot.

Even the "perfect" recall of the hypnotized subject is of dubious veracity. Psychologist Bill Putnam demonstrated that a hypnotized subject may describe more details in recalling a videotape of an accident, but their recall contains more errors. Increased detail doesn't mean increased accuracy, but more effort creating the semblance with more complexity. When hypnotized, people are far more suggestible than usual and may be able to conjure up "recalled" images on demand to suit their inquirers.

Psychologists have long thought that humans possess a fixed filing system in the mind, something like a computer's memory storage, with each item stored in a unique location. However, a system like this, which can't possibly register all the different ways we can pick up a cup or write or speak identical words and phrases or handle all of our encounters with different combinations of objects in space and time, is simply inconceivable.

In 1930 the physician A. A. Lowe treated a patient who had suffered a stroke. He recovered the ability to speak in well-formed sentences, but he had a particular handicap: "when given a sentence or paragraph to read . . . , he left out many words and combinations of words, giving the distinct impression of agrammatical reading."

5-14

Mickey M., in parts.

Lowe tried to find the nature of the problem. He showed the patient nouns such as *child, shirt, box*. The patient read *dad* as *father*. The patient understood the concept but could not speak the actual printed version. He made similar mistakes in reading *girl* for *child* and *wicked* for *vice*.

Lowe argued that this patient's abilities resulted from "reading" —making up—the semblance rather than reading the words. Lowe gave him nonsense syllables, such as *lem, sim, fic,* and *tek* to read.

He read *sto* as *story*, *fal* as *fat*, *ser* as *serve*, and *tla* as *atlas*. However, when he had a word in a context, such as *clear as mud* or *off guard*, he understood and spoke correctly. On-line he tried to make up the semblance.

Perhaps there is no sign of a "storage area" existing in the brain. The neural connections are like an enormous network of interconnected wires, but nowhere do they terminate in one location as one would expect if there were a memory file in the brain. Memories aren't photographic; they do not store individual events; rather, they can be lumped together, erased, or altered by later experiences.

We remember the semblance, not the signals. As our minds adapt to fit our changing situations and needs, so our perceptions and memories change as well. If we are very hungry, a shopping center nearby is recalled as a source of food, rather than as a place to idle away time looking at clothes. Once our hunger is sated, we may then remember that we wanted to check out a sale at one of the boutiques.

The hard points in the brain select basic signals from the world, colors, edges, and corners. The ability to organize information, to be creative, to be competent, even to remember, is the ability to link these "fragments," using the maps that seem to exist inside the nervous system.

A unit of memory is called a *chunk*. In perceiving and remembering bits of information, chunking is the process of using a code to organize individual items into units of memory. GEAIMNN is a sequence of seven bits that you can probably retain only briefly. MEANING is a sequence of the same seven bits, but you have a code (in this case, the English language) that can organize them into a chunk (in this case, the word *meaning*).

The mind continually processes the world, and what is a semblance one time may eventually chunk into a signal. To a child letters were once distinct, but we don't have any idea how many *e*'s there are on a page or how many pages we have read. "What's in that book?" someone asks. "Nothing," you say, consigning thousands of letters, millions of dots of ink, recipes, racetrack and stock reports, quiet diplomacy, sewer bursts, to oblivion.

The ability to chunk information greatly expands the storage capacity of memory because small signals combine into larger chunks that are then more easily remembered. Knowing a code increases the capacity of memory and the ability to remember.

Read this quickly: 1392781243729. Now write down what you remember; most likely you remembered only about seven of the numbers. Now, here is a code to follow: begin with 1, then multiply it by 3; repeat this multiplication five more times. With these instructions, you need not memorize any of the numbers; the code tells you where to begin, what to do, and where to stop.

Chunking allows us to recall a large amount of information, in other words, to build up complex semblances based on subtle signals from the world. With feature detectors in perception, we saw how a prewired capacity to see small elements such as line ends or vertices could lead to the ability to discriminate classes of objects. In memory, whole events, eras, or abstract concepts are tied to simple perceptions or symbols.

Think of the swastika, symbol of Nazi tyranny. To the average three-year-old, it is a meaningless pattern, perhaps to be recalled, perhaps not. It will take on significance as soon as the child learns about the events of World War II. To the European old enough to have survived World War II, the swastika has an enormous amount of significance, calling up memories of dreadful times of war, loss, grief, death, and horror. To promote their power and presence, the Nazis deliberately used the tendency to link memories to simple forms by making sure their swastika symbol was widely displayed.

Now it is nearly impossible for someone who has associated the swastika with Nazis to think of anything else when seeing one. Chunks of memory linked together build up, step by step. Each time a link is repeated, it is strengthened, and the neural organization behind it becomes more fixed, less flexible. A flash of red in the corner of your vision as you sit at your desk may signal that your wife has just driven up and into the garage. Each time this sequence of events occurs—red flash, wife enters—the more likely you are to interpret that brief glimpse as meaning your wife is home.

After this link is well established in your mind, a different red car driving up or something else that just happens to make a similar flash will automatically trigger "she is home." Although the sign was misinterpreted, you judge and act based on the memory chunk that sign has brought into action. A small sign becomes equivalent to a complex perception. Higher levels of semblances may also be called up—your wife is home, you haven't started the dinner yet, she will lecture you on your share of responsibility around the house.

But how you interpret that red flash depends on who you are, what you are doing, and your past experience. And as we mature, the nature of our signals becomes more complex. A mass of fur and movement and eyes and smell in childhood is reduced to "old dog" later on. What was a million little edges and bevels and reflections is a boring mirrored wall later on. We crunch the signals as we automate more and more, as we age. This can lead to efficiency; it can lead to boredom too.

Memory in Place: Semblances and Signals

In 1932 Frederic Bartlett destroyed the idea of memory. He noticed in his experiments that people's recall of figures and events was not accurate. He realized that the transformations memory performed on elements generally altered them to be more like the previous experiences of the person recalling them.

He tried an old school game in which one person created a drawing, then passed it along to the next person and so on, each person adding to the picture. When an exotic drawing of a face was drawn by a sequence of people, it was transformed into an entirely normal drawing of a face.

From experiments like this, Bartlett developed the notion of the *schema*—a mental template into which we fit our experiences. Investigators of the memory schema have discovered several types of distortions in recall. Memory is selective—information not in the currently active schema cannot be recalled; it is interpretive—the active schema leads to supposition about the meaning of events, which is stored with the representation of the event; and it is integrative—different ideas and events are combined into one schema and can no longer be processed separately.

Schema are components of the semblance, the dream of what is happening. When remembering, we seem to use our dream of what occurred to guide our mind, and this leads us to interpret events along the lines of our memory. Quickly read the following story and then, before reading on, jot down what you remember of it.

With hocked gems financing him, our hero bravely defied all scornful laughter that tried to prevent his scheme. "Your eyes deceive," he had said. "An egg, not a table, correctly typifies this unexplored planet." Now three sturdy sisters sought proof. Forging along, sometimes through calm vastness, yet more often very turbulent peaks and valleys, days became weeks as many doubters spread fearful rumors about the edge. At last from nowhere welcome winged creatures appeared, signifying momentous success.

You probably remembered next to nothing of this passage. Now read the story again, but this time consider the situation: The story is about Columbus's voyage to America. Psychologists Dooling and Lachman found that people who had been given this context remembered much more than those who had not. The main function of context is to provide a way of organizing information beforehand, therefore making it more memorable. A title usually announces an overall context and makes part of what is read more accessible.

This phenomenon underlies why, as noted earlier, after naming fruit that begins with the letter a, people were able to name more quickly fruit that begins with the letter p. The schema of "types of fruit" had been called to the front of the mind. What we call "context," the current schema in place, can affect what is remembered.

And, while signals spark semblances, semblances work as well to select signals. Elizabeth Loftus showed people a reddish-orange disc. Some were told it was a tomato; others that it was an orange. Later they were asked to select the color that most closely matched the color they saw. Those who had been told the disc was an orange selected a color close to orange; those who had been told the disc was a tomato selected a color closer to red.

In an even more provocative experiment, Loftus showed that, after viewing a film of an accident, people were more likely to report having seen broken glass in response to the question, "How fast were the cars going when they smashed into each other?" than if asked a question less suggestive of high-velocity impact. There was no broken glass in the scene.

The on-line system of memory has far-reaching implications for our traditional means of judging criminals. Eyewitness testimony has enormous power in court. But we do not remember what we see; we remember what we think we have seen, given the current information and situation. Additionally, other experimenters have found that we are unable to disregard information in making judgments, even when instructed to do so, another practice that is common in jury trials. Everything that happens goes into the mind, and it all affects our dreamt-up world.

The rough, reconstructive nature of memory is sufficient for everyday life. We do not need to know complete details, nor are we capable of recalling literally every detail of an experience, even what a penny looks like. But when details are important, perhaps a matter of life and death, the reconstructive nature of memory can become a problem.

5-15

Some memories are
close to us, some
locked away.

Memory is influenced not only by previous knowledge but also by events that happen between the time an event is perceived and the time it is recalled. Your hopes for the future are based on the past. Your mind is "made up" by past experiences, not of course by any direct experiences of the future. We are always behind the world in our projections and estimates.

This makes us presume many half-witted things: We imagine we are more attractive, younger and slimmer than we are, more vital, and that we have longer to live than we do. Most people don't plan for the inevitability of their death, they don't anticipate growing old. Almost every tailor says that his male clients always have their pants tailored too tightly around the waist because they believe that they are going to regain their previously slim shape. And we believe that if bad things haven't happened to us, they won't ever happen, and if bad things have happened to us, they will happen again. Our same old brain is based, in large part, on assumptions from the past. After all, what do we know?

Penfield Revisited

But what about Wilder Penfield's "breakthrough" findings of specific memories in specific parts of the brain? In retrospect, it seems Penfield was subject to the same misconceptions as the rest of us. When faced with a complex, full-fledged experience evoked by an electrode in the brain, he responded with a likely semblance of reality—experiences in the brain must be real, stored events. Thus, he didn't even ask if they might be reconstructed events.

One of Penfield's patients, when the electrode was applied, heard her mother calling in a lumberyard. A record of the past? No, it was not. The woman later stated that she had never in her life been near a lumberyard. Other patients' "recollections" turned out to be influenced greatly by the conversation between the doctor and patient in the two minutes preceding the electrical stimulation. The doctor may have said something about building a home or a stack of lumber.

We compute our memories on the fly. Penfield's probe seems to have stimulated signal systems in the brain, and since we don't experience isolated "hard points," these stimulated signals were interpreted immediately into little dreams—experiences as real as life but not connected to past events in the physical world.

We usually have one story line in mind at a time. This semblance has such influence that it alters the representations we have of our past experiences. When students were persuaded to adopt a different opinion on an issue, their memories of their previously held positions changed to accord more closely with their current opinions. To operate most effectively within our semblances of the world, we can only use one mind in place, as I will describe it, at a time. Have you ever said, "I don't know what I ever saw in ———," regarding a past mate? You view your experience through your current semblance, which doesn't include being enamored with your past Mr. or Ms. Right.

We think of ourselves as consistent, and of our view of the world as so, but we're not and it isn't. From time to time, place to place, group to group, our ideas, opinions, and semblances change. If you are trying to recall certain items, say, names of birds, what you remember will depend on where you are and what you are doing. If you are out hunting ducks, you would be likely to think of other game birds—geese, quail, pheasants. If, on the other hand, you are on an Audubon Society field trip, you may be more likely to think of robins, blackbirds, and finches. What is a bird in our mind changes from instant to instant. All judgments are made in terms of the current state of affairs in the mind. A robin is not so typical a bird when ducks and geese are at the top of your mind. Semblances are made up "on-line," as we go, and are themselves influenced by the signals coming in from the world that are active in the mind.

So our memories, as exact, recorded, fixed images of the past, are an illusion. We believe we are stable, but this is one of the built-in illusions of the mental system. We believe we remember specific events, surely. Yet we don't. We make them up on the fly. We change our minds all the time, from our estimate of the odds on a bet, to how we view our future. And we are unaware that the mind is doing this.

Memory, like the rest of our mind, did not arise to provide us with an objective and comprehensive database composed of the contents of the world. Rather, our general concern is adapting our behavior. We may wish to avoid someone who once caused us pain. Previous experience with that person produced changes in us. We pick up information about other people who we think may also cause us pain by noticing similarities between them and the person who has hurt us before. We are not retrieving specific information, but "tune" differently, perceive and act differently. Our biology adapts all the time with experiences: Our leg muscles expand when we walk more, our stomach when we eat more.

But do our leg muscles "remember" the marathon, does our stomach remember the beef? No, and neither do we remember what has occurred. Rather, the brain changes with experience, and thence we adapt and adjust. There are no *real* memories as we know them. We reinterpret the hard points in memory over and over in our life, assembling our past anew throughout our lives, throughout changes in experiences.

Certainly, all our experiences contribute to our view of the world and affect the semblances we create. But to believe we have a complete memory of events is an illusion, as our view of our consistency is an illusion. The mind evolved to keep us adapting, not to know ourselves, so even events we are sure that we remember perfectly are just a *re-semblance,* the mind's I deciding on the fly. Memories are a dream.

19

The Dream
of the Dream

Every night spirits are released from this cage,
And set free, neither lording it nor lorded over.
At night prisoners are unaware of their prison,
At night kings are unaware of their majesty.
Then there is no thought or care for loss or gain

—RUMI

I'm in a classroom rather like the one in which my senior-year high-school English class was held. A boy stands up and leaves the room. I expect something bad to result from this action, but class goes on. I walk down the hall to my room. It is a rather generic room, with white walls. There is a mirror on the door; I see I am wearing leg warmers that make my legs look elephantine.

I become concerned that I have been away from class too long and have broken the rules. I go back out into the hall. There is a note hanging from the doorknob which says that I have returned to my room to rest. My mother is in the hall. I think of my leg warmers and look down to see they have fallen about my ankles. I am satisfied that looks sufficiently normal. We walk away from the class-room. I am pleased to realize that "here," which I think of as Europe, they don't have as strict standards about attendance as they do at colleges in America, and I comment on this to my companion, who is now my friend D. Their jackets say "E.Y.E.," and I think that this is from the name of the school, which is "E.Y.," with the E added for amusement value.

I like the idea of a jacket that says "EYE." I see many also have the Stanford logo and figure there is some kind of cooperative arrangement between the two schools. I need to find a bathroom and do so. There is a mess, paper and water all over. As I try to clean it up a bit, water flows into an open space in the floor leading to a cavern below the toilet, and the toilet automatically flushes. Back in the hall again. There are more and more people around. D has a record in his hand. I think there's a radio station here with the DJ booth being above us in the wall. Someone asks me if I'm in line. I tell her no, I don't want to be here at all.

I walk away and hear an announcer's voice in English. I think this must be an American radio station. Now I'm browsing in a store. I decide to look at shoes, because this will be my last chance while I am in Germany. I quickly see there are Rockports for the same price in marks as I paid in dollars (39). That excites me, but I redirect my attention to what I need, since I already have those sandals.

Two guys come up, and I am in their way. I feel nervous and get up to go. I realize I've left my purse, and one guy hands it to me, saying, "Sorry." I think it's odd he said that. My purse is distorted, and I think it matches my confused state of mind. I try to walk around the rack to the other side, but end up going all the way around the perimeter of the store. I am then awakened by a sound in the bedroom.

Dreams during the night are the result of our world-modeling activity. They occur when our brains are active, but we are asleep to the outside world, cut off from sensory input. Dreams are fascinating examples of the operation of the mind when isolated from the influence of the external world, in vitro, as it were. The convincing nature of dream experience shows that we see a world made for us by our brain functions, not the world "out there."

Dreams are hallucinatory experiences that occur during sleep. The conventional view, however, throughout the early history of

Western psychology, was that sleep was a passive condition, which could be induced by the reduction of sensory stimuli in the environment. The brain would essentially turn off, having nothing to process. Dreaming, then, was thought of as a lighter stage of sleep in which the mind was partly awake but disoriented.

In 1953 Eugene Aserinsky and Nathaniel Kleitman made a chance observation in the course of studying the sleep patterns of infants: Periods of quiet sleep seemed to alternate regularly with periods of eye movements and bodily activity. These regular periods of rapid eye movement, called REM sleep, are studied by attaching electrodes near the subjects' eyes. People of all ages experience REM sleep every night. When test subjects are awakened just after periods of REM sleep, they give vivid reports of their dreams some 90 percent of the time. When awakened after other stages of sleep (collectively called non-REM, or NREM), they report dreams less than a third of the time. William Dement and other researchers have studied the relationship of REM sleep to dreaming. He has produced evidence for a precise correspondence between REM sleep behavior and dream gaze changes. One subject who showed many side-to-side eye movements reported dreaming of a tennis match!

REM sleep is extremely curious; many contradictory phenomena occur at once. The eyes move rapidly, of course; breathing and heart rate become irregular; there is sexual excitement—erection in the male and vaginal engorgement in the female; and the vestibular system is activated. During all this activation, all other commands for voluntary movement emanating from the brain are blocked from reaching the muscles at the spinal cord. You might dream that you are running, but your legs do not move. Breathing, heart rate, and cerebral blood flow are activated, but the rest of the body is paralyzed.

Here's how it works. Immediately preceding and during REM sleep, there is increased "spiking" activity in cells of certain areas of the brain stem. The active cells "wake up" the cortex and send messages that inhibit the muscles of the body that are not essential to metabolism (with the notable exception of the eye muscles). These "REM-on" cells also have direct connections to eye-movement neurons. The cycle of sleep stages repeats three or four times a night, although the same stage is slightly different at each occurrence.

Not only do all humans dream several times a night, but all mammals have REM sleep.

What are dreams like? The brain is at least as fully active in the REM state as it is when we are awake. The world of dreams can be as vivid and real to us as the world we awaken to in the morning. Our physiological processes cover a greater range of variation in REM sleep than in waking, and our experiences in dreams also range more widely, from dimness and vagary to brilliance, clarity, and vitality seldom attained in waking life. That the dream experience seems real while it lasts is attested to by nightmares, in which we feel real fear even though only threatened by phantoms of the mind. Our astonishment when we become aware we are dreaming shows us the faith we have in our illusions. Oliver Fox, writing of a lucid dream he had in 1902, in which he was faced with the puzzling sight of the cobblestones in a familiar street all pointing in the wrong direction, exclaimed, "Then the solution flashed upon me: though this glorious summer morning seemed as real as real could be, I was 'dreaming'!"

Dreams differ from waking in a few clear ways. One, as already noted, is the variability of the intensity of the experience of dreams. The content of the dream experience is highly unstable, changing from moment to moment. While we dream, our sensory impressions are not anchored by input from the physical sense organs, leaving them free to change with the drift of a thought.

That it is much easier to forget dream experiences as compared to waking ones is undeniable. The reason for this is obvious when considered in terms of evolution. What is likely to befall an animal that recalls dreams as clearly as waking experiences? Suppose you dream that your husband died and you remarried your boss. It wouldn't be too terrific if you acted on this memory the next morning! So we have an ability to recall dreams, generally with some effort, but we also possess the ability to distinguish between dreams and waking life.

Our capacity to remember our nightly journeys in those strange realms made the origin of dreams one of the great mysteries of life. All peoples have beliefs about where dreams come from and what they mean. Dreams are real experiences, which feel as real as waking life. It is not surprising that many prescientific societies believe dreams are the true experiences of the spirit wandering in other worlds as real as this. In some cultures the dream world is thought of as a meeting place where man can communicate with spiritual beings or powers. In others, actions committed in dreams are considered as consequential as waking actions, to be rewarded or punished accordingly.

In dreams anything can happen—horrendous crimes, terrible disasters, wondrous magic, and holy miracles. The appearance of the deceased in dreams may have motivated the development of the human concept of life after death, as Idries Shah suggests in his book *Oriental Magic*. Before amusing ourselves too much at the expense of such "primitive" thinking, let us consider that people who consider their dreams as other worlds are just interpreting signals as semblances.

Freud's theory holds that dreams are created by unconscious wishes, often uncivilized ones, such as the desire of a man to have sexual relations with his mother. To Freud, much—if not almost all—dream content could be connected to the sexual urge. Without these frustrated drives of the id, there would be no dreams, especially for Freud, as dreams are supposed to guard sleep—keep unacceptable impulses from awakening us. But are dreams in truth so tied to unconscious drives?

In 1977 Allan Hobson and Robert McCarley proposed their "activation-synthesis" theory of dreams. Dreams, they said, are by-products of the REM process, which is driven by the lower parts of the brain. Cells in the brain stem become highly activated in REM sleep and send a barrage of messages upward to the cortex as well as down the spine to inhibit the motor system. The muscles are prevented from moving, external sensory input is blocked, and cortical motor, sensory, and association areas are kicked into action.

This is called, in the trade, "bottom-up" brain activity—perceptual and motor areas are turned on by random impulses. The dream is the interpretation of the impulses and is a confused and confusing sequence of bizarre and meaningless sensations and actions. Falling, sexual excitation, flying, paralysis, events of the day, are all intermingled. The dream is then the brain devising a partially coherent story from all the noise. The content of a dream is no more meaningful than an inkblot.

The activation-synthesis theory is a provocative new perspective. It has been highly influential in helping modern researchers break from neurosis-based ideas to model dreaming on brain processes. However, activation-synthesis also falls short in explaining dream experiences. As Stephen Laberge said: "Anybody who has ever awakened from a dream exclaiming with delight, 'What a "wonderful" plot that was!' knows that sometimes dreams are more coherent than 'the forebrain making the best of a bad job' would suggest." At least they seem so to us. Why?

Freud's theory postulates that dreams reveal the conflicts and neuroses of the dreamer, hidden in arcane symbols. Hobson theorized that dreams are only significant because of the little fragments shown to us by random activation. Consequently, the meaning we project into the otherwise senseless sequence of events is just the interpreter working on a confusion of images and feelings. Also contradicting Freud, Hobson declared that the meaning of dreams is transparent, not symbolic. In Hobson's dream, a cigar can well be a cigar, not a penis.

While it is completely unconvincing to think that dreams *evolved* to serve as letters from the unconscious mind about our condition, dreams can convey much more meaning than an ink-blot, or any other impersonal projective test. Dreams are like artworks, revealing something of the structure of the artist's mind, as individual as the life of the dreamer.

What happens to us in dreams is composed from recent events, active concerns, motivations, and anxieties. If you go to sleep hungry, you are more likely to dream of food. If you are on the lookout for a rare bird, you may well sight it in your dreams. If you have a terrible fear of fire, you may be plagued by dreams of fire. Dreams are bizarre, transient, and peculiar because we try to make some kind of semblance out of the goofy salad going on inside us.

Why dream? What useful purpose does dreaming serve? Nobody really knows. The purpose of REM sleep must include a rationale for why all mammals experience it, so the reason cannot be purely psychological. So far, scientists have been able to determine that REM sleep assists adaptation. Only mammals are capable of complex learning, such as when rats learn to alternate turning right or left in a maze to find food. Also, people who learn difficult tasks in the day show increased amounts of REM sleep that night.

REM sleep stimulates the nervous system, exercising connections and keeping the brain fresh and ready for waking life.

Newborn babies spend 50 percent of their sixteen to eighteen hours a day of sleep in REM, perhaps warming up their preprogrammed behaviors. Hobson believes that REM sleep may help us—and all our mammal relatives—to put in place and rehearse the famous four Fs of adaptation—feeding, fighting, fleeing, and sex. It is so important for reproduction for us to practice the last, he suggests, that natural selection ensured that we experience a powerful sex drive during each and every REM period. Consequently, penile erections and vaginal engorgement occur in REM sleep, some vindication for Freud's prime processor.

However, the best answer to why we dream is because we have brains. Because it is essential to survival for us to have a map of the world "ready at mind," our brains model worlds whether they are based on current information from the senses or on internally generated activation of collected experiences and current concerns. In both cases the world we inhabit is assembled from pieces of experience produced by the various modules of the mind. It is not easy to tell a dream from waking, which should alert us to how distant we are from direct knowledge of the world around us.

There is dissension between the activation-synthesis and the interpretative view, whether psychoanalytic or not. I think they divide along the lines of different levels of signals and semblances. Remember, as in memory, that low-level signals can chunk together to make higher-order units.

In the great preponderance of dream life, the signals are straightforward elements of waking life and simple representations of the brain's state during sleep. They include features needing integration into the mind's representation of the world. People move, paint their homes, others die, new products at work appear, horns beep, relationships change, concepts change, seasons change; there are new TV programs, movies, books, children, classes, foods, noises; the news changes, the sports listings change, the new fall colors for dresses are different; we lose things, forget things, and much more.

Housekeeping goes on daily, in the mind as in the home. Yet there are central issues of life about which many people are concerned that do not have too much to do with the minor changes in our life's signals. And, of the six or so dreams per night and the countless images we produce, very few are thought of, interpreted, and remembered. Reported, remembered, presented dreams are extraordinarily few compared with the wealth of material from which they are selected. This "manifest dream" may be, like the rest of our "dreamt" daily world, a product of our semblance processing, knitting together the large pieces of the world, not the signals from the brain stem.

It is the difference, I believe, between putting the edge detectors together to make the *as* and *ds* of a word, and knowing what *adapt* means to an analysis of the mind. One is important but low level and certainly occurs—we can't know what *adapt* means without processing an *a*. However, knowledge of adapting depends on other concerns—our interest in the mind, our interest in evolution, and more. Similarly, an image in a dream may well get selected for our conscious thought as a result of our continuing preoccupation with an issue in our life, such as loss, fidelity, fear. It isn't meaningless, this process, just a different part of the process.

In the course of a Freudian analysis, a patient may produce a series of similar but not identical statements that appear to be recollections of memories to which the patient pays no attention. In a successful analysis, these connect to memories when they suddenly are reconnected to their emotions. Freud said these scenes "are not productions of real occurrences . . . but products of the imagination which find their instigation in mature life." Freud believed that dream work in psychoanalysis is a further reconstruction of memories in a way that connects emotions to events adaptively.

So during dreaming, thoughts translate into images, as in the Hobson description. However, during the telling or the reconstruction of the dream, the process is like that of Penfield's patients, weaving the signals into a known semblance. The dreamer interprets the dream itself instantly and thus "dreams" the same dream twice. The argument between these two viewpoints is, in my view, about two levels of a very complex, multilevel process, the process of knowing the world in all its elements.*

*I am indebted to an interesting paper entitled "Hierarchies, Boundaries and Representation in a Freudian Model of Mental Organization," by William Grossman, Michigan Psychoanalytic Society in March 1988. I also thank Owen Renik for drawing this paper to my attention.

How do we experience the world then? The world of experience is highly evolved, selecting a few signals from the outside and linking them to survive; the mind is specialized to keep us au courant in our one local world: one language, one culture, one locale, one style of life.

We sift constantly through signals, making decisions, inferring from information, deciding what a person is talking about, sorting through different hypotheses, deciding if a situation is an emergency, if resources are scarce, if that noise needs action, if something is larger than another or brighter or smaller.

This complex, incoherent process produces a dream of the world, one in which we usually do the right thing. While we don't understand why the process works, we do know that the mind evolved to create semblances from meager signals; those semblances recombine to make up the dream in which we live. It is part of the reentry system described earlier.

It is difficult to accept that our experiences are a dream, because most of the time our mind responds through its "hard points," specific systems that extract specific features of the outside world. These keep us on track, keep the dream fitted and refitted continuously. The same processes hold in perceiving different parts of the world as in remembering them, as well as in the night dream itself, where random events are assembled by the same logic.

So our broad but shallow mind tries to link everything together, from linking edges to make a square to linking falling, flying, sex, business worries into a dream. Our routines are recruited from emergencies, so we must always make fast judgments and incorporate all information, for conditions might change. We're constantly on-line, reinterpreting our experience and our life. This ability to invent instant semblances of the world is a capacity that we exercise every night in our dreams.

Although no one can give a complete framework, it seems that evolution offers us a beginning set of selections of the world. We pick up a sound or a light byte, then elaborate on it, creating the dream, the semblance we live within. And the world of experience is thus dreamt, whether it be of a house, a remembrance, or a dream itself. We live inside a very small world, one highly evolved to work. And most of the time it does.

VI

Is This the Person to Whom I'm Speaking?

Just asking for a donation wakes up the whole system.

So every moment a fresh purpose occurs to the heart,
Not proceeding from itself, but from its situation.
Why, then are you confident about the heart's purposes?
What make you vows only to be covered with shame?

—RUMI

Why do we promise with all our heart to do things which we never do, when it unquestionably destroys our friendships? Why do we do many things that "we" don't approve of?

When we are talking to someone, the one talking to you, who may well be honest, sincere, and concerned, may not be "in place" later on when it's time to act. Someone else, maybe excited by something else, may be "minding" the store. This staffing of the mind, so adaptive in most situations, also leaves us liable to unwonted influence. And we change personality as well, shifting centers of action and judgment without knowing that we're doing so. The unconscious shifting of the mind's works is what salesmen as well as scoundrels try to take advantage of.

Here we look at how our recruitment system can make us vulnerable to sales pitches, cult leaders and judging others. Our minds shift drastically because of all this conscious, as well as unconscious, influence. First we look at how sometimes we are not aware of what is happening to us, and then other times we are more aware of what is happening than we know. Such is the ever-shifting system inside us. We need to recognize that, like Lily Tomlin's obnoxious telephone operator, Ernestine, "Is this the person to whom I'm speaking" is not always a joke.

20

Mind in Place
and Mind
Out of Place

You're at home on a quiet Sunday afternoon. The doorbell rings. It is a cordial and concerned couple. They are committed to the beautification of the state. They show you a three-by-five card that they hope you will display in a window of your home. It says "Keep California Beautiful." You accept it and put the card in the window.

You don't think much about it, but placing the card changes something within you, something important, something that makes you, unaware, more vulnerable to new influences. Two weeks later another couple rings the doorbell. This time they are wearing "Driver Safety" buttons and are lugging with them an eight-by-six-foot sign. It says "DRIVE CAREFULLY" in big black letters. They ask if you would put it on your front lawn, even though it would block your view of the street and darken the whole house.

Now, you and I would believe that you'd never put the sign up. And indeed, almost nobody who hadn't been visited by the "Keep California Beautiful" couple agreed. But of those people who were visited after the first group, 60 percent agreed to put the huge sign up.

I wouldn't believe that anyone would do such a stupid thing either, if in the mid-sixties I had not been helping one of the research assistants who went from house to house. Of course, I didn't know who had been visited previously, but as I made my rounds, I was simply stunned at how easy it was to convince some people and how impossible it was to convince others.

I now know why it happened. When the homeowners agreed

to put the three-by-five card up, they shifted a new and unsuitable mind into place. The experience of displaying a small card in the window got a "foot in the mind" and shifted them to think of all the useful social projects and programs available and what they could be doing. When the next one came along . . .

Why Good People Do Bad Things So Easily

Supposedly model citizens go awry because we all have numerous minds, containing different "rights" and "wrongs." No one is all good or all bad. In some new situations, different people emerge: Nice men and women abuse their children, a nice middle-class boy suddenly becomes the shaven-headed follower of a "wise man." The serial killer who seemed to be a mild-mannered model citizen is almost a standard story now. Yet none of us is all that far away from "changing our minds" and selves.

Recruitment of minds underlies some brainwashing techniques. The American public was amazed when U.S. POWs returned home from the Korean War. Many of them naturally stated their dislike of the Chinese Communists, but there was an extraordinary amount of praise for some of their achievements: "They've done a fine job with the people of China"; "Although communism isn't good for the United States, it's a good thing for Asia."

Unlike the North Koreans, who brutally treated American prisoners, the Chinese were gentle. Instead of physical maltreatment, they targeted the prisoners' mental states, shifting the mind in place. The captives were first asked to make relatively unexceptionable statements: "The United States does indeed have problems with poverty"; "In a communist country, unemployment is not a serious problem." They were also asked to write essays, in the guise of students, recapping the communist position on many issues not connected with the war: distribution of wealth, health services for all, and the like. So they wrote, with their captors' approval, fulsome little turgid screeds about the greatness of Mao and the sanctity of the humble workers.

They paid the price for writing their piles of rubbish. Their work caused a gradual and gentle shifting of mind in place, which then worked wonders. When the boys returned home, their attitudes toward the enemy had undergone a startling change, unlike that of prisoners of any other war in which the United States had been a part.

Sometimes the coincidence between ordinary shifts of mind and exceptional public events is overwhelming. In the late 1970s, I had two experiences so close together that they're still linked in my mind.

I knew of the work of another psychologist, who was, as was common to social psychologists of that era, researching how people change their minds. This time, somewhat like the "driver safety, foot in the door" study, his assistants visited people, appealing for charity. One group received a standard pitch; a second received the same pitch, but the solicitors added, "Even giving a penny will help." Of those who heard the standard pitch, 20 percent donated, and their average donation was under $3 (this was the seventies). Of those who heard the second pitch, 62 percent donated. That's not so surprising, since many people would seem to be able to come up with a penny. More donations would surely result, as the higher percentage of donors indicates, but one would expect these donations to be small, in line with the suggestion of a penny gift, so that the average donation would be lower. It wasn't. The average donation was over $5! Those persuaded into donating by this "penny pitch" donated as much or more than did the others. Why?

When one of the squadron of simpletons that makes up our mind is shifted into place and prepares to act, all evidence indicates that it doesn't always know (or, more probably, care) how it got there. The "donation docket" shifts in easily when you are asked to give a penny, but once it is active, the program causes you to donate normally. This happens because our minds don't always communicate with one another. This separation of minds is what makes us so fragile, so liable to change.

I had all this evidence on the drifting, shifting, weakling nature of our minds in my mind one day in 1977 when the mayor of San Francisco asked me to lunch to advise about raising money for a church-run citizens group that was trying to help addicts in the "Tenderloin" district of the city. This area of San Francisco is an older, somewhat run-down zone near the center of town, filled with older homes, street people, and streetwalkers. The mayor, an attractive and energetic politician named George Moscone, was to be assassinated the next year by the ex-cop supervisor Dan White. However, that is another story.

We went to Bardelli's, an old-time restaurant with a posh ambience near the Tenderloin. There were four of us at lunch, all but me dead now: the mayor, a pastor, me, and a fourth. The clergyman was saying how much he appreciated the efforts of the other man, because he could get the most hard workers out on the streets helping the poor and the addicts. "His people," the pastor said, "are working long hours, helping the poor, helping and helping more. Jim here is the man who has the method, and we'd like you, Doctor, to see if we can apply the way he works to the rest of the volunteers."

The mayor asked Jim how he had managed to convince hundreds of citizens to volunteer and work so hard, when everyone else could get only a few people at a time, and those for only a few hours. Jim said that he began the technique of building up his mission by approaching prosperous-appearing prospects on the street during their lunch hour, asking them to help the poor. Most of the office workers walked past or otherwise refused, but Jim had instructed his operators to then say: "Help them for just five minutes at work by folding and mailing a few envelopes." Then they'd offer five addressed stamped envelopes and the letters, as well as a note about future work opportunities.

Everybody, Jim announced proudly, did something. "And they came back for more. You know, once I get somebody, I can get them to do anything." The clergyman beamed, and the mayor smiled hopefully. I was to see if his methods of fund raising and volunteer assistance had "wide application for the city's relief services."

I agreed to find out. I spent some time talking to Jim and observing his co-workers and interviewing them. But after working for a week with Jim and observing what went on at the church center, I was not convinced that he was the right person for all this charity work, even though he had his own successful mission. His methods reminded me too much of the pennies for donation, the foot in the door, the Chinese system. Something about it, and I only wish now that I could have put my finger on what it was, unsettled and bothered me, more than it should have, or so I thought. Anyway, I decided to turn down any further work on the project.

The mission went on, obtaining its new recruits in ways similar to Jim's description. But then things started to go wrong, and there were articles in the press questioning the value and even the propriety of the mission.

In response to the mounting criticism, Jim left San Francisco and went to Guyana, a small South American country, to set up a new community of his followers, which he named Jonestown.

Jim Jones's followers were not the only ones to meet a horrible end, although theirs was one of the most horrific. Joining a cult is easy, as has been demonstrated by followers of Rajneesh, by the Moonies, and others, since the mind in place is easily recruited; but it takes the rest of the person along, and it can (at extremes) cause great tragedies like the mass poisoning at Jonestown.

21

Interpreting
Our Selves

Mind shifts are unquestionably disastrous when we are conscripted unaware into a cult. But this same mental process goes on inside us all the time. While Sigmund Freud well described the process of transference—the patient's transferral of his or her feeling toward parents to a therapist—this recruitment phenomenon inside the mind (which I label "mind in place") isn't limited to the therapeutic encounter. Reactions and judgments, originally evolved for emergency work, are recruited for other purposes. These routines swap in and out of consciousness, bringing about distortions.

"Minds" moving in and out of "place" seems to be the way the mind recruits its operators. The process is similar to the way software works in a modern computer, where different programs are swapped in and out of a working memory. They enter, take over, and operate, and when they leave, they leave no traces. The collections of reactions are the minds we use to navigate through life. While there are many minds, there are many more situations in the world, so we recruit one mind for many situations. The squadron of simpletons is recruited for different jobs. This process underlies our problems making judgments, making decisions, making do.

In his recently translated *The Art of the Novel,* the Czech novelist Milan Kundera recalled, after observing a friend for decades, how one good woman's mind shifted and so acted poorly, due to her very heroics:

> [She] had been arrested in 1951 during the Stalinist trials
> in Prague, and convicted of crimes she hadn't committed.
> Hundreds of Communists were in the same situation at

the time. All their lives they had entirely identified themselves with their Party. When it suddenly became their
prosecutor, they agreed, like Josef K., "to examine their
whole lives, their entire past, down to the smallest details"
to find the hidden offense and, in the end, to confess to
imaginary crimes. My friend managed to save her own life
because she had the extraordinary courage to refuse to
undertake, as her comrades did, . . . the "search for her
offense." Refusing to assist her persecutors, she became
unusable for the final show trial. So instead of being
hanged she got away with life imprisonment. After
fourteen years, she was completely rehabilitated and
released.

This woman had a one year old child when she was
arrested. On release from prison, she thus rejoined her
fifteen year old son and had the joy of sharing her humble
solitude with him from then on. That she became passionately attached to the boy is entirely comprehensible. One
day I went to see them, by then her son was 25. The
mother, hurt and angry, was crying. The cause was utterly
trivial: the son had overslept or something like that. I
asked the mother, "Why get so upset over such a trifle? Is
it worth crying about? Aren't you overdoing it?"

It was the son who answered for his mother: "No, my
mother's not overdoing it. My mother is a splendid, brave
woman. She resisted when everyone else cracked. She
wants me to become a real man. It's true all I did was
oversleep, but what my mother reproached me for was
something much deeper. It's my attitude. My selfish attitude. I want to become what my mother wants me to be.
And with you as a witness, I promise her I will."

What the party never managed to do to the mother,
the mother had managed to do to her son. She had forced
him to identify with an absurd accusation, to "seek his
offense," to make a public confession. I looked on, dumb-
founded, at this Stalinist minitrial, and I understood all at
once that *the psychological mechanisms that function in great
(apparently incredible and inhuman) historical events are the
same as those that regulate private (quite ordinary and very
human) situations* [italics mine].

I wrote a drier version in my *Multimind*: "The same neural processes that evolved to judge brightness, length and taste now have to judge prices, politics and personalities."

Minds shifting produce inconsistent people in different situations, as the working mind "in place" executes its job as if it had always been there, then disappears, to be replaced with another "recruit," one with different memories, priorities, and plans. And "we," our conscious self, hardly ever notice what has occurred. We know what is *on* our mind—whether we're seeing trees or rain, smelling smoke or hearing rock—but we have no capacity to know what is *in* our mind—which mind "program" is acting for us at any given time. So our standards change without our awareness.

Let's follow the computer analogy for this "mind in place" concept. Computers can do many things. Mine can create drawings on screen on its own, it can do accounting, it can do word processing (it is doing this now), and it can play games. But it can't do all these things at once, because it has a limited central processor and memory. So one program occupies the system at a time; hence, the limited working memory may contain one program, such as a spreadsheet. When one is finished with the program, another, perhaps a word-processing one, may be loaded into working memory.

When one program is, then, "in place," it reckons with its own set of priorities. Commands are different for these different programs, and the data they access are different, although some programs can access another's data. Now, in both the brain and the computer, working memory is limited, and the number of programs is great. While our own assortment of "minds" is as different as a graphics program and a database are, they still have different priorities regarding selection of information, reactions, memories, and judgments. In extreme circumstances, we can quite easily shift to different multiple personalities. This shifting of minds makes our adaptable mind surprisingly vulnerable to cults, to drugs, and to advertising as we will see.

The tendency of the mind in place to overreact to vivid information can cause violence and even kill. The suicides of prominent people are often given front-page space in the newspaper. And, immediately after a highly publicized suicide, the number of suicides and commercial airline crashes and automobile fatalities also rises.

In more ordinary experiences, out-of-place minds can make us misjudge people or can make moods spread to color other thoughts, then pass away. Some people act "possessed" for longer or shorter periods; others can think certain thoughts only when drunk or angry or elated or depressed. Here's a basic, well-studied, precise example.

You go to place a bet on the ponies. Your horse is listed at 4 to 1, but you think the odds are better than that, so you bet. On your way to the bettor's window, you believe the odds are, say, 3 to 1 or so, so it's a good bet. However, after you place your bet, your mind has moved; you now think your horse has almost an even chance to win! Nothing has happened. The race hasn't been run yet. But your mind has moved, shifted, as a result of placing the bet. This research study was done at a racetrack, interrupting bettors before and after they had placed their bets. How many times does your mind similarly shift without your knowing it? And how does this shift change your priorities?

One researcher found out how much people were willing to pay for their involvement in their decisions. Psychologist Ellen Langer sold lottery tickets for a $50 prize. Each ticket cost $1.00. Subjects were either handed a ticket or allowed to choose their own. Later, ticket holders were asked how much they would sell their ticket for. Those who had been handed a ticket asked for an average of $1.96, while those who chose their own wanted $8.67. Why? Choosing the ticket shifts the mind in place to one that attaches fantasies and expectations to the ticket, which becomes more central, more valuable, and more a part of the person.

I've always wondered why a mother, after losing a child to a drunk driver, and having no more children, becomes so inexhaustibly active in the prevention of future drunk driving. Or, why, after a relative is lost due to hospital mismanagement, family members become so very earnestly engaged in reforming hospital practice in the country. I don't think it is only altruism at work, or "working through" the loss, though of course there may be some of that. I believe the changed attitude is due to the shift of mind recruited and amplified by the difficulty. After hearing about a tragedy and becoming involved in it, the person highlights the issue—drunks on the road, doctors who are unqualified. The excitement of the loss amplifies the mind in place. Thus, a parent may now redirect his or her mind to Mothers Against Drunk Driving or an AIDs awareness group. This "conversion" may well benefit society, but recruitment of minds in place also makes joining cults surprisingly simple.

Divorces are often tough and unpleasant, even mean. We often hate those we once loved. A person who once caused us great positive excitement now is now seen as being quite negative and the excitement now magnifies all that is unacceptable. And we can easily be seduced by a loving message, join an organization, and find ourselves in a hateful cult, hating the outsiders who threaten our love. The mind in place not only shifts, but its "volume" is turned up by the arousal, and we are not aware of this.

In a test of how we usually interpret emotion, two psychologists injected epinephrine (which causes arousal) into students who were told it was a vitamin. Half the students were with a euphoric person who tossed paper airplanes and shot baskets into the trash can with wads of paper. These students reported feeling euphoric. The other half of the students confronted an insulting and irritated person and later reported being angry. The psychologists, Stanley Schachter and Jerome Singer, concluded of this famous early 1960s study that emotional experiences can depend upon the interpretation of arousal. Many people have tried with little success to replicate the result of this experiment. Since it is no longer permissible to conduct experiments with epinephrine injections, there will be no further replication attempts. However, many other studies indicate that our interpretations of ourselves can have profound effects on our emotional experiences.

While these laboratory experiments are subject to argument,

there are plenty of real-life examples of unexplained feelings causing problems. After a surgical procedure, an individual's mental state seems to be more unsettled than would be expected. I don't mean the understandable worry and difficulty that are associated with the surgery itself, nor the discomfort following and the possible painful aftereffects. Something seemed to happen to people I knew weeks later, when the painkillers were not necessary, when they were out of trouble.

Recently I asked a surgeon to conduct telephone interviews with his patients about their feelings every week after successful abdominal surgery. Right after surgery, of course, they are medicated and their feelings are numb. Then, a bit later, the pain is strong, but the relief from completing the surgery and having a successful operation seems to makes people feel okay. But later still, attitudes change. Of the twenty-three patients interviewed, twenty had a great increase in worry and feelings of worthlessness and despair after six or seven weeks.

I believe these bad feelings are due to the nonconscious internal disruption and the process of slow healing that follows surgery. Weeks later, we have no way of knowing what is going on inside ourselves. We have little sensory apparatus for detecting wound healing inside, since we aren't prepared, via our evolution, for the internal activity/arousal after surgery. Once one is far enough away from surgery, the only explanation for the painful feelings would be that something else is wrong.

What is wrong, we ask ourselves silently, noting signals of which we are consciously unaware. Maybe it's my marriage. Maybe it's my work. Maybe it's my weight, I always feel ugly. But maybe it's the silent screams inside, as hormone levels change and wounds, invisible, seam together. Importantly, the depressed feeling occurs only a few weeks after surgery, not right afterward, when the effect of surgery is fresh in mind. This diffuse, unexplained, and thus irrational arousal is what gives emotions their bad name. And certainly we can see how they can make us vulnerable in specific situations. You may not understand why a couple you know ever got married; they were always so incompatible. She was so intellectual, he so earthy; she so cool, he so hot. She says: "It was the war." That is how she explains it. She was aroused.

And many people find that exercise with a partner of the opposite sex is very provocative. Why? People who exercise and then see porn have more sexual excitement than those who view pornography without exercise beforehand. Because of "mind in place," becoming sweaty and aroused can transfer to sexual excitement—working out is great for making out. But it may not be so good for a long-term relationship, because the wrong mind was in place, making its hot and desirous decisions. All the rest of the "yous," cool and worrying about taking out the garbage and cooking dinner, have to live with a choice made by a different mind for a long time. This shift of mind into sexual attraction is why discos are so noisy, stimulating, and fun. But the person you meet there isn't necessarily the dominant personality or mind in place in the marriage.

One woman wrote to me: "I've had three divorces now, and each time I get involved, it is with someone quite exciting. Yet after only a few months of marriage, it all seems to fall apart. I've been to psychotherapy, been to marriage counseling, and tried everything." She then asked for suggestions. I wrote, asking her for more details about her life, but we found nothing that might cause the dilemma. Then, in an answer to another letter, I noticed her letterhead: She worked for an exercise club. I asked if she had met all her ex-husbands at work. She had! I counseled her to forget these exercised men and to restrict her search to someone she met elsewhere, and she did. Her work situation seemed vital to me because of the "war bride" effect: The excitement of the situation *transfers* to the mind in place, and everything seems exciting, even dudes in exercise shorts.

The effect extends to many emotional areas. A divorce researcher noted a prevalent but sad transfer recently: "One of the girls in my study told me when she was fifteen, 'Violence is something that involves my father, but I'm free of it.' At nineteen, in a serious relationship with a man, she said, 'He hits me—that's how I know he likes me.' I nearly cried."

Part of our problem, in all of these situations, is that we've incorrectly interpreted what is going on inside us. While unconscious interpretations usually work very well, we can, surprisingly, misinterpret ourselves because we don't realize that we dream up the world, moment to moment. Our own emotions can fool us, our ideas of violence can fool us, we can mistake the love offered by "friends" and become cult members. Such is the adaptability of the mind.

VII

Getting to Know "Yous"

Getting to know "yous."

There are so many simpletons going about their business that it is no wonder that our mental system evolved to keep us out of touch with them all and to interpret ourselves in a simple way. Below a full consciousness there are several levels of awareness, and it is not necessary, or even desirable, for us to be conscious of everything in our world. If we knew everything that we "know," we'd go crazy—there's too much. So, some things seem to seep in to the mind, beneath the threshold of conscious awareness.

We evolved a set of automatic rules to interpret events in the world, and ourselves. We may not like the priorities of our limited mind system—one limited to keeping out of trouble, minding the store, and organizing our actions around the short-term contingencies of our environment. But this is the system that "got us here." Whether it can get us into our future is one issue we have to take up.

Events shift and even jerk us around unawares. Your family has finally decided to go on that skiing holiday after six years of going to Miami for your winter week away from home. For several weeks prior to the trip, you spend most evenings poring over the lavish brochure of the picturesque Frozen Rivers Resort Village, looking at the views of the Rockies in winter, the long slopes, brilliantly clothed skiers schussing down the beautiful powdered inclines, and later the hot toddies at the lodge in front of a crackling fire. It will be heaven. The week before your trip, you go to a party and mention your vacation to the woman standing next to you. Unfortunately, you are talking to an orthopedic surgeon. She recoils as if you've slapped her and says: "You have to be crazy to ski. Just last weekend a young man came into the hospital in an ambulance and had to be wheeled up in a chair to surgery. He had slipped on the slopes and fallen head over heels over 2,000 feet. He had to get emergency treatment in the mountains, and I had to amputate one leg. I'll probably have to do the other. He will be paralyzed, anyway. And just for a weekend in the snow, going down a mountain, going nowhere."

You're not exactly delighted when you introduce the surgeon to your husband and see her begin her routine.

If you were to look at yourself as a bunch of simpletons in the coolness of mind, you would think: "There's more than one slippery slope here. Obviously, she sees all the injuries and has to fix them, and her viewpoint is quite prejudiced. I know there is only a very small chance of getting injured. After all, James has gone skiing every winter weekend for the last fifteen years without getting hurt, and I've only known one person who has gotten hurt in my whole lifetime. And meeting her and listening to her doesn't really alter anything; it only gives me access to a world I know has to exist. The story just shifts my mind into another set of judgments. We can't expect any additional chance of injuries thanks to this conversation. She hasn't told me, for instance: 'There will be a severe snowstorm and hurricanelike winds this weekend, so I'd delay the trip for a week if I were you.' That would be realistic information, and we could change our plans. Her remarks don't change anything at all except my own mind."

But your simpleton takes control, and you bolt to the nearest telephone to call the airline to inquire about their "Fun in the Sun" package tour for the family. And now most of "yous" hope and pray, with all your heart, that the plan isn't sold out, and although you are not a truly religious individual, you pray again, with even greater intensity, that there are no airline pilots at the party who are going to talk to you about the safety records of their airline.

The automatic shift of simpletons is caused by access. Like a real news event or a personal shock or even a sudden mood change, an incidental event automatically shifts your thinking, even when you aren't aware of it. Let's analyze this case: Your meeting with the surgeon shifted your anticipation of the trip from the joys of the slopes, the toddies and the fires, to the possible dangers of skiing—the broken bones, broken necks, paralysis, even possible death. And now, solely as a result of a random conversation, you will always believe it was your fault if something happened to one of your children on this holiday. It's impossible to go on that trip.

Similarly, your opinion of people and of your goals and life actions can shift drastically because of the access you have to information. In the case of the skiing trip, such access didn't yield any information of value, yet we often can't distinguish the valuable from the merely chance. The media, with their featuring of dramatic news, magnify this problem.

The same thing happens with public policy: Margaret Thatcher kept news coverage of the Falklands war off British television, lest the access to the killings inevitable in war interfere with her policy. This access changed the shape of the Vietnam conflict, when the devastation of war was brought into homes via television. Today it influences drug policy, when a particularly lurid murder or bust receives attention, and it certainly affected our ideas about the Gulf War. The mind adapts, whether it would seem rational to do so or not.

22

On Rationality
and Adaptation

We use that same old ever-adapting brain to judge events in the world. Proposals to double the U.S. government's budget for taking care of the homeless to $760 million was politically impossible in 1989 and 1990. In contrast, a mere 1 percent overrun in the $38 billion Midgetman nuclear missile received little government scrutiny; and the cost was approved. Yet the increase is the same—$380 million. The Midgetman overrun is viewed as a slight change from the original estimates, while the same money in the homeless budget constitutes a doubling. We judge the degree of change, not the actual dollar amount, let alone the relevance.

Crack is one of the most important problems. It is addictive and will kill thousands of people each year. We've greatly increased our budget to combat it. But suppose I told you of a substance six times as addictive as crack, which killed 4 million Americans in the 1980s? We have no large budget to fight it. The substance is tobacco, which slips into the mind's routine. It will kill millions in the 1990s too, thousands more than crack will. Cigarettes, however, have killed millions for years, so we don't need to think about them; our mind finds it easy to ignore the continuing problem, just as it does a continuing noise or a continuing heavy weight.

Since the mind evolved to incorporate all information, before and after an event, into a semblance, we're open to subtle manipulations in advertising. Whereas it is clearly unethical for companies plainly to misrepresent their products ("New Doitall cures all cancers instantly!"), it is not so plain how we should regard advertisements that imply a relationship by making two statements in one breath. An energetic woman on television tells you, "Brand

X is a revolutionary new vitamin. I feel great all day!" The obvious implication is that she feels great because she takes Brand X vitamins. But the advertisement does not say this. The logical connection is not spoken, so the company that makes Brand X is not liable for false advertising. However, the human mind is not a logical instrument, but one that absorbs everything so as to compute likely events in the environment.

Advertisers would not make such advertisements if endorsements were unsuccessful. Nor would there be any point in showing healthy young men and women smoking their cigarettes in the fresh outdoors if the mind could easily distinguish between the simultaneously presented concepts of smoking and a vigorous, healthy life. We are not inherently rational, and our memories are not snapshots of the past. As we've seen, memory, like other processes of mind, serves us by maintaining our consistent dream of the world.

The failure of adaptation is more precisely a failure to update the system that has until now held us in good stead—the oversupplied thousand-forms-of-mind brain, part of which gets selected in the world and then educated. For the mind has evolved well to adapt to the world of our fathers and mothers, a stable world where, if our family farmed, we would do so; if they practiced slash and burn, we would do so; if they hunted antelope, we would do so; if they built stucco, we would do so; if verbs at the end of sentences were, we so would do.

Many psychological scientists have studied our constant misjudgments of events. This research, most often called deviations from rationality, offers a striking set of demonstrations of how the mind can make mistakes. While this research has become influential, very often inciting calls for better judgment or better training of rational judgment, this prescription is as useful as trying to improve our future by knowing all the *T* terms in *Cultural Literacy*. In truth, this work demonstrates that the mind is well adapted for the average world in which our ancestors lived. Remember, decisions are based on what would work best in a stable world, not one where all changes. The problem is that our world is now transformed: In strategic ways it has changed more since World War II than it changed between the time of Christ and that war, as

Eisenhower said. It is a "new world," as in the title of a book Paul Ehrlich and I wrote in 1989.

With enough manipulation anyone can cause individuals to make mistakes, and the mind is certainly biased so that its quick reflexes cause errors when information is presented by clever psychologists. It is important in any research, to separate the studies of the mind from the stunts. I am for improving judgment, but giving the Nobel prize to someone who showed that human judgment deviates from normative econometric theory says more about the way we look at our mind than the value of the work.

A mind built up with countless specific adaptations can never be rational. We piece together the results of a small set of probes to judge the world, picking up a few signals and making quick assessments of what is outside, in the case of marauders, and inside, in the case of memories and dreams. Such a mind will never be rational; but it will always try to adapt. And it cannot always be correct either. If we consider a mind that has evolved to meet most situations adequately, say 95 percent of them, we may have a better idea of what being correct is. Consider these sentences:

- *Dhis is 95% correct.*
- *Although 99% does sound awflly good, it produces a sentence that is only as accurate as this one is.*
- *Joanne, your mother and I will not, after all, be attending the new play at the theater next Thursday.* This sentence, which could be 100 percent accurate, might also be 99 percent accurate if the word *now* was intended, rather than *not*. A 1 percent inaccuracy completely changes its meaning.

If evolution gave us a system that is right most of the time, much more than 99 percent, one can still find holes, given the enormous amount of information to be processed. Looking at our mistakes, in carefully controlled studies, does little to help us understand how and why people, for the most part, get through life, avoid dangers, eat when they are hungry, achieve a balanced diet, respond adequately to their boss, remember who their children are, keep their balance, maintain their weight, remember their last conversation, learn mathematics, wear the right pair of socks, wash adequately, and the like.

Stanford psychologist Lee Ross and his colleagues set up an experiment in which they randomly assigned the role of "questioner" for a quiz to one student; to another, the role of "answerer." The questioner was to compose a set of challenging questions from his or her store of knowledge and to pose these questions to the answerer. Later both students rated the general knowledge of both the questioner and answerer.

Notice that the questioners had an advantage. You can ask anyone any question to which you know the answer: Did Nostradamus precede Spinoza? Is spina bifida a hot holiday resort? Is Diego Garcia a cigar? Is there a megillah vanilla ice-cream franchise in Tel Aviv? Anyone, no matter how much he or she knows, can be made to look stupid. What is cute about this study is that the observers did come to believe that the questioners, by virtue of their ability to pose impossible questions, were indeed smarter than the answerers. (Incidentally, this was Ross's way of getting back at his peers, since the genesis of this experiment came from Ross's feeling of rage at his Ph.D. examiners, who asked him all sorts of difficult questions that he could not answer.)

There are many different studies on the way the mind misjudges events: When people are asked to judge the relative frequency of different causes of death, they overestimate the frequency of well-publicized causes such as homicide, tornadoes, and cancer, and they underestimate the frequency of less remarkable causes such as diabetes, asthma, and emphysema. Judgments are biased by how easily people recall specific examples.

This inclination was also demonstrated in an experiment by Tversky and Kahneman in which they read lists of names of well-known people of both sexes. In each list the people of one sex were more famous than those of the other sex. When a group of observers was asked to estimate the proportion of men and women on the lists, they overestimated the proportion of the sex having more famous people on the list. For example, if the list contained very famous women (such as Elizabeth Taylor) and only moderately well-known men (such as Alan Ladd), subjects overestimated the proportion of women on the list. Available memories affect our judgment.

Because the mind's systems focus on what to do next, concrete or vivid information is very influential in judgment, from canceling a skiing trip to making important governmental policy decisions. The president of the United States changed his position on the Israeli invasion of Lebanon only after seeing a child harmed in the war. The photo determined his judgment. Richard Nisbett and Lee Ross described an acquaintance of theirs, who, like the woman who did not go skiing, note the same misjudgment:

> [She] often testifies at congressinal committees on behalf of the Environmental Protection Agency. . . . She reported that the bane of her professional existence is the frequency with which she reports test data such as EPA mileage estimates based on samples of ten or more cars, only to be contradicted by a congressman who retorts with information about a single case: "What do you mean, the Blatzmobile gets twenty miles per gallon on the road?" he says. "My neighbor has one, and he only gets fifteen." His fellow legislators then usually respond as if matters were at a stand-off—one EPA estimate versus one colleague's estimate obtained from his neighbor.

Ross also asked people to judge others in another study. Some were told that their judgment was good, others that it wasn't so good. Afterward, he told them that it was an experiment and their "feedback" was random. However, people incorporated the information anyway: Those who were told they were good raised their self-estimate, and those who received bad evaluations lowered it. That the mind computes on-line means that we adapt to new information even when we don't need to. Again, a system that usually would be helpful misleads here.

Yet many, especially critics of our education system, still believe that, were we more able to spout a set of names about who won what war, all would be well. The view that we should rationally judge alternatives is, first, impossible, as has been explained; moreover, it is absurd with an understanding of how the mind was constructed and how it actually operates. Most analyses of the mind are as well directed as a group of music lovers who assert that all life has led to the creation of opera. A case could be made, grants dispensed, but the premise is shifty. We could consider the delicacy of the larynx and the raising of the upper palate, producing a better voice, that occurred in the evolution between Neanderthal and Cro-Magnon, 45,000 years ago. Surely this shows the import of opera singing! The case could go on to consider the delicate motor control of the fingers and the evolution of the delicate hand itself, as needed for bowing the violin or the keys of a wind instrument. Surely the hand was developed for this purpose. Upright posture could work so that the audience would see the emotional expression. Manufacturing an argument is easy for anyone, as most historical arguments show. Evolution doesn't leave us a good record, but it's easy to fill in the gaps.

In this argument, modern opera is the ultimate goal; in others, the goal is rationality. Analyzing the mind's mistakes as deviations from ideal rationality as a research and intellectual strategy is like analyzing toddler's talk as it deviates from the sound of an aria by Kiri Te Kanawa.

Because the mind tries to keep the world tiny and limited, it works to exaggerate small changes in the world and to ignore large ones. It ignores large changes because our ancestors could do nothing about major shifts in the world except move or die. In a small world, like a darkened room, small shifts become significant. Such an approach was excellent for discerning minuscule shifts in a small village, but it is terrible in a crowded environment or in a long-term relationship.

While the nerve circuits short-circuit reality well and often, the modern problem is the misapplication of mental routines where they are not appropriate. But we can't know how to reeducate ourselves and our children without first identifying these routines. To make a personal change, we have to be able to observe the automatic workings inside ourselves.

23

Observing the
Conscious Self

Most of our interpretations take place unconsciously, automatically, and work by rules evolved over millennia. As the mind is divided into processes that make comparisons, ignore information, shift reactions into place and then out, so consciousness is divided, spread out on different levels. The trick in managing the mind is to bring the automatic reactions into consciousness. For instance, the discovery that emotions have a separate pathway into the brain suggests a different means of mind management, understanding that there are reactions that you can never control. However, you can avoid them, especially by replacing one routine with another.

Let's start with simple actions. What are you going to do now? You can stop reading. You can continue reading. Maybe you'll hear something that makes you angry or maybe a loud noise will roust you up from the book. How do you decide, what do you decide?

The part of the mind where different decisions cross is consciousness. Some sections are automatic, such as driving a car; some are even more basic, such as the recoil of the hand when it contacts a flame. Some are unconscious, as when we frown when someone whom we dislike comes into view. Our actions aren't simple: We don't always do what we want, nor do we always know what or why we're doing something. Our own name, *Homo sapiens sapiens*, means the twice-knowing human (except that we don't always know everything we know, let alone twice).

Consciousness is a word with many meanings, including being awake, being aware of what is going on around us or of what we are doing or of ourselves. Being conscious is being aware of being

aware. It is one step removed from the raw experience of seeing, smelling, acting, moving, and reacting.

Because of our ever-adapting mental system, human beings can change radically, from moment to moment. This, of course, stood our ancestors in quite good stead as long as they lived within an environment with little change. Yet our particular set of transportable simpletons can also make us shift from a good schoolboy to a killer or to a creative genius. The mind is in transit all the time, from one action to another. Most of the time the evolved adaptations smoothly serve us; when they don't and there is a discrepancy, there is always consciousness.

It is in consciousness that restructuring lies. And consciousness, far from being in control all the time, is usually not needed if the mind's recruits are executing their billet. Consciousness comes in late; it is potentially powerful but it is usually a weak force in most of our minds, easily overridden by circumstances, by eloquent people, by lower forces of the mind, by automatic routines.

Writers and scientists have taken very different positions on the nature of consciousness. On the one hand, there is the concept that with consciousness, free will, determination, and learning we can do anything, accomplish anything, change everything, and heal ourselves. It is a good placebo belief, this unconditional optimism, and it often works. But when pushed to its extreme, it can lead to hopeful attempts to change that become hopeless or even harmful, as in, "Well, if I have cancer, I must have had the wrong attitude." On the other hand is the hominerd hypothesis: Reason is all; our mind, as we have it, is what we are stuck with, and the best we can hope for is some kind of eloquence as we realize we're the pawns of fate. Maybe computers will save us.

Many systems determine consciousness. Although language, poetry, philosophy, and the building of computers may seem to be the most important functions we have, what the brain, and hence consciousness, is doing most of the time is quite different.

Consciousness is involved when deliberate, rather than automatic, control or intervention is needed. The main operations of the brain do not really include thought and reason, but blood flow, blood chemistry, and the maintenance of the *milieu intérieur*. Pain interrupts philosophical dialogue; the longing for food eventually disrupts concentration; disruptions in the weather, which disrupt brain functions, also disrupt thought. Very few of our decisions get shunted up to consciousness; only those that need a top-level decision about alternatives. We thus live our lives without knowing how we are doing it and what is happening to us. The simpletons just go about their work.

So, William James's famous statement on the workings of consciousness can be seen as more prescient than even his fans have given him credit for:

7-3

Squadron of simpletons

Our normal waking consciousness, rational consciousness as we call it, is but one special type of consciousness, whilst all about it, parted from it by the filmiest of screens there lie potential forms of consciousness entirely different. We may go through life without suspecting their existence; but apply the requisite stimulus, and at a touch they are there in all their completeness, definite types of mentality which probably somewhere have their field of application and adaptation. No account of the universe in its totality can be final which leaves these other forms of consciousness quite disregarded. How to regard them is the question—for they may determine attitudes though they cannot furnish formulas, and open a region though they fail to give a map. At any rate, they forbid a premature closing of our accounts with reality.

If I could have said it better by this time, I would have. James portrays well the mind as a squadron of adaptations whose activation underlies consciousness and influences our attitudes ("definite types of mentality which probably somewhere have their field of application and adaptation").

Our normal waking consciousness builds us a model of the world, based on sense and body information, expectations, fantasy and crazy hopes, and other cognitive processes. If any of these factors is radically altered, an altered state of consciousness may result.

If sensory knowledge is eliminated, either through anesthetics or sleep or sensory isolation tanks, and our brains are still activated enough to construct a world model, we dream. In the normal course of a day, we undergo profound alterations in our consciousness: At minimum, we sleep, we dream, and we wake. We are consciously aware only of a small part of what our minds are taking in at any one time. And consciousness can split.

A nineteenth-century psychologist, Pierre Janet, suggested to one of his patients under hypnosis that she write letters to certain people when she came out of her hypnotic state. Later, when she was shown the letters, she had no recollection of having written them and accused Janet of forging her signature. The act of writing had been dissociated, "split off," from normal consciousness. Of course, many of the demonstrations of hypnosis show how easy it is to split consciousness and control.

Although the word stems from Greek word for sleep, *hypnos*, hypnosis bears only a superficial resemblance to sleep. There are many ideas about what hypnosis is, but behaviorally and physiologically, it is not sleep. Hypnotized people act as if they register information on some levels but not on others, thus leading to apparently contradictory behavior.

Hypnotist Martin Orne reported an experiment with a subject who spoke only German until age six. When hypnotized, he regressed to age six and was asked whether he understood English. He answered, *"Nein"* ("no").

> When this question was rephrased to him 10 times in English, he indicated each time in German that he was unable to comprehend English, explaining in childlike German such details as that his parents speak English in order that he not understand. While professing his inability to comprehend English, he continued responding appropriately in German to the hypnotist's complex English questions.

The blunt split of consciousness in multiple personalities is the extreme case of separated minds in place, shifting in and out. For most people the separated selves, while independent, are probably like members of a team: They are individuals but know about each other and take direction from the coach. In multiples, extreme trauma, usually in childhood, often causes the conscious restraints on the mind to break down, revealing the separate selves.

We all experience mind splits. Have you never felt "out of it" and just snapped back, with no recollection of the time? Reading a sentence, we are consiously aware of meaning, but we're not usually conscious of the spelling of the words, hence the difficulty of proofreading (did you notice that *consciously* was misspelled earlier in this sentence?). And we're not conscious of grammar unless wrong it being.

Although unconscious minds produce contradictory interpretations of experience, consciousness provides us with a unique, consistent interpretation. We only see one interpretation of the reversible Necker cube at a time. And since we automatically notice mistakes in grammar, we unconsciously analyze the syntax of what we read and hear. It all works automatically.

Do you remember when you first learned to drive a car? "Let's see. Press the left foot down on the clutch. Move the stick shift into first gear. Let the left foot off the clutch. Press on the gas with the right foot." While learning to operate a car, it is very hard to think about anything else—including driving somewhere! But once the movements become automatized, you can carry on a conversation, sing, or admire the scenery without being conscious of operating the car. Shifting gears, even the total activity of driving, becomes automatized.

This takes place when a series of movements or actions is repeated, as in writing a sequence of letters to make a word. Automatization occurs in difficult skills that are practiced or repeated, such as sports and musical activities. Familiar actions are accomplished "without thinking," meaning without much involvement of consciousness, leaving us free to notice new events. This is just as Evolution intended. She wouldn't waste her resources giving us access to our internal workings if it didn't lead to increased reproductive success.

Conscious processes occur one at a time, take effort, and are inefficient. They are more flexible than unconscious processes. At any moment the content of consciousness is what we are prepared to act on next. This system gives events that affect survival quick access to consciousness. Although hunger will not intrude as dramatically as does pain, the need to eat will be felt strongly if you do not eat.

7-4

Doing something the first time is difficult; later it becomes automatic.

When we *know* that we are aware of something, we are conscious of it. But we can be aware of something without being conscious of it—subconscious awareness. During sleep, when attention to the environment is shut off, we are nevertheless aware of sounds. If the sounds have a particular significance, consciousness can be aroused; we awaken when our name is called but not someone else's. When a sleeping person listens to recordings of names, he or she shows a profound cortical response to his or her own name but not to others'. A mother sleeps through the noise of sirens in the streets, but awakens at the far softer sound of her baby crying. She must be aware of the environment, allowing only the important stimuli to enter consciousness. Moreover, there is much evidence that different, separate centers of the mind can respond to events, even when we are not conscious of events.

Strange as it may seem, the signal-gathering apparatus of the mind can receive information well outside of consciousness. From our accustomed perspective, this sounds absurd, but from the understanding we are developing here, it is a necessity, because many of our partial selves operate beneath our awareness, only sometimes informing our conscious selves of their activities.

Many mind processes are not accessible to conscious awareness under any circumstances. Consider speaking: You are conscious of what you say but not of how you say it, conscious of the ideas you want to express but not of the process that converts ideas into words. A great deal of knowledge about how we do things is unconscious in this sense.

How can we recognize a person by his or her face? You might think we distinguish the differences in the features—Joe has a large, lumpy nose; Sue has high, arching eyebrows; Mikhail has a red forehead birthmark. However, the ability to discriminate faces is complex, one that would stretch the capacities of the most sophisticated computer. The ability to assign a name to a particular face selected from a crowd of hundreds is more astonishing than the ability of merely distinguishing one from another.

People who have incurred damage to specific brain areas lose the ability to identify faces, a disorder called prosopagnosia. Such

Need to Know

people can still discriminate among faces (one has thicker brows, someone else a smaller mouth), but they cannot recognize them as belonging to the people they know. One man with this disorder said that if he did not recall the dress his wife was wearing, he could pass her right by at a party without knowing who she was.

Facial recognition proceeds outside of conscious control. We cannot determine who someone is by a verbal description of the features of his face or, as in prosopagnosia, where we lack the module of mind for recognizing faces, even by seeing the distinct features.

The following discussions highlight two kinds of unconscious processing, blindsight and subliminal perception. These phenomena demonstrate how we may be affected by a lot of information that we don't even know we are receiving. But this process of acquiring knowledge without awareness of doing so happens throughout our mind's working. We take much of our knowledge for granted, without being conscious of how we know it.

Blindsight

In the early seventies, many researchers in neuropsychology, including me, were surprised by the discovery that animals with destroyed visual cortexes could direct their eyes toward novel visual stimuli. We would expect that without the visual-processing part of the cortex, the creatures would be completely blind. To find out if humans had this capability, researchers studied war veterans who had suffered gunshot wounds in the visual areas of their brains.

These veterans were shown flashes of light that were localized in the blind zones of their visual fields (the visual field is the total area visible to an eye that is focused on a single point) and asked them to look toward the flash. First the researchers anchored the head and asked the patient to fix his gaze on a point. Then they flashed the light and afterward asked the subject to move his eyes toward where the light had been.

The men wondered how they could look at what they could not see. But when they agreed to try, they were able to guess to a certain extent where to look. Shortly after this study became well known, a brain-surgery patient known as D. B. came to the attention of Lawrence Weiskrantz, who had been studying the effects of cortical damage on the vision of animals.

D. B. had had a surgical procedure to remove a small tumor from an area within his visual cortex. As a result he lost vision in a large part of the left half of his visual field; he was not conscious of seeing anything in that area. Soon after the surgery, D. B.'s surgeon, Michael Sanders, noticed that D. B. was showing signs of being able to locate objects in his supposedly blind spot. He could reach for an outstretched hand, although he could not see it.

Sanders and Weiskrantz tested his ability by having him point to markers placed on the wall within the range of his blind field and by having him guess if a stick held up in his blind field was vertical or horizontal. He appeared to do these tasks with ease, though again he said he could not see the markers or stick. He was incredulous when told how well he had done.

This was *blindsight*. Further studies with D. B. demonstrated that he could identify the position of objects in his blind field, determine their orientation, and even discriminate an *X* from an *O*. Curiously, while performing the challenging task of detecting faint stimuli in both his blind and sighted regions, D. B. reported fatigue only when the task was in his sighted field. He commented that he didn't get tired when using his blind field because he "wasn't doing anything."

Perhaps unconscious processing doesn't feel like work in the same way that conscious problem solving does. How can a person see without a visual cortex? A clue lies in the finding that blindsight is generally more sensitive to oscillating, flickering stimuli than to fixed, steady ones. Such sensitivity helps one detect novel events and find objects.

Blindsight is one way that information inside us is unavailable to consciousness—and influences actions—although we may deny it. We're worse off than Freud thought, because many actions proceed without our knowing anything about them. Blindsight is an ability to retrieve information unreachable by the conscious mind.

Blindsighters can learn to detect the presence of an object in their blind area and learn to focus on it These people don't know how they do it, but they can still learn strategies for gaining information, such as making several eye movements before guessing the location of an object in their blind field. Although they are unaware of any sensory input from the object, their "guesses" are better than chance.

This learning isn't too different from our normal way of learning skills. For instance, when learning to type, we quickly start to find the keys automatically. We "guess" where the keys are; and the more we practice, the better we are at guessing and the less aware we are of what we are doing. The best typists are completely unconscious of the process of seeking the letters on the keyboard.

Subliminal Perception

By any ordinary standards, it may seem strange or mysterious that humans should be able to perceive things without being conscious of them. If they are important enough to be processed by the brain, then why should consciousness not need to know about them? But this is backwards thinking. Brains existed, and worked well, long before humans and before self-awareness. A better question might be: Why are we aware of what we are aware of? What special purpose is served by allowing a stimulus to enter consciousness?

Events that enter consciousness require immediate action, or a decision between alternatives. However, the brain must continue to monitor the environment with a much wider scope than that permitted by consciousness, so that it can select what is relevant and requires attention. There are many indications that we evolved to react to information at a level below consciousness—researchers have found that people show changes in skin resistance, heart rate, and other measures of emotional reactivity in response to stimuli that cannot be consciously perceived.

A growing, controversial, body of research literature shows that we may be profoundly affected by these subliminal stimuli. Subliminal stimuli are sensory information below the threshold of conscious perception, that is, that one cannot report having perceived. In the laboratory they have affected electrical potentials in the brain, physiological responses, sensory thresholds, memory, decision making, perception, dreams, and emotions.

In the simplest demonstrations of subliminal perception, a person is shown a picture so quickly that he says it is not present, but he can nevertheless guess at a better-than-chance rate the nature or color of the object shown subliminally. We can know more than we know we know.

We may find the results of investigations into subliminal influences on perception and behavior somewhat disturbing. In addition to all the information that obviously affects us, many signals may be received by one mind that affect others without us being aware of them. Subliminal stimuli affect emotional life and even the way we perceive and behave. They sneak in beneath our awareness; therefore, it may be very important for us to understand their effects. After all, we cannot defend ourselves against influences that we don't know about.

People tend to prefer the familiar. If given a choice between two objects that are otherwise equally desirable, people will usually choose the one that is more familiar to them. Bob Zajonc has demonstrated that this preference for the familiar extends to images shown so quickly that they cannot be seen. When geometric shapes are flashed to a person faster than he can recognize them and the person is later asked to pick from a set the figures he likes best, he chooses the figures he has been exposed to before, while insisting the question is absurd!

An electrical shock too slight to be felt, applied in a series of easily detectable shocks, increases the perceived intensity of the shocks that follow it. The stimulus, although unavailable to consciousness, still affects the perceptual mechanisms involved in judging the strength of a sensation. Here we see how the little minds operating behind the scenes have their say in the composite dream we experience as the world.

For instance, subliminally presented unpleasant events decrease sensitivity. When a song you don't like comes on the radio, you turn down the volume. In the same way, the brain, when it detects something it doesn't like, turns down the signals it is receiving. Subliminal stimuli can influence mood states: In one study subliminal suggestions for alertness increased the heart rates of subjects who were performing difficult arithmetic under time pressure. Hidden suggestions, then, can influence cardiac response to stress. Faint signals from the environment may thus affect the way we respond to stressful situations.

Subliminal messages also affect behavior. People who were asked to write stories about pictures wrote shorter ones if the card displayed the subliminal message "Don't write" than if it did not or if it said "Write more." If the subjects could see the imperatives, they had no effect on the length of the stories written. Presumably, when the subjects had conscious access to the commands, they could use that consciousness to override the messages.

The conscious mind can exert its power of veto only if it is informed of the actions of the simpletons below. This makes sense—you can't redirect your hired help if you don't know what they are doing.

Mommy and I Are One: Psycho-therapeutic Uses of Subliminal Effects

The late psychiatrist Lloyd Silverman stirred up a great hubbub of controversy among psychologists by claiming that subliminal stimulation could be beneficial to psychotherapy. Silverman's subliminal psychodynamic activation, or SPA, studies began when he found that certain subliminal phrases, such as "Destroy Mother," could intensify the psychopathology of schizophrenics. The same phrase when presented above perceptual thresholds produced no deleterious effect. Later Silverman turned to the question of whether subliminal stimuli could decrease pathology and increase adaptive behavior.

He chose as his therapeutic stimulus the phrase "Mommy and I are one," because he believed it would evoke pleasant feelings of unity with "the good mother of early childhood." Although this proposition may seem silly to mature adults, we have seen that attachment to the mother is a fundamental "part of the program." "Mommy and I are one" is useful in a wide variety of therapies, not just for schizophrenics. Subliminal presentations of this phrase have improved people's progress in overcoming phobias, losing weight, and learning mathematics.

Not all researchers have been able to duplicate Silverman's findings, and many are consequently reluctant to accept them. The question may be the choice of the subliminal phrase or the technique of presentation. It is difficult to determine when you are dealing with an effect that you cannot consciously evaluate. Something is happening here, but we don't know what it is—do we?

Does subliminal perception have applications in teaching and therapy, or is it a scientific curiosity? Thousands of tapes are currently on the market, offering subliminal help in reading, sexual performance, sleep, thinking, and almost anything else. There is no quality regulation of these products, and since subliminal effects may not work at all without the right circumstances, it is no wonder some consider them quack medicine.

Nevertheless, the subliminal influence has become very popular with the media, which sensationalize its dangers. A hysterical response has arisen from parental worry that rock music is controlling the minds of today's youth with backwards subliminal messages. One of the most unwholesome cases in recent years concerned the hard-rock group Judas Priest. The parents of two boys who killed themselves after listening to one of the band's albums believe that the suicides were caused by a backwards message in the music that said, "Do it, do it, do it," implying that the listener should kill himself. The idea of this "backwards masking" is that when you listen to certain recorded speech or lyrics backwards, you can make out words in the gibberish. Somehow you are supposed to be able to decode these messages unconsciously when the music is played in the usual manner.

However, there is no evidence that the human mind can understand backwards speech or be influenced by it, even subliminally. Furthermore, the "discovery" of backwards messages in rock music is itself a fascinating illustration of the way we dream up the world. Take any recorded speech and play it backwards, and you will find that you can discern words and meanings in the noise. What you hear is also likely to reflect your current preoccupations. There is a simpleton who finds meaning in speech—its best guess of what is being said. That's fine if something *is* being said, but otherwise, you receive the weird guesses of that simpleton.

There are many unnoticed influences on the mind. Elements in our environments of which we have no conscious awareness affect our brains and minds. The changes of the seasons affect mood and thought—even adding extra light in the winter can change the mind's working. We've seen that pheromones such as androstenol, sprayed on a mask, can alter judgments of people and that we prefer things we don't even know we have seen, just because we have been exposed to them once. These operations of the mind work automatically for the most part, giving events the attention and emphasis that natural selection determined to be important long ago. However, we will not help ourselves by becoming hysterically paranoid about being controlled by invisible forces.

Because it is difficult to know ourselves with all these different special-purpose systems swinging in and out, we need to learn how to apply our consciousness to observing the different selves within. Although consciousness is a relative newcomer to the mental system, probably making its entrance following the great brain expansion, it can help us to change the way the mind works.

Our normal process of self-knowledge is destined to be wrong and to blockade real self-understanding. "We" never make up our minds: they have been made up long ago. Our minds don't even know themselves. And the oneness we feel is an illusion too, for we are not the same person from day to day or moment to moment. Our mind contains a special system, hidden from our view, that quietly preserves the illusion of unity. By making better use of our consciousness, we can overcome this delusion to some extent and rework the mind to operate better in the world we have made.

24

Knowing the
Individual
Simpletons

We have difficulty addressing or calling up the "person to whom I'm speaking" within. Because of the system that we first described in Libet's work, oftentimes the different centers of action arise on their own. That's why we don't seem to live up to "our" expectations. It's a matter of which "we" is answering the call. Once we understand that consciousness is normally a weak force in the mental system, we can see how it can be strengthened, by bringing the automated routines to consciousness, using self-observation.

Your husband burns the toast. It's the last piece, and he did it the previous Thursday morning as well. Of course, you're disappointed. And you want to give him a piece of your mind. You begin to describe how you were looking forward to the toast, and now you have go off to work yet again without it. Why can't he simply watch the toaster more carefully, or even just set the darkness gauge a little lighter? He's a little abashed and a bit put out. A simple argument, so far.

But now you are about to give him a piece of your mind that you didn't know about. All of a sudden you're thinking, automatically, almost how you don't like the way he's treated your friends when you're at dinner; he seems to patronize them. And he didn't make the car payment. He's too tired to be affectionate at night, too often, you think.

Now, if you know that your selves shift in and out, you don't automatically have to go along with "your" thoughts. These other thoughts have appeared because an emotional self has shifted into

place, a result of the agitation caused by the burnt toast. You notice this shift and recognize that you don't need to think this way. It's just a problem with the toast, and you don't have to let it become a major crisis.

You observe, "There's that stupid mind shift again. I'm not going to bring up past problems, even though I want to." You may not be able to resist the moves of your mind the first or the second time it happens, but after a while, you will be able to play the mind's game, learning to shift yourself from mind to mind instead of allowing the automatic routines to take over.

Here's a letter I received, with an obviously fictitious name:

Dear Dr. Ornstein:

My husband and I constantly argue. He thinks I am too easy on our son, and I feel he disciplines all the time. He hates to go to the theater, and I can't understand why he lends an ear to that annoying and catcalling music he calls opera. The other day he told me that I am untrustworthy because he thought I was flirting with a gas station attendant, but I think he is dishonest because he cheats on his expense account and claims deductions from the IRS which he didn't take. We fight with respect to the proper way to act all the time. Which one of us is right?

P. Stein

Dear Phyllis Stein:

Relax and stop the ceaseless arguments with respect to who is right. Neither of you is. Neither of you faces reality and knows a truth, nor does anybody or any animal, for that matter. Instead, our mind cleverly "blinds" us to most of the world out there. Some of the blinding of unimportant options is done by the way the nervous system works, and some of it is based on our ideas and intentions of the moment. People look out upon different things in the world, they remember what happened differently, and their reality is actually different.

Everybody has blind spots; there's even a physical one in the eye. There are sounds we don't hear but our dog can; different people can remember faces well, others names; some people remember evenings by what people wore, others by the food, still others by whom they were attracted to. There is no color in nature, no sound, no smell, only movements of waves and molecules. It is we who create the music in the mind, it is we who experience the shift in the composition of gases as perfume.

We build up a world that is different from each other's, individual to individual, culture to culture, species to species. Our minds are blind, but they also bestow a world to us. But what is important to realize is that your arguments are both right and both wrong.

R. Ornstein

We overlook our mind's moves because the mind adjusts to events without our noticing it: We may become accustomed to intensifying noises in the street and then tune them out in the same way we become accustomed to a spouse's growing complaints, which we ignore as well, until it becomes too late. Weight gain, financial gain, marital strain—all are analyzed in the same way.

It's not as if we actually know ourselves, either. The conscious self, does not, it seems, have direct access to the rest of the mind but, following the voluntary action studies, seems to watch how and when the "other minds in place" move in and out. Then it must guess what to do, much as a general must choose his personnel. The self has to make guesses about its own internal state as it must about others. And usually these guesses are pretty good.

When there is a problem, the well-adapted self-knowledge system goes awry. Older people whose hearing is failing, especially those who don't want to admit it, become paranoid. Such a response can develop in a half hour, as shown by an experiment where these conditions were manipulated. Students hypnotized toward deafness and then given a posthypnotic suggestion to disregard that deafness became dramatically more paranoid.

We misjudge our internal processes and are, for instance, attracted to people in exciting situations (people meeting under dangerous conditions fall in love, or at least lust, quickly), we ignore how weather, postoperative pain, normal hunger and thirst all affect judgment.

Here's how someone transferred habitual routines into his marriage, eventually losing his wife. A brilliant attorney carried his legal beliefs home and into the bedroom. "I got so tired of negotiating about sexual positions," the wife recalled. He couldn't stop doing this, even after years of therapy. "And the more successful he became in law, the worse it was for us in bed. Why did he have to make love like a lawyer?"

Knowing that there are different selves shifting in and out allows us to observe the automatic reactions of the mind. We can observe *which* factor—external, food, personal, social, environmental—is causing a given reaction. Under the stimulus of self-observation, the mind begins to change, and the links between action and reaction loosen.

Many of our reactions still are recruits from the basic characteristics of the senses. Vivid events cause us to attend; slow continual changes escape our notice. In December 1988 the Pan Am crash in Lockerbie, Scotland, caused the world to notice. But in the two days after the media reported the tragedy, more people were killed on the U.S. highways than died at Lockerbie. And that is true for each and every two days until the present time too.

But we aren't interested in stories about continuing problems. Just show us the new disasters, please. Tragedies mount, so much now that we need to redefine what exists in our world. If we thought that we could consider events in the world reasonably, our news media would make sense; but we evolved to operate differently. We would need to begin with ourselves.

Self-observation is not the normal kind. You have to learn to observe yourself *as if you were another person*. When you observe this way, you don't keep explaining why you did something, as we usually do. You simply record your experience: He said, "Exact quote"; I flushed and became angry. You develop a detachment from what is happening and start to think of your *selves* as "him" or "her," going about their business, as if they were other people. When does the "sharp cookie" come into play? When the "whine and dine," when the "reckless recluse" or the "frivolous floozie"? Giving them good names helps (and you don't have to tell anyone else about them).

This kind of observation is necessary if you are to learn how and when to switch. You can switch only to someone who already exists, and you have to know who he or she is—that self may not be who you hope is there. The shifts to someone already in existence makes the change easy. A woman who is good with her children but tense and nasty with co-workers may only have to swing in a bit of her "home concern" at the office to get on better and get ahead. She may not need complex retraining in how to get on with other people; she may know it very well. But she doesn't swing it in the right time. That she can solve problems at home indicates that she is simply not bringing the right mind to the office. She may have thought that work required more aggression or a different self. It doesn't, at least not exclusively.

Because the mind contains so many different systems, strengthing the role of consciousness can be accomplished through self-observation. The observer—you—simply watches your actions and notices what is happening. It's easier when you start by observing the outside world. Techniques for this have been developed over centuries and are easy to use. These exercises are called "just sitting" in Zen, "mindfulness" in yoga, "self-observation" in Sufism.

Self-observation isn't as exotic as it may sound. Just take some time to listen to all the sounds in and outside your room: the noises of the buildings and traffic, static on the radio, creaks in the walls. They are ever-present but never noticed. Because the mind adapts, you miss much of what goes on around you. Try to connect again with what is happening outside, not what you need to know. These first observation attempts help us to begin to eliminate the automatic shifts of mind.

When you begin self-observation, use the explanations of the mind's routines in this book to help pinpoint the areas you need to change first. You might want to keep a journal of your daily activities, marking especially days that you haven't been able to use the right mind. Keep records too of the rest of your life—who you are, who shifts in control of each of your social, emotional, and business activities. Then look to see if there is a pattern in this journal of the self.

Many people find that they suffer from too much arousal, which disrupts work and personal situations. It's important to find "arousal absorbers" that are fun for you, which you can use to switch out when you need to. It's all very well to have your mind reason with you, but it doesn't always win because of the emotional arousal caused by these thoughts. You might find rock or Bach good mood switchers, or you might need to engage in physical activity of some sort. You might try to reward yourself with delayed arousal absorbers: "If you keep your cool, your reward will be listening and singing along with Motown on the way to work," as a safety net, rather than relying on the impossible, complete self-discipline. The simpletons need to be let out occasionally.

7-6

Some memories are close to us, some locked away.

Said one of my interviewees: "I remember when I was working in middle management and was very stressed out. When I got home in the evening, before I did anything, I would shut myself in a room, draw the curtains to keep the neighbors out, take my clothes off, and turn on the Rolling Stones and dance like a loon with total abandon. It works, but you have to know no one is going to come barging in, because you do look pretty weird."

You've had a bad day at the office and snap at your children as you try to unwind; they, of course, crave attention. You say, "Give me just ten minutes on my own, and I'll be with you. Right now I'm an impossible person to be with because I've had a dreadful day." If you don't take that time to gain control of the mind in place, you will carry over the set of reactions appropriate to your hassled work into your home, and you will carry on miserably. Stop. Do something different and wipe the slate clean.

This is important because small changes can create huge effects in the mind. A sudden improvement in mood, for instance, swings a different mind into place. A few moments of peace at home can get you started in the evening on the right mind. Because moods alter memories, thought, and action plans, doing a little to change mood can work wonders.

Creativity is part of evolution, and it works in a way similar to natural selection, in which there are random variations, some of which prove useful and are "selected" by the environment. People generate many ideas, almost at random, a few of which are appropriate and become selected. Chance plays a great role in both the generation and the evaluation of ideas. *Generation* of ideas is the primary stage. People who have many ideas are more likely to have creative ones. A useful creative idea is rare. Campbell emphasizes:

> [The tremendous amount of nonproductive thought] must not be underestimated. Think of what a small proportion of thought becomes conscious, and of conscious thought what a small proportion gets uttered, what a still smaller fragment gets published, and what a small portion of what is published is used by the next intellectual generation. There is a tremendous wastefulness, slowness and rarity of achievement.

Thousands of small and wrong ideas help prepare the way for an occasional useful one. Thomas Edison supposedly evaluated his progress on an invention by saying that he now knew a hundred ways that wouldn't work. Creativity involves hard work and the relentless generation of ideas and thoughts to produce a few that pass evaluation. *Evaluation* is the assessment of an idea's worth. It is perhaps more important to recognize a good idea than it is to possess one.

But people are not monolithic, so they're not totally creative or noncreative. There are, however, certain human characteristics that may facilitate creative expression. It seems that people who think unusual thoughts often lead lives different from the rest of us. Isaac Newton spent almost sixteen hours a day locked up in his rooms at Cambridge working on his ideas; he had lots of wild ones on cosmology as well as those that transformed physics. If you spend too much time being like everybody else, you decrease your chances of coming up with something different.

We think of some people as being creative or being dull, without realizing that creative people aren't creative all the time and dullies aren't dull all the time and in every way. Think of it this way: Language is creation; every sentence we utter is an on-the-spot invention. All children as they grow up can recognize millions of sentences and exclamations that they have never heard before.

Remember the woman at the party who met a surgeon whose experiences scared her off her wonderful vacation? One way to have avoided this would have been to say, simply, "Let's boogie." Do for yourself what Alfred R., the near-suicide, had done to him: Prescribe a mental bypass, and get rid of the SOB.

Sometimes events can put you out of your mind in a positive sense. To control this response, you need to be able to visualize a set of activities that you genuinely enjoy, activities that can help you switch out when you need to. It doesn't matter what they are; watching birds, Ping-Pong, dance marathons, restoring cars, sewing, walking in your special place in the woods—all of these can help if you cultivate them.

But you have to secure this refuge inside yourself, a haven to retreat to before your difficulties arise. In this way, you can avoid much of the stress in your life and don't have to learn how to reduce it. A haven also helps you build up your self-esteem, so that when defeats occur, as they always do, they don't affect "all" of you.

It's important, early on, to recognize what happens when the wrong mind is allowed to control a situation. Things go quickly from bad to worse. Sometimes the only positive course of action available is retreat from the situation altogether, before things

Sideminding It

7-8

Internal controls.

escalate to full-scale war—even if that means locking yourself in the bathroom for a moment until the right mind (or at least a better one) comes to the fore. Obviously, if your three-year-old is about to run into a busy street, you are not going to stop for a few minutes of deep breathing. But very few situations demand this kind of immediate action—fewer than we might think. Taking the time to understand how mental routines run automatically, and can run away with you, will pay off. You will be able to make a real, attainable, and lasting change once you gain such understanding.

Shifting to a Positive Mind in Place

Surprisingly small shifts in the mind's operations can change us greatly. They can be disastrous, as in the case of Jonestown, or they can be, if not wonderful, a strong positive force. The reason is that when anything happens to us, getting drunk, getting laid or laid off, we shift the mind in place, becoming for all intents and purposes, a different person.

Being in a good mood, optimistic, can increase longevity and can increase chances for success. The trick is to manage the small, controllable events close to oneself and then deal with the larger ones. Doing so changes the system so that, once in a better mood, you have access to more positive feelings and creativity. Moreover, the better mood itself is health-enhancing.

Human beings would be overwhelmed by the world if we experienced it raw, so we select unconsciously. We live inside a set of illusions. Most of us think that others have a good opinion of us, that we're well liked, good looking, and the like. Most of our opinions of ourselves are overvalued. The only people who don't overvalue themselves are the mildly depressed, the true realists.

Someone tells you that you are kind, insincere, intelligent, slothful. Most healthy people remember the kind and intelligent. Somehow, the rest slips through. There is a built-in process toward remembering the positive and screening out the negative. Healthy people remember their successes better than their failures and imagine they can influence events more than they really can.

Can you know yourself well and accurately? Probably not, since self-perceptions center on a small part of the mind, one that usually is involved in controlling actions, not controlling knowledge. The mind makes up its own story about reality from a narrow trickle of information received, reduced, and filtered through our senses. These constructed beliefs, many based on denial and illusion, have adaptive value. So, many of the "irritational" defense mechanisms are adaptive. Denial of threatening information often allows us to avoid unnecessary anxiety.

The kind of illusion we create has consequences for us. If you are in a difficult condition but have an illusion that you can control it, *even if you can't,* you will feel less stressed. Over-optimistic illusions may also be adaptive after a crisis, enabling one to deny the implications of trauma and get through a calamitous time. And keeping the optimistic parts of the mind going also pays off. Of patients undergoing surgery, the group that expressed greater optimism had lower death rates.

Optimism seems to shift the mind in place. We should therefore focus on having successful experiences, no matter how small. Choose something that *you* want to change and select a small step that you are confident you can achieve. Finding ways to increase your confidence may pay rich dividends.

A bright outlook can even help patients adapt to open-heart surgery. The psychologists Carver and Scheier assessed bypass surgery patients before the operation. Those with a more hopeful and positive outlook showed fewer complications during surgery, their lung function returned speedily, they sat up in bed sooner, and they were able to walk around the room earlier than their gloomier counterparts. Six months later, those who expected an improved quality of life, a quick return to work, hobbies, and exercise, tended to get just what they expected.

Our own shifts in our minds change greatly how we live. It's important to use as much of this information to get our selves under some kind of conscious, willed, command because small prompts can shift the entire mind in place.

VIII

Why There Will Be No Further Evolution Without Conscious Evolution

Our evolution to date.

Important as the struggle for existence has been and still is, yet as far as the highest part of man's nature has been and even still is, there are agencies more important. For the moral qualities are advanced, either directly or indirectly, much more through the effects of habit, the reasoning powers, religion &c., than through natural selection.

—CHARLES DARWIN, *The Descent of Man*

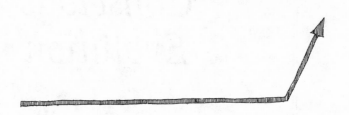

Slow changes sometimes aren't noticed until too late.

When we enter into the world, we have to live in one place of all the possible places. No brain could be prepared for that, so it comes into the world oversupplied with neurons and incompletely organized. During the long period of infancy, our early environment "selects" the specific minds to survive in a fixed world. But now we live beyond this early set of adaptations for increased survival. Increased survival means, in the evolutionary sense, more offspring. In the modern sense, it means overpopulation, more and more individuals on an earth with finite resources. Thus, our adaptation is in a new era: Can we change ourselves in time so that our triumphal increase in population and our increasing waste don't choke or kill us?

We are going to need a lot of help in the next few decades to refashion and rethink our world. Some of it will be political, some technical, some social. I believe that the psychological understanding can assist in all areas. This book is about the origin of our thought, not a manual of action or a specific program for the future. On the other hand, the analysis here lends a different perspective: We can't and don't have to change everything but might be able to pinpoint changes in parts of the mind, not the whole.

Our progress depends more on consciously directing adaptations than on improving rationality. In so doing, we need to change our social emphasis, to that period when the mind gets wired up, and to understanding the altruistic basis of much of human action, again firmly rooted in evolutionary theory. The problem for us to decide is which of the recruits to develop and which to cast off.

I want now to discuss why we are currently failing to understand the modern world and why it is so urgent that we take a new and conscious role in our own mental evolution.

25

Ready
for the
Tiger

Everything has now changed except for our way of thinking.

—ALBERT EINSTEIN

Think of yourself in a world as it should be for your mind. In the world of a tribe with 200 to 300 individuals to support, marauding animals, perhaps another tribe competing, your concerns would be very, very different from those today. In this ancestral atmosphere, how could events across the earth have anything to do with your plans or your life?

When we reached our current state of mind, there were scattered thousands of human beings; now there are billions. Thousands of years ago in Mesopotamia, the seat of civilization, there may have been a few scattered groups armed with spears. What effect would one attack by a group on another have on the tribes living in North America? When would they hear of it? When would they know of it? Never. Would they worry that the attack would endanger their future? Obviously not. But now one country in the Mesopotamian region has developed chemical, and perhaps nuclear, weapons. Iraq's invasion of Kuwait certainly affected many lives thousands of miles away. We knew about the proceedings of Operation Desert Storm minute by minute, and its importance to our future was great.

Sense, perception, memory, thought, and social judgment evolved in a stable, small, simple, and slow world, now long gone. We can't smell radiation or easily sense low levels of acid rain or electromagnetic fields. The "problems" pose unprecedented, even incalculable, dangers.

Previously unimaginable travel, such as to the moon, is now possible. Nuclear power and nuclear weapons, unimagined by our predecessors, now threaten our existence. Much of what is newly invented or created is done by a lone genius or a small group. Our technology can leap way ahead of the ability of the remaining billions of us to adapt.

About 25,000 years ago, humanity was at most a few million people, surviving mainly by hunting and gathering. With the first major human revolution, the development of agriculture 10,000 years ago, settlements grew up along the fertile floodplains of the Nile, in the Fertile Crescent of the Middle East, and around the Ganges delta and Huang Ho (Yellow River) in Asia.

The growth of the human population, the measure of our reproductive success, is astonishing. At the time of the agricultural revolution, the total human population was less than 10 million. Today, almost that many people are born *each month*. The intensity, the production, the very weight of the throng of human beings on the planet were not forces present in that world that made us, the small world we evolved to know. At the time of our final evolution, all humanity lived in tiny scattered tribal settlements; now more people live in a few square miles of Tokyo than all who then existed. In the small world of our ancestors, if someone cut down a forest 10,000 miles away, no one believed it would affect the clean air they were breathing. Such a thought would be like believing that a change in a canal flow on Mars would affect your job plans next year. Idiotic. Impossible. Or how well can we judge when each one of a flotilla of submarines off our coastline has more explosive power than has been fired in anger in all of our history?

How could a chief of a small tribe be prepared for the idea of 2 billion people dying in half an hour when he had seen only a few hundred during this lifetime? Now humanity at large affects us, as never before, and humanity at large is, indeed, very, very large. Because the mind is so well adapted to the world it enters, it is failing right now. As does each generation, we evolved to adapt to the world of our parents. I was born into a world that had half the people, no televisions, computers, nuclear weapons, space travel, faxes, smog, acid rain. How was I to know what the world of the future would be like? How were my parents to know? How were my teachers?

The tribal mind transferring the world to the offspring won't hold in our future. Compounding the problem, we change the world much more in five years now than did many of our ancestors in a millennium, and we're ready for the tiger.

Everyday Life: How Adapting Can Lead Us Astray

Adaptation is doing the best job in any circumstances, be it selecting the quicker of two routes, identifying the greatest threat, picking the ripest fruit, or finding the safest place to sleep. This ancestral system of simpletons (what I've called the SOB) is what makes us such avid and dazed shoppers today. Shifting the mind in place is the job of advertisers,. who shift adaptation, attention, and more to get us to do what they want. You look at a set of expensive liqueurs in a shop. One sells well above any other in its class. Why? It is more expensive, costing $23.95 compared with $19.95 for most others so it should be perceived as too expensive.

The reason for that liqueur's popularity is the way the mind adapts to relative judgments. The distributors have an ad campaign listing Christmas gifts under $1,000, which includes a lizard-skin leather pouch, a custom silver-framed portrait, a $450 pen, and the now amazingly cheap $23.95 liqueur.

We miss much because we adapt to it. A slowly increasing weight problem or a slow turn toward drugs by our children is shunted into the background. Where, for instance, does the constitutional right to bear arms reach its limit? Technology changes slowly and constantly, but we don't. Rifles and semiautomatic weapons seem okay to some, just an extension of our basic rights. Will it stop when you can buy a tactical nuclear weapon with a call to an advertiser in the back of the sports pages?

As I am writing this book, I get hungry. I see that a local Chinese restaurant has a special of three dishes for $15, delivered. I know they have good hot-and-sour soup, so I order. But then I notice that one of the dishes has to be soup or salad; the à la carte price for the hot-and-sour soup is $3.50, for the salad, $4.95, so I

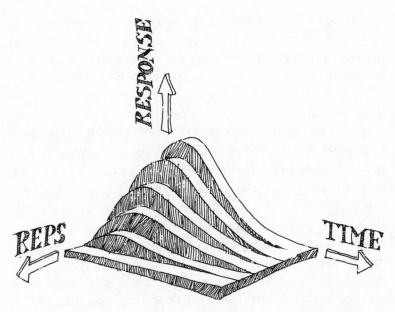

RESPONSE REPS TIME

8-3

When a noise
repeats, we stop
listening.

order the salad. I've found a bargain. But I wanted the soup and the salad is terrible and I didn't even want it. I am not, dear reader, in my right mind.

The same routines happen in home life. When we consider expenses with a large base (such as a $65,000 home-remodeling budget), small increases are easy to explain away (an extra $5,000 for furniture or kitchen appliances). But expenses on a small base, such as purchasing books, are much more difficult to justify, even if they are for much less: "You mean you spent $25 for a *paperback?*" The same thing happens in business budgets.

Prior judgments anchor future ones because they shift our simpletons around. Suppose an engineer is about to start a job at a new company. What do you expect his salary will be? If the person next to you says $25,000, your estimate of his salary is going to be very different than if the person next to you says $60,000. If the person says $25,000, your estimate is going to be much closer to $25,000, say $30,000, than if the person says $60,000, at which point you might declare that $50,000 would be adequate starting salary.

And, on a more basic level, you may notice the change if you are accustomed to carrying a 2-pound briefcase home from the office, and suddenly your workload sends you home with a 3-pound one. However, if you are hauling wood, you will be very unlikely to notice the difference between a 50- and a 51-pound load.

Of course, these errors are rare and are instances of the ability to simplify the world. The ability to generalize saves effort. We need not waste time discriminating the sound of one car horn from another to get out of the way; different-sounding telephone rings all signal the same thing. Moreover, we are conscious of only a few things at once.

Since the mind evolved to select a few signals and then dream up a semblance, *whatever enters our consciousness is overemphasized.* It does not matter how the information enters, whether via a television program, a newspaper story, a friend's conversation, a strong emotional reaction, a memory—all is overemphasized. We ignore other, more compelling evidence, overemphasizing and overgeneralizing from the information close at hand to produce a rough-and-ready reality.

The killing of one hostage on the cruise ship *Achille Lauro* attracted worldwide attention; millions of Americans changed their travel plans. Yet more people were being murdered each day in the United States than all those ever killed by terrorists; people still traveled in this country. In this case of terrorism, the wide dissemination of the event mirrors the workings of the mind: The tragedy was covered by the world press. Such distorted focus continues. I was in England a few years ago when the San Francisco earthquake hit. I was amazed to find the English media preoccupied by the catastrophe. Everyone asked me how I could return to San Francisco, even residents of New York and Lagos! A few days later, a stronger and damaging earthquake hit in the Pacific but caused little reaction. We become inured to common disasters, to continual bombings, to the ongoing problems of poverty, the homeless. SOB.

The reaction of the media to such events demonstrates the selective process of the mind. When we hear of a danger, it is impossible to get it out of our mind. Psychologist Dan Wegner described how a vacation was ruined. He was about to go on a trip south when a medically minded friend drew attention to a skin problem, mentioning that it might be skin cancer. Now, could you forget it? For the rest of the trip, Wegner believed every minute of exposure to the sun brought danger; every chance to have fun was dampened by the thought, "That's not important; I may have cancer." Of course, he didn't have cancer (and went on to write a great book about this experience called *White Bears and Other Unwanted Thoughts*), but unwanted images, feelings, and ideas flood our mind form many sources. The mind trades off accuracy for speed. We must usually rely on incomplete information to make judgments, to reason, and to solve problems.

This recruitment of reactions can have tragic consequences as well. In the early summer of 1990, five brutal and senseless drug-connected murders in New York City within a short time began to raise concern about the amazingly easy availability of handguns in the United States. Finally, this awful sequence of deaths would cause people to wake up, to notice, maybe to do something about the problem. However, like much that goes on inside the mind, this concern was quickly shunted off the front pages and out of our collective "mind" by the Iraqi invasion of Kuwait. The chance for protecting innocent citizens was lost again.

Was the invasion of Kuwait related to the handgun murders? No, nothing in the invasion lessened the risk of handgun murders in the streets. If anything, the risk was increased by the diversion of U.S. military forces away from enforcing drug laws and confiscating assault weapons to Saudi Arabia. The media simply responded to stronger stimulus, much like a neuron that fires in response to a strong stimulus while it is already responding to

8-4

We can respond to a firecracker quickly but ignore constant bombing.

something else. It is the SOB at work: The nervous systems of those making decisions as to what is news or public policy are the same nervous systems as the rest of us have.

Most people do not mind the slow increases in the prices they are paying for milk, bread, wine, meat, and other items they buy every day. However, the increase in car prices causes great dismay, even though car prices have increased less than the average of the Consumer Price Index. We don't notice the slow monthly price increases in an item such as milk, but a car, which we buy only every three or four years, carries the accumulated price increase— and we notice quickly.

The more sensational the event, the more it seems to attract our thought processes. The "wilding" maiming of the Central Park jogger, a little girl falling down a septic hole, a dead hostage dangling in the air in Iran—all command our attention. Moreover, our own situations influence our judgment: People out of work overestimate the rate of unemployment.

Airbags save lives. But they will save very few lives over the next several years. One television commercial showing a collision between two airbag-equipped cars is extremely effective. A life saved by an airbag attracts far more attention than one saved by a reduction in the pollution produced by the automobile with the airbag. However, reducing that air pollution would save hundreds more people than airbags in every car would. Ensuring that people inflated their tires properly would save more fuel than the 55 mile-per-hour speed limit, but we do not attend to it.

Little is done about the chronic dangers of highway safety or the 500 murders per week or the 100 billion cigarettes smoked each year—because they are familar problems. A single "new" event, such as a terrorist strike, is immediately on the front page of newspapers all over the world. We conscript jet fighters to apprehend terrorists who have killed a single man, but little is done to protect the lives of many who are permanently injured and lost to society. It seems senseless, absurd, and bizarre, but the mental system ignores common daily dangers, even dangers that threaten death, waiting for the tiger.

Accidents are one means, unfortunately, of gaining access; they automatically shift your simpletons in place, making people prey to misjudgments in marriage, business, and politics.

When an airplane goes down in another country, we worry about our own safety at home. Only when a crazed gunman kills children with a rifle designed for war, do we think about banning such weapons. When a celebrity is stricken with breast cancer or AIDS, it becomes a national concern. When you are frustrated in traffic, you become frustrated about progress at work or the state of your marriage as well.

The Human Journey

The first major change in the world was the development of agriculture. When people began to settle down to till the soil, they started on the road to growth, to cities, to overpopulation, to smog, and to nuclear weapons. The trip down that road was slow at first. Even in the 10,000 years from the agricultural revolution to the Middle Ages, there was no *fundamental* change in the nature of human lives.

The Industrial Revolution produced many more innovations: wide availability of printing, factories, steam engines, mass production, railroads, electric power, telegraphs, and more. In this new era, development piled on development, and the pace of change picked up. Human society moved faster and faster until it took off into a new and unknown world. Where there were once only prairies and deserts, now farms and factories thrive. Where there were swamps and forests, the land now contains laboratories, learning institutions, and launching pads.

All of these transformations are merely part of our very brief history on earth. To be generous, these last 20,000 years, since the caves at Lascaux and since farming and all the rest, are an insignificant amount of evolutionary time. In this period, which seems quite long to us, there has been *no time* for biological evolution to improve the development of our mental capacities, our ability to meet the challenges of the environment, our ability to think, reason, and to create. We are only 2,000 generations from Neanderthal, and only 750 generations from Lascaux. No time, this time.

We in the modern world are thus the same people who evolved when our species numbered small groups roaming around the savannas of East Africa, evolved to flourish where the world of one's parents would be almost the same as the world of the child.

The system we recruited had the primary aim of reacting quickly to immediate danger—those who did lived long enough to produce us. Those who acted more thoughtfully and with due deliberation of the proper course, who could avoid panic when confronted by mild threats—who acted rationally, that is—probably lived shorter, and thus less generative, lives. The survival argument against rationality in primeval conditions is that payoff is very lopsided: Fail to respond to a real danger, even if that danger would kill you only 1/10,000 as often, and you will be dead. A few years later, you will be deader in evolutionary terms, for fewer of your genes will be around. However, an overreaction to danger produces only a little hysteria, a little stress, and maybe a little embarrassment—probably little or no loss of reproductive ability. Maybe the excitement would even recruit a little more reproductive effort!

Running from every snake or tiger or loud noise probably doesn't disrupt life too much. Not running, while it might kill you only slightly more often, can eventually produce major changes in the population. The same numbers hold in this example as for the height difference cited earlier. If panic in response to a threat in all cases improved survival by even 1/10,000, those who panicked would be 484 million times more populous than those who did not. And so it was good to respond emotionally and quickly to the average dangers threatening most of our ancestors. Rationality is a great idea and ideal, but we never had the time for it; we don't have time for it now, and thus we don't have the mind for it.

The World and the Mind

So the human mind is the way it is because the world is the way it is. That's what the evolved systems organize the mind to do—mesh with the world.

I remember watching the medieval system in action on a visit to Fez, in Morocco: An old man working filigree on a copper tray, his son finishing the polishing of a tray with the lines for the final work inscribed, a younger one rounding and polishing the edges of another one, the grandchildren rough-cutting and hauling the unfinished sheets to the workshop. I am sure at home that the bread baking and cooking procedures were being taught.

The world for almost all of humanity during all of our history was small, a tribal realm bounded by at most a few hundred kilometers. Of course, some tribes were nomads and lived through

Ready for the tiger—or the lion or the bear or the crocodile.

periods of migration. Yet it was the same tribal mind-set, the same set of circumstances all over again.

The ancestral system of adaptations flourished when the world was stable. And it is this stability that is so changed in the modern world. The world we adapted to is no more. To recast our statement: The mind is the way it is because the world *was* the way it *was*, some 40,000 years ago. Give or take a dozen millennia, 40,000 years ago, our evolution reached its current form. Forty thousand years is almost no time in earth history and allowed no time for us to adapt biologically. It is but 2,000 generations.

But 40,000 years is longer than everything in our culture's *entire history*. There were no cave paintings, writing, farming, religion, factories, refinement of metals, let alone plastics and technology, so long ago. Hell, forty or so years is everything

263

nowadays. Consider the number of human beings on earth. In my own lifetime, the world has been transformed as much as in all of human history before it. It took, roughly speaking, from the time of the first humans until about the time of my birth in 1942 to produce the first 2.65 billion human beings living on the planet at one time. It has taken only my own lifetime to add the same number. And the pace of change is increasing; producing the first billion humans required about a million years; producing the most recent billion, fourteen years.

As has been pointed out, our own understanding of ourselves is processed by our mental procedures, so we don't always know ourselves directly. We hold a well-organized and simplified version of our environment, of the nature of other people, and even of our own lives and our own beliefs in our minds.

Understanding ourselves as a set of minds that come into place, then move out, makes it possible for each of us to see ourselves as a team, not a unified individual. Thus, we promise with all our heart to behave better, to be tidy, to obey the law, but we can't always change our behavior, despite our best intentions. There are real limits to change, but they need come from a different understanding of ourselves, as a squadron of simpletons, not one single-minded individual. Consciousness is real and is potentially powerful, but it usually needs training, or it can be overwhelmed by other factors.

The adaptable mind enters the world and in the womb and early in life has its particular squadron selected, learns language, learns what to eat, and develops the skills—maritime, domestic, equestrian, agricultural—and the mechanisms, mental and physical, to live in the world. Carnivorous, vegetarian, polygamous, monogamous, brutal, tranquil—we select and learn it is impossible to identify it all.

For most human life the adaptation to the world was well established by biological evolution, producing an oversupply of minds. In infancy and later, the culture selects those minds needed for that culture from the palette of possibilities. The mind so selected is then prepared further. From about age three or four to about thirteen in many societies, children undergo an intense indoctrination/memorization period. Catholics are confirmed at thirteen, and most tribal rites of passage happen by then as well.

This process seems to a great extent universal: Every culture studied and reported in the *Human Relations Record* uses memorization to convey its knowledge. Bushmen need to know the history of every object and every exchange of their tribal families before they are ten or twelve.

Can We Adapt?

There is currently quite serious concern about the nature of human consciousness and our ability to adapt to the modern world. Many people feel that the development of their own consciousness is of high priority because humans now have a greatly increased ability to control and manipulate the earth, an ability far beyond anything we had during the long millennia of our biological evolution. The destruction of the entire earth is no longer an impossibility.

Human beings have gone outside their original savanna residence and now live all over the earth and, for brief periods, away from the earth itself. From the moment our ancestors stood upright, they began to explore unexpected places and to create unanticipated conditions. As a result, we have had to and must continue to adapt, and do so constantly, to unprecedented challenges.

The key difference between our need to adapt now and that need for earlier generations is that, throughout history, while environments changed, there was rarely a period in which the mesh between the older and younger generation would not cover adaptation to the changes. Beginning with *Homo erectus*, beginning with the brain breakthrough, humanity began to change the environment to suit ourselves, what René Dubos thoughtfully termed *creative adaptation*. Clothing, fire, dwellings, and agriculture all enabled people to live where none could before. Yet for many centuries the change in complexity of life remained slow enough to accommodate: the iron age, farming, even the early Industrial Revolution all caused disruptions, diseases, changes in the way of life. But they all could be accommodated because the speed of change occurred over generations.

Now humanity is changing the world beyond the generation-to-generation adaptation time. Now human inventiveness is overwhelming human adaptiveness. Once an invention becomes widespread, such as electronic or jet planes, everyone is under pressure to adapt to a new situation. As a result of the way we evolved, our ability to judge lags behind our ability to create.

The dangers in the current era are of a different kind than those confronted previously. As mentioned, no one has been prepared by evolution to view 15,000 murders before puberty, as the average child does, on television and in the movies, according to recent studies. What does such exposure do to the mind as it gets wired up? How do we distinguish what is the truth of our real world from what is a travesty? No one is biologically prepared for the destruction that is following acid rain. When would anyone have had to worry about what they burned, when there were at most a few million people on earth? When did we have to worry about the water supply being clean?

No one is prepared biologically for the complexity of the crowds, the noise, and the pollution of the urban surround in many of the world's cities. And there is no time for the glacially slow processes of evolution to produce the changes needed to prepare us. Our own brain took more than 500 million years to "create." We don't have that kind of time.

8-6

Sometimes the complexity of modern life overwhelms our simpleton system.

26

Conscious Evolution

New organs of perception come into being because of necessity. So, necessitous one, increase your need.

—RUMI

S o here we are now, courtesy of countless historical accidents. If *Australopithecus* had not stood up, if the brain had not grown so rapidly, most likely as an adaptation to the heat of savanna life combined with many other developments, we'd not be here. Had your upbringing not selected you to read English, you couldn't read about it here. But however we got here, all our history, all our evolution, all the accidents that led to us are all over. Now it is our turn to guide our future evolution. Our inheritance has given us adaptations to many worlds and enough brain for further conscious development.

Our biological evolution is, for all practical purposes, at its end. There will be no further biological evolution without conscious evolution. We have to take command of our evolution now and begin a massive program for conscious changes in the way we think, the way we relate to others, the way we identify with the rest of humanity. The pace of change is far too great for us to try to adapt unconsciously. We have to take our very evolution into our own hands and do for ourselves what biological evolution has done for all life: adapt to an unprecedented new world.

Our great brain gives us the extra capacity to become aware of ourselves, to an extent greater than any other animal. It gives us the capacity to imagine a future, to change the world. All animals adapt to the world they find. Human beings do so too, but we also change the world for our own benefit. We have changed the nature of plant life, the very shape of animals; shelters have allowed us to live where no human could, technology now enables us to do things that were impossible a few years ago.

The End of Accidental Evolution

267

All human beings have, within themselves, entirely unparalleled adaptations, new adaptations that need to be nurtured deliberately in our schools, in our training, and in our lives. Conscious change can't do everything, since the inherent automatic moves of the mind exist for a good reason, but with a slight shift in our priorities, we may be able to adapt much more than we'd believe, and adapt in the right direction.

Our normal upbringing, focusing on the individual mind and priorities, may work against, not for, a solution. A shift toward a view of humanity as one animal, toward relinquishing the "every man for himself" attitude, might enable us to take those "selfless" steps that could begin to solve our collective problems. Human beings now have a greatly increased ability to control and manipulate the earth, an ability far beyond anything we had during the long millennia of our biological evolution.

We need a new curriculum about the nature of the human mind now, and we need to require politicians to pay attention to the long-term consequences of their actions. We need to update our education continually, in schools, in the home, and in the media, and teach a new upbringing. We need school curricula to teach us about why our mind is primed to be ready for the tiger, to react quickly to emergencies, whereas small, slow changes in the world are the real threats. Humanity, its development and its limits, should be what is taught early on, along with geography and the like.

Although our future will always require us to adapt to an unprecedented world, if we take the pains to communicate the major changes in the world, the developing mind will "pick up" much of the information needed. Instead of tribes or families, we need to bring up our children to identify with humanity itself. Instead of focusing on specific countries, we need to understand how we live on one globe and communicate that to our children and to adolescents, who are "making up their adult mind" about their role in the culture. We need a global patriotism instead of a local one. Instead of news that focuses on specific exciting stories, media that focused on the continuing problems could change people's minds.

How do we convey the message about what we are doing to the earth? It will involve changes in how we communicate. We need a new way to perceive slow changes, and we need to train our children to look at the changes that build up slowly. We need to petition the media to work on stories that escape the individual eye, not enhance those sensational murders.

We also need to understand that the different simpletons within must be addressed. Because of our innate preference for new events and for commotions, people will always need exciting stories to watch. But the news media can pick exciting stories that also trace the major changes in the world.

Surely, when people are suffering from environmental pollution, we can run stories on the consequences of pollution to individuals. The emphasis on individuals is key, since the mind responds best to representative examples. Villages in Romania may be prototypes of what could happen to the rest of the earth, and we should see what went on. Someone dying from the effects of acid rain or skin cancer is no less an object of sympathy than someone shot dead in the street in a drive-by shooting. We need to dramatize and attend more to the continuing tragedies of our time than to the isolated "whale trapped by ice floe" stories. But we also need to recognize that one simpleton always wants to hear about the single hostage killed, the whales trapped in Alaska, the little girl in a sewer. We shouldn't fight that need but must learn to communicate the message in a way that makes audience—the human animal—respond. This is why an alliance of psychological and environmental scientists with the media may pay off.

Creative Adaptations

The human mind contains many different adaptations awaiting their wake-up call, issued by experiences in childhood, in schooling, and in the news that surrounds us.

Think of it: a huge brain, preadapted to select from many different "programmings," a neural selection system that wires up the nervous system differently depending on where it lives. This amazing assemblage of adaptations allowed humanity to survive and flourish anywhere on earth and, as the biblical injunction had it, to be fruitful and multiply. It is the root of the triumph of humanity, this ever-adaptable and adapted mind.

One way we need to change is to concentrate on the developments that take place during the special periods of youth, when we adapt most readily. In early life (and remember that the mind cannot be prepared exactly for the world in which it lives), the mind absorbs a vision of the surrounding local "world." We then identify with the group we see, play with, talk to, and hear stories about in our youth. This adapting to the world of our parents is great for a tribal situation, but the sense of deep-seated differences between peoples, reinforced by our different languages and accents, stays with us forever.

If we are to change society, we need to know that changes can come most completely, if slowly, by changing the "information world" of our young. If we expose children to materials showing how all humans are in the same boat, then our children may well develop a new kind of adaptation, one that will make the next generation as different from us as we are from preliterate, pretechnological peoples.

This focus on changing the adaptations of the mind shifts the emphasis from critical training in rational skills to areas where new growth can blossom. Intervening during the period when the infant makes its first adapation to the world will pay off much more than we might have thought. It is in this period that we should be spending most of our resources for a new kind of affirmative action, since the language and mental abilities in infancy are, for all intents and purposes, equal among all groups, and it is in this critical early environment that we can help people most.

We also need to attend to the other critical periods in development, especially those particular times when our adult goals are formed, during the period from about ages twelve to eighteen. During adolescence there is a second refinement of the mental system, an all but final reorganization for adulthood. Career choices are made, goals are set, and we decide who we want to be. Our society in the future needs to focus on providing materials for a new curriculum at that time, and to do so deliberately.

Can human beings really develop so differently? Can attention to the kinds of adaptations we make in infancy result in a different kind of humanity? The difference upbringing can make is clear in animal studies, where drastic changes can be accepted. Ronald Melzack shows how exposure in infancy can affect the way the mind gets organized. In *The Puzzle of Pain*, he describes a study in which puppies who never saw their elders whimpering when shocked grew up different from those who did and from normal puppies. Those that didn't see any pain reactions did not flinch in adulthood when they were shocked. These Spartan puppies could withstand the pain, while the rest acted like regular dogs. It wasn't training or retraining, just exposure in infancy that changed a function as basic to us as pain.

Perhaps the most important place to begin is with a new altruism. One difference is in how we identify with others and in how we identify them. In essence, all animals are altruistic; no animal lives a completely selfish life. All organisms work on the principle that "it is all relatives." Altruism is very deeply ingrained into the system. There is a convergence of research work in psychology on healthy altruism and on the need for a kind of altruistic, in-the-same-boat, one-world view that gives me more hope than I might ordinarily have.

Human beings are one step beyond straightforward biological altruism; there is something very distinct and very different about the human animal that makes it possible for us to identify with groups larger than those with whom we are genetically close. In infancy we most likely develop an identification with our kind beyond those who share our immediate genes. In a system similar to that which prevents incest, identifying those whom we know early, each child thus learns whom his or her group comprises. It can be small or large. And it's that capacity for cooperation, the capacity to bond together in families, that has made it possible for human beings to reproduce to the degree we do.

It is this bonding together into something greater that seems to be important. This concept has been understood by the elite group that has been responsible for all the world's religions. Yet this understanding now needs to become the property of many, not the few, because of both scientific evidence and of social necessity.

Basic to many is a sense of the welfare of all people. The problem lies in how we identify "all people." Many Native Americans refer to themselves as "the people"; "the Arab world" is all people for others; the Chinese consider themselves the people of the earth.

What is considered to be "all people" is very different at different times. One person's terrorist is another person's freedom fighter. Some people consider the people they are concerned about their family; some people consider the people that they are concerned about their tribe, their company, their team, their army, their nation, their religion. More and more people, because of the real changes on earth, are beginning to consider their people to be all of humanity. And they need to.

A long process of gathering ideas about how we are going to form our future is needed, because our future is much more dependent now on what many other people do in the world and is much more precarious than we might think. Do we need to have such disasters as AIDS, war, pollution before we change? We don't have time to wait for some more compelling impetus for change, since our capacity for disasters increases as humanity's power grows and our numbers increase. Ancient processes of thought and reckoning, ones we now teach, need refreshing.

I hope that, by understanding that the survival questions that face us are much more collective than individual, we may be able to wire up the next generation of people in a very different way. They would be connected to this understanding simply by receiving the right kinds of information in infancy about who our "relatives" are.

Not only has the population of humanity swelled up; the changes we are making on the planet are so enormous that it behooves us to convey a very different message, to convey a message that unites the concerns of religion with the concerns of science. It means that none of us are alone.

Within religious traditions, however encrusted they are now, is a different perspective on life, could we but connect it with the rest of modern knowledge. We need, now, to free such thought from the strictures of the churches and make it the property of many individuals. For example, religions emphasize compassion and generosity and humility; society needs these threads interwoven in all our decisions. These virtues need to become the basics of our education. Surely, most of us feel uncomfortable seeing someone else in pain or misfortune. By being able to help others, we may be able to eliminate that guilt and discomfort. Helping others also changes our perspective on our everyday problems. Thinking of those who are less fortunate resets our idea of where we are in reality. There even seems to be direct benefits to feeling compassion. David McClelland did a study in which he showed immune-system changes in people who simply watched a movie about Mother Teresa helping the ill. Once again, like most of evolution, there may be a biological basis for helping the group, that is, for helping humanity.

The Mind as a Group that We Might Someday Lead

For millennia individuals have been attracted to the idea of "higher selves" or "mystical experiences." We now need to be aware that these experiences are important for our future and recognize that they are within the range of all.

We can remake our minds by shifting the mind in place. The traditional term for controlling our selves or taking hold of ourselves is *will*, an unfashionable term nowadays. If there is a will, it will reside in the selection of the differing minds that we call into play. The paradox of our shifting minds is resolved this way: Conscious control is a small and weak force in most minds, a force that we can develop by self-observation.

The development of consciousness lies not far away in a bedazzled or dazed mystic trance, but in conscious selection. This is the third kind of evolution we possess. Natural selection begins blind. Neural selection in youth is more or less an automatic transfer of the world to the mind. Conscious selection is the way we can take our evolution in our own hands by developing the ability to select parts of the mind.

The awareness of individuality was a great advantage when survival threatened an individual's existence; one could locate and isolate an enemy animal and use it for food. This basic need for individual survival is no longer quite so basic for many in the West. Most of us now buy our food; we do not need to hunt for it. This is a time when the need for conscious evolution is becoming a necessity for all humanity, not just a few individual isolates fasting and praying in a hilltop monastery. The traditional descriptions of humanity as blind or asleep, as an automation, all speak to a view that we usually are the prisoners of our automatic selection routines.

There is a continual conflict between the proponents of reason and intuition, between the lawyers and the dancers, the generals and the poets. I believe that we may be able to understand these abilities as different sections of the thousand forms of mind, as Rumi mentioned.

There is a much more attainable, more vital aim: to organize the diverse human selves and understand that what is classically and somewhat archaically termed the "sacred" and "profane" are simply different components of the human endowment, those routines that are basic and those that are more abstract and far seeing.

Thus, instead of assuming that there must be conflict or a continual struggle, we might think of the group of simpletons inside ourselves as different parts of the mind having different roles in life. The lower, "profane" selves certainly exist. Human beings share with other animals biological needs basic to survival: thirst, hunger, and temperature regulation, anger and arousal. But human beings do not live by bread and circuses alone. The relationship between these selves is different than what we suppose.

Not everything gets swept away in a wonderful transformation; we still have the rest of our evolved selves with us. If our normal set of minds evolved for survival, we should know that our judgments will always be biased this way—sex and the family are very important priorities, and they comprise a large portion of our mind. This built-in system of adapting mainly for survival— getting food, getting security, getting laid—explains why conscious adaptation may seem to go against the well-evolved mind moves. Many of the classic "mystical" methods work by fighting bodily needs to loosen the mind's attachment to the body—a soul encased in a "mortal coil." Countless regimes try to free the conscious mind to go elsewhere: Monasteries emphasize a release from all worldly desires, often forcing a restriction of diet and stimulation. The fasting, the chanting, the privations, the destruction are all ways to loosen the automatic mind moves, connected so deeply for biological adaptation. This unsophisticated and baseless torture is not needed.

Medieval Turkish aspirants spun in a circle; Buddhists concentrate on breath; yogis may gaze at a mandala or at a vase, contemplate a meaningless phrase, such as "Show me your face before your father and mother met." What could be a state of "no mind" or of "mysterious darkness"? Meditations like these direct consciousness away from external events to internal ones, to separate oneself for a short period from the flow of daily life and to "turn off" the active mental selection routines. Most involve separating the practitioner from daily, ongoing activities. He or she usually sits alone or with a small group in a special place, in a naturally isolated area, sometimes near a waterfall.

And self-observation, like a developing neural group that strengthens connections, enhances the capacity for change of mind. Associations can be made between voluntary acts and their consequences. Through self-observation we know our own squadron of simpletons, even though they can be embarrassingly contradictory, conflicting, lazy, automatic, brilliant, generous, greedy, and the like. That awareness can lead to a weakening of the automatic selection of the "minds in place." And to a strengthening of conscious selection.

And we need, desperately, to be able to go beyond our unconscious mind shifts. Conscious intuition is a faculty to select the right part of the mind for the job. This capacity to comprehend instantly and to direct the mental system is the often unrealized aim of "conscious development."

The survival problems now facing us are collective rather than individual: how to prevent destruction of the earth; how to relate and understand diverse and divergent ideas, doctrines, and peoples, all of whom have their own "reality." What have been called spiritual perceptions or higher consciousness refer to a view of reality in which individual actions combine into something more organized.

And this happens in ordinary experiences as well. Players on a team create something greater than their individual efforts; people in a company can do the same. The concept of these "levels" of human reality should not really be so strange. We are used to acting in it when we say, "I've been a fan of this team for twenty-five years."

In a similar way, there is another level of understanding reality of which everyone is already a part. We don't have to destroy all the mind, all those simpletons that help us, in order to progress. What we need to do often enough is to be able, through self-observation, to switch in and out the simpletons we need. We don't need to mortify the simpletons, but we do need to conscript the right recruits when we need them.

The mind manipulates this unruly concatenation of selves, so we can never transcend our evolved set of special-purpose minds.

This gives us our mixed nature of "beast and angel." We need to carry all the selves along. "Enlightened," we would remain the same person, not some kind of sanitized white-robed ascetic. We'd understand that we have to satisfy many agendas at any one time and know which mental routines are useful at any moment. Thus, we'd still start at a sudden loud noise, relish a dinner, and enjoy family life, while adding a different organization of our selves. Some of the group of simpletons that we might someday lead may not be nice guys, some may have conflicting needs, but they need to be pointed, consciously, in one direction.

This is why an understanding of the automatic nature of the mental system enables a different approach to our future. One can't review evidence such as has been considered in this book without feeling that one acts in just the same rotten way as everyone else, that one has precious little room to maneuver, that we are all in the grip of our ancient adaptations for much of our life, no matter how high-minded we are, no matter how much we wish to change. We can never eliminate our "base nature" completely, any more than we can rid ourselves of heartbeats. Part of the humility that is supposedly learned by asceticism, by self-denial can also be discovered from studying the modern research on the separated simpletons inside the mind.

No matter how much we prize our individuality, almost all human beings act automatically in the same way. Our motives for action follow the same pattern. Everyone thinks they're unique, but we all have the same magnificent and inexpressible feelings when we see the sunrise, fall in love, hold our child for the first time, lose a loved one suddenly. They are the squadron of the mind. We all want more than we have, we remember the good old days fondly, we are fooled by the dramatic. We think alike. We get angry the same way, we feel love the same way, we feel hatred the same way, we see colors and forms the same way.

If we view humanity as one animal, the picture is different than our normal one, the demand is different and the possibilities are different. This human animal grew in size more than 500-fold since the time of Moses and grew in power several million fold. However, humanity's conscious management of its increased power has not expanded commensurately. Like any maturing organism, humanity's faculties developed at different rates and in different eras. Humanity has grown in size, strength, and dominion, but not in its consciousness.

Religious groups need not concern themselves, as they have historically, with the processes of biological adaptation: farming and food production, reproduction and propagation, housing, social organizations, service of all kinds to a specific community. Advice on whom and how to marry, how to organize society, how to consider relatives and kinsfolk, now interferes with evolution. Now religious leaders propose such ideas as "God is within you" to justify a life locked in poverty.

I hope we can now begin to unite the insights of the rational, the emotional, the intuitive, and the spiritual. "The kingdom of heaven is within" and "Angels are the faculties hidden in the mind of man" are ways of describing this unity. Raising consciousness means to become conscious of the different selves within and how they are partial, while also keeping aware of the larger venues of perception.

The most significant worker in adapting classical spiritual thought to the modern world is the Afghan author Idries Shah. In his many important works, Shah has translated and written stories of the Sufi tradition showing how the different "minds" within can operate, and spelling out our current dilemma.

Many concern the joke-figure Nasrudin, whose antics mirror those of humanity. Nasrudin allows us to see our situation through the lens of humor, summing up much of what is known about the inflexibility of the normal human consciousness and the current need to change thinking. In one story that I often quoted, Nasrudin is taking a plane from a Middle Eastern country to London along with his flock of followers. The four-engine plane takes off and all is well for a while. Then one engine fails, and the captain says "Do not worry. We will be late into London, by a half hour." Everyone is calm. The second engine fails, and Nasrudin's flock gets worried. The captain says that they will be two hours late. Nasrudin is soothing; everything is all right. Then the third engine fails, and the captain says that the plane will limp along and will be several hours late. Nasrudin, in this story the fountain of conventional thinking, says: "Let us pray that this plane does not go down. For if it does, we'll be here all day!"

Until recently, these fables were considered to be only moral or social tales, or even just folk homilies. But, as a modern version of the perspective of Rumi, they serve as a blueprint of the different selves inside ourselves. Shah points out that the basic components of previous spiritual systems have been transferred to the modern economy—safety, group membership, control of diet, and the like. One should take full advantage of the developments of modern society and, in an age of specialization, specialize in what is important. Contemporary people, interested in understanding themselves, are free of past strictures.

However, developing instant comprehension, paradoxically, takes time and is a process too subtle for those who demand everything immediately. In this the process is not much different than professional training: One does not become a nuclear physicist by merely gaping at exploding stars and by wishing it so. It takes years of training and effort. Is it reasonable to think that developing a faculty of mind akin to language would be easier?

It is a subtle but also quite difficult procedure to shift our minds in place and suspend our usual ways of action. And it looks different than the concepts put forth by church groups, ashrams, and the like, since it depends on a view of the mind as adaptation, not a hierarchy of functions. An understanding of the mind may well liberate us from society's different compartments, which have held our selves in custody. We need to develop our own evolution now, to move from the evolutionary operations detected by Darwin to those proposed by Rumi. With our immense brain, uncommitted in our infancy, we contain realms of undeveloped possibilities beyond the world we were born into.

It is vital now for our normal perspective on our life to shift. Our minds have grown up with an idea of the world as circumscribed by a few miles and by a few score of individuals. Now our world is one of billions, of space travel, of weapons of mass destruction, one in which all people are of the same tribe, in that we all now share the same fate.

There are countless technical and social fixes proposed to the continuous problems of modern life, and I do not reject any of them. We need all the pollution regulations, gun controls, peace initiatives, appropriate technology, recycling and precycling that we can develop.

However, it is an understanding of our mental system that may well provide the clues to those who wish to effect changes— for we do have some extraordinary abilities, as well as the accumulated limitations of millions of years. At least now we know somewhat more about what our mental limitations are!

Because we've changed the world so much, we need as a society to direct new kinds of adaptation consciously in all periods of life, in infancy, in youth, in society at large, in the planet, in spirit. I can't say that humanity will do it, but it is clear that unless we understand our roots in ancestral worlds and our adaptation to that world and how our adaptations cling inappropriately now, we have no real hope of changing. There will be no future for life unless we can take our own minds into our own hands and change in an appropriate direction.

The human mind, with its deepest roots in ancient routines for the analyses of simple signals, evolved to respond to dangers such as the tiger, and more recently the product of a rapidly expanding brain, can and will adapt even further, moving deeper within, into the many adaptations humanity has always possessed.

To echo the evolutionists Darwin and Rumi, there is grandeur in this view of the mind, with an endless supply of possible capabilities, waiting to be called in response to the new necessities of the new world we've created. Undertaking conscious evolution, with an understanding of the complexity of our myriad minds within, may be easier, closer at hand, and more liberating than we might normally think.

AFTERWORD

This is the story that begins Idries Shah's monumental adaptation of spiritual thought to the modern world. In it, published almost thirty years ago, we can see the themes of fresh adaptation and the layers of minds inside us.

Through all our different experiences, we can develop a way to select the right mind, not the mind we would usually choose. In more traditional terms, this yields an internal stability, detachment from the different minds within, and an increase in ability to select the right one. The story, "The Islanders," examines the different kinds of adaptations and simpletons within.

Once upon a time there lived an ideal community in a far-off land. Its members had no fears as we now know them. Instead of uncertainty and vacillation, they had purposefulness and a fuller means of expressing themselves. Although there were none of the stresses and tensions which mankind now considers essential to its progress, their lives were richer, because other, better elements replaced these things. Theirs, therefore, was a slightly different mode of existence. We could almost say that our present perceptions are a crude, makeshift version of the real ones that this community possessed.

They had real lives, not semilives.

We can call them the El Ar people.

They had a leader, who discovered that their country was to become uninhabitable for a period of, shall we say, 20,000 years. He planned their escape, realizing that their descendants would be able to return home successfully, only after many trials.

He found for them a place of refuge, an island whose features were only roughly similar to those of the original homeland. Because of the difference in climate and situation, the immigrants had to undergo a transformation. This made them more physically and mentally adapted to the new circumstances; coarse perceptions, for instance, were substituted for finer ones, as when the hand of the manual laborer becomes toughened in response to the needs of his calling.

In order to reduce the pain which a comparison between the old and new states would bring, they were made to forget the past almost entirely. Only the most shadowy recollection of it remained, yet it was sufficient to be awakened when the time came.

The system was very complicated, but well arranged. The organs by means of which the people survived on the island were also made the organs of enjoyment, physical and mental. The organs which were really constructive in the old homeland were placed in a special form of abeyance, and linked with the shadowy memory, in preparation for its eventual activation.

Slowly and painfully the immigrants settled down, adjusting themselves to the local conditions. The resources of the island were such that, coupled with effort and a certain form of guidance, people would be able to escape to a further island on the way back to their original home. This was the first of a succession of islands upon which gradual acclimatization took place.

The responsibility of this "evolution" was vested in those individuals who could sustain it. These were necessarily only a few, because for the mass of the people the effort of keeping both sets of knowledge in their consciousness was virtually impossible. One of them seemed to conflict with the other one. Certain specialists guarded the "special science."

This "secret," the method of effecting the transition, was nothing more or less than the knowledge of maritime skills and their application. The escape needed an instructor, raw materials, people, effort and understanding. Given these, people could learn to swim, and also to build ships.

The people who were originally in charge of the escape operations made it clear to everyone that a certain preparation was necessary before anyone could learn to swim or even take part in building a ship. For a time the process continued satisfactorily.

Then a man who had been found, for the time being, lacking in the necessary qualities rebelled against this order and managed to develop a masterly idea. He had observed that the effort to escape placed a heavy and often seemingly unwelcome burden upon the people. At the same time they were disposed to believe things which they were told about the escape operation. He realized that he could acquire power, and also revenge himself upon those who had undervalued him, as he thought, by a simple exploitation of these two sets of facts.

He would merely offer to take away the burden, by affirming that there was no burden.

He made this announcement:

"There is no need for man to integrate his mind and train it in the way which has been described to you. The human mind is already a stable and continuous, consistent thing. You have been told that you have to become a craftsman in order to build a ship. I say, not only do you not need to be a craftsman—you do not need a ship at all! An islander needs only to observe a few simple rules to survive and remain integrated into society. By the exercise of common sense, born into everyone, he can attain anything upon this island, our home, the common property and heritage of all."

The tonguester, having gained a great deal of interest among the people, now "proved" his message by saying:

"If there is any reality in ships and swimming, show us ships which have made the journey, and swimmers who have come back!"

This was a challenge to the instructors which they could not meet. It was based upon an assumption of which the bemused herd could not now see the fallacy. You see, ships never returned from the other land. Swimmers, when they did come back, had undergone a fresh adaptation which made them invisible to the crowd.

The mob pressed for demonstrative proof.

"Shipbuilding," said the escapers, in an attempt to reason with the revolt, "is an art and a craft. The learning and the exercise of this lore depends upon special techniques. These together make up a total activity, which cannot be examined piecemeal, as you demand. This activity has an impalpable element, called *baraka*, from which the word 'barque'—a ship—is derived. This word means 'the Subtlety,' and it cannot be shown to you."

"Art, craft, total, *baraka*, nonsense!" shouted the revolutionaries.

And so they hanged as many shipbuilding craftsmen as they could find.

The new gospel was welcomed on all sides as one of liberation. Man had discovered that he was already mature! He felt, for the time at least, as if he had been released from responsibility.

Most other ways of thinking were soon swamped by the simplicity and comfort of the revolutionary concept. Soon it was considered to be a basic fact, which had never been challenged by any rational person. Rational, of course, meant anyone who harmonized with the general theory itself, upon which society was now based.

Ideas which opposed the new one were easily called irrational. Anything irrational was bad. Thereafter, even if he had doubts, the individual had to suppress them or divert them, because he must at all costs be thought rational.

It was not very difficult to be rational. One had only to adhere to the values of society. Further, evidence of the truth of rationality abounded—providing that one did not think beyond the life of the island.

Society had now temporarily equilibrated itself within the island, and seemed to provide a plausible completeness, if viewed by means of itself. It was based upon reason plus emotion, making both seem plausible. Cannibalism, for instance, was permitted on rational grounds. The human body was found to be edible. Edibility was a characteristic of food. Therefore the human body was food. In order to compensate for the shortcomings of this reasoning, a makeshift was arranged. Cannibalism was controlled, in the interests of society. Compromise was the trademark of temporary balance. Every now and again someone pointed out a new compromise, and the struggle between reason, ambition, and community produced some fresh social norm.

Since the skills of boatbuilding had no obvious application within this society, the effort could easily be considered absurd. Boats were not needed—there was nowhere to go. The consequences of certain assumptions can be made to "prove" those assumptions. This is what is called pseudocertainty, the substitute for real certainty. It is what we deal in every day, when we assume that we will live another day. But our islanders applied it to everything.

The words "displeasing" and "unpleasant" were used on the island to indicate anything which conflicted with the new gospel, which was itself known as "Please." The idea behind this was that people would now please themselves, within the general need to please the State. The State was taken to mean all the people.

It is hardly surprising that from quite early times the very thought of leaving the island filled most people with terror. Similarly, very real fear is to be seen in long-term prisoners who are about to be released. "Outside" the place of captivity is a vague, unknown, threatening world.

The island was not a prison. But it was a cage with invisible bars, more effective than obvious ones ever could be.

The insular society became more and more complex, and we can look at only a few of its outstanding features. Its literature was a rich one. In addition to cultural compositions, there were numerous books which explained the values and achievements of the nation. There was also a system of allegorical fiction, which portrayed how terrible life might have been, had society not arranged itself in the present reassuring pattern.

From time to time instructors tried to help the whole community to escape. Captains sacrificed themselves for the reestablishment of a climate in which the now concealed shipbuilders could continue their work. All these efforts were interpreted by historians and sociologists with reference to conditions on the island, without thought for any contact outside this closed society. Plausible explanations of almost anything were comparatively easy to produce. No principle of ethics was involved, because scholars continued to study with genuine dedication what seemed to be true. "What *more* can we do?" they asked, implying by the word "more" that the alternative might be an effort of quantity. Or they asked each other, "What *else* can we do?" assuming that the answer might be "else"—something different. Their real problem was that they assumed themselves able to formulate the questions, and ignored the fact that the questions were every bit as important as the answers.

Of course the islanders had plenty of scope for thought and action within their own small domain. The variations of ideas and differences of opinion gave the impression of freedom of thought. Thought was encouraged, providing that it was not "absurd."

Freedom of speech was allowed. It was of little use without the development of understanding, which was not pursued.

The work and the emphasis of the navigators had to take on different aspects in accordance with the changes in the community. This made their reality even more baffling to the students who tried to follow them from the island point of view.

Amid all the confusion, even the capacity to remember the possibility of escape could at times become an obstacle. The stirring consciousness of escape potential was not very discriminating. More often than not the eager would-be escapers settled for any kind of substitute. A vague concept of navigation cannot become useful without orientation. Even the most eager potential shipbuilders had been trained to believe that they already had that orientation. They were already mature. They hated anyone who pointed out that they might need a preparation.

Bizarre versions of swimming or shipbuilding often crowded out possibilities of real progress. Very much to blame were the advocates of pseudoswimming or allegorical ships, mere hucksters, who offered lessons to those as yet too weak to swim, or passages on ships which they could not build.

The needs of the society had originally made necessary certain forms of efficiency and thinking which developed into what was known as science. This admirable approach, so essential in the fields where it had an application, finally outran its real meaning. The approach called "scientific," soon after the "Please" revolution, became stretched until it covered all manner of ideas. Eventually things which could not be brought within its bounds became known as "unscientific," another convenient synonym for "bad." Words were unknowingly taken prisoner and then automatically enslaved.

In the absence of a suitable attitude, like people who, thrown upon their own resources in a waiting room, feverishly read magazines, the islanders absorbed themselves in finding substitutes for the fulfillment which was the original (and indeed the final) purpose of this community's exile.

Some were able to divert their attention more or less successfully into mainly emotional commitments. There were different ranges of emotion, but no adequate scale for measuring them. All emotion was considered to be "deep" or "profound"—at any rate more profound than nonemotion. Emotion, which was seen to move people to the most extreme physical and mental acts known, was automatically termed "deep."

The majority of people set themselves targets, or allowed others to set them for them. They might pursue one cult after another, or money, or social prominence. Some worshipped some things and felt themselves superior to all the rest. Some, by repudiating what they thought worship was, thought that they had no idols, and could therefore safely sneer at all the rest.

As the centuries passed, the island was littered with the debris of these cults. Worse than ordinary debris, it was self-perpetuating. Well-meaning and other people combined the cults and recombined them, and they spread anew. For the amateur and intellectual, this constituted a mine of academic or "initiatory" material, giving a comforting sense of variety.

Magnificent facilities for the indulging of limited "satisfactions" proliferated. Palaces and monuments, museums and universities, institutes of learning, theaters and sports stadiums almost filled the island. The people naturally prided themselves on these endowments, many of which they considered to be linked in a general way with ultimate truth, though exactly how this was so escaped almost all of them.

Shipbuilding was connected with some dimensions of this activity, but in a way unknown to almost everyone.

Clandestinely the ships raised their sails, the swimmers continued to teach swimming. . . .

The conditions on the island did not entirely fill these dedicated people with dismay. After all, they too had originated in the very same community, and had indissoluble bonds with it, and with its destiny.

But they very often had to preserve themselves from the attentions of their fellow citizens. Some "normal" islanders tried to save them from themselves. Others tried to kill them, for an equally sublime reason. Some even sought their help eagerly, but could not find them.

All these reactions to the existence of the swimmers were the result of the same cause, filtered through different kinds of minds. This cause was that hardly anyone now knew what a swimmer really was, what he was doing, or where he could be found.

As the life of the island became more and more civilized, a strange but logical industry grew up. It was devoted to ascribing doubts to the validity of the system under which society lived. It succeeded in absorbing doubts about social values by laughing at them or satirizing them. The activity could wear a sad or happy face, but it really became a repetitive ritual. A potentially valuable industry, it was often prevented from exercising its really creative function.

People felt that, having allowed their doubts to have temporary expression, they would in some way assuage them, exorcise them, almost propitiate them. Satire passed for meaningful allegory; allegory was accepted but not digested. Plays, books, films, poems, lampoons were the usual media for this development, though there was a strong section of it in more academic fields. For many islanders it seemed more emancipated, more modern or progressive, to follow this cult rather than older ones.

Here and there a candidate still represented himself to a swimming instructor, to make his bargain. Usually what amounted to a stereotyped conversation took place.

"I want to learn to swim."

"Do you want to make a bargain about it?"

"No. I only have to take my ton of cabbage."

"What cabbage?"

"The food which I will need on the other island."

"There is better food there."

"I don't know what you mean. I cannot be sure. I must take my cabbage."

"You cannot swim, for one thing, with a ton of cabbage."

"Then I cannot go. You call it a load. I call it my essential nutrition."

"Suppose, as an allegory, we say not 'cabbage' but 'assumptions,' or 'destructive ideas'?"

"I am going to take my cabbage to some instructor who understands my needs."

BIBLIOGRAPHY

Ahern, G. L., and G. E. Schwartz. 1985. Differential lateralization for positive and negative emotion in the human brain: EEG spectral analysis. *Neuropsychologia* 23 (6):744–55.

Ainsworth, M. D. S., M. Blehar, E. Waters, and S. Wall. 1978. *Patterns of attachment: A psychological study of the strange situation.* Hillsdale, NJ: Erlbaum.

Ainsworth, M. D. S., and B. A. Whittig. 1965. Attachment and exploratory behavior of one year olds in a strange situation. In *Determinants of infant behaviour, 4,* ed. B. M. Foxx. London: Methuen.

Albert, M. A., and L. K. Obler. 1978. *The bilingual brain.* New York: Academic Press.

Antonovsky, A. 1984. The sense of coherence as a determinant of health. In *Behavioral health,* ed. J. D. Matarazzo, S. M. Weiss, J. A. Herd, and N. E. Miller. New York: Wiley.

———. 1987. *Unraveling the mystery of health.* San Francisco: Jossey-Bass.

Antrobus, J. 1990. The neurocognition of sleep mentation: Rapid eye movements, visual imagery and dreaming. In *Sleep and cognition,* ed. R. R. Bootzin, J. F. Kihlstrom, and D. L. Schacter. Washington, DC: APA

Asch, S. E. 1946. Forming impressions of personality. *Journal of Abnormal and Social Psychology* 41:258–90.

———. 1951. Effects of group pressure upon the modification and distortion of judgments. In *Groups, leadership, and men,* ed. H. Guetzkow. Pittsburgh: Carnegie Press.

Baars, B. J., and M. E. Mattson. 1981. Consciousness and intention: A framework and some evidence. *Cognition and Brain Theory* 4:247–63.

Baddeley, A. 1986. *Working memory.* New York: Oxford University Press.

Barash, D. 1986. *The tortoise and the hare.* New York: Viking-Penguin.

Beck, A. 1976. *Cognitive therapy and the emotional disorders.* New York: International Universities Press.

Beloff, J. 1978. Why parapsychology is still on trial. *Human Nature* 1(12):68–76.

Benton, A. L. 1980. The neuropsychology of facial recognition. *American Psychologist* 35:176–86.

Berlin, B., and P. Kay. 1969. *Basic color terms: Their universality and evolution.* Berkeley and Los Angeles: University of California Press.

Biederman, I., 1987. Recognition-by-components: A theory of human image understanding. *Psychological Review* 94:115–47.

Borgeat, F., J. Boissonneault, and L. Chaloult. 1989. Psychophysiological responses to subliminal auditory suggestions for activation. *Perceptual and Motor Skills* 69:947–53.

Boynton, R. M. 1971. Color vision. In *Woodwater and Schlossberg's experimental psychology.* 3d ed., ed. J. W. King and L. A. Riggs. New York: Holt, Rinehart and Winston.

Bransford, J. D., and M. K. Johnson. 1974. Contextual prerequisites for understanding: Some investigations of comprehension and recall. *Journal of Verbal Learning and Verbal Behavior* 11:717–26.

Bridges, K. M. B. 1932. Emotional development in early infancy. *Child Development* 3:324–41.

Brown, A. M. 1990. Human universals. University of California, Santa Barbara. Typescript.

Brown, J. 1977. *Mind, brain and consciousness.* New York: Academic Press.

Buss, A. H., and R. Plomin. 1984. *Temperament: Early developing personality traits.* Hillsdale, NJ: Erlbaum.

Buss, A. H., R. Plomin, and L. Willerman. 1973. The inheritance of temperaments. *Journal of Personality* 41:513–24.

Calvin, W. H., 1986. *The river that flows uphill: A journey from the Big Bang to the big brain.* New York: Macmillan.

Campbell, B., 1982. *Humankind emerging.* Boston: Little, Brown.

Campbell, D. T. 1960. Blind variation and selective retention in creating thought as in other knowledge processes. *Psychological Review* 67:380–400.

Carver, C. S., and M. F. Scheier. 1988. *Perspectives on personality.* Boston: Allyn and Bacon.

Chase, W. G., and N. A. Simon. 1973. The mind's eye in chess. In *Visual information processing,* ed. W. G. Chase. New York: Academic Press.

Chess, S., and A. Thomas. 1987. *Know your child.* New York: Basic Books.

Chomsky, N. 1980. *Rules and representations.* Cambridge: MIT Press.

Cosmides, L., and J. Tooby. 1986. From evolution to behavior: evolutionary psychology as the missing link. In *The latest on the best: Essays on evolution and optimality,* ed. J. Dupre. Cambridge: MIT Press.

Craik, F. I. 1989. On the making of episodes. In *Journal of Verbal Learning and Verbal Behavior* 12:599–607.

Curtis, H. 1983. *Biology.* New York: Worth Publishers.

Darwin, C. [1859] 1968. *The origin of species.* Reprint. New York: Penguin Books.

————. 1872. *The expression of the emotions in man and animals.* London: Longmans.

Deecke, L., T. Bashore, C. H. M. Brunia, E. Gernewald-Zuberbier, G. Gernewald. 1984. Movement-associated potentials and motor control: Report of the EPIC VI motor panel. In *Brain and information: Event,* ed. R. Karrer, et al.

Deecke, L. 1987. The natural explanation for the two components of the readiness potential. Commentary on Libet. *Behavioral and Brain Sciences* 10, 781–82.

Deecke, L., B. Grzinger, and H. H. Kornhuber. 1976. Voluntary finger movement in man: Cerebral potentials and theory. *Biological Cybernetics* 23:99–119.

De Lumley, H., 1969. A paleolithic camp at Nice. *Scientific American* 220(5):47–59.

Dement, W. C. 1972. *Some must watch while some must sleep.* San Francisco: W. H. Freeman.

Dement, W. C., and N. Kleitman. Cyclic variations in EEG and their relation to eye movements, body motility and dreaming. *Electroencephalography and Clinical Neurophysiology* 9:673–90.

Dement, W. C., and E. Wolpert. 1958. The relation of eye movements, bodily motility and external stimuli to dream content. *Journal of Experimental Psychology* 55:543–53.

Deregowski, J. B. 1973. Illusion and culture. In *Illusion in nature and art,* ed. R. L. Gregory and G. H. Gombrich. New York: Scribner.

————. 1981 *Preconscious processing*. Chichester: Wiley.

Dubos, R., 1968. *So human an animal*. New York: Scribner.

————. 1978. Health and creative adaptation. *Human Nature* 1(1):14–21.

Eagle, M., 1959. The effects of subliminal stimuli of aggressive content upon conscious cognition. *Journal of Personality* 23:578–600.

Eibl-Eibesfeldt, I. 1970. *Ethology, the biology of behavior*. New York: Holt, Rinehart and Winston.

————. 1971. *Love and hate: The natural history of behavior patterns*. Trans. G. Strachan. New York: Holt, Rinehart and Winston.

————. 1972. Similarities and differences between cultures in expressive movements. In *Non-verbal communciation*, ed. R. A. Hinde. Cambridge: Cambridge University Press.

————. 1980. Strategies of social interaction. In *Emotion: Theory, research, and experience,* ed. R. Plutchik and H. Kelerman. New York: Academic Press.

Ekman, P., W. V. Friesen, M. O'Sullivan, A. Chan et al. 1987. Universals and cultural differences in the judgments of facial expressions of emotion. *Journal of Personality and Social Psychology* 53(4):712–17.

Elsasser, W. M. 1979. A contribution to the theory of memory. *Journal of Social and Biological Structures* 2:229–34.

Erdelyi, M. H. 1986. *Psychoanalysis: Freud's cognitive psychology*. New York: W. H. Freeman.

Estes, W. K. 1980. Is human memory obsolete? *American Scientist* 68:62–69.

Fantz, R. L. 1961. The origin of form perception. *Scientific American* 204:66–72.

Fialkowski, K. 1986. A mechanism for the origin of the human brain: A hypothesis. *Current Anthropology* 27:288–90.

————. 1987. On the origins of the human brain: Preadaptation vs. adaptation. *Current Anthropology* 28:540–43.

Fodor, J. 1983. *The modularity of mind*. Cambridge: MIT Press.

Fonagay, P. 1977. The use of subliminal stimuli in highlighting function differences between the two hemispheres. Paper presented to Experimental Psychology Society, Birbeck College, London.

Fox, O. 1962. *Astral projection*. New Hyde Park, NY: University Books.

Freud, S. [1900] 1955. *The interpretation of dreams.* Reprint. London: The Hogarth Press.

———. 1913. *New introductory lectures on psychoanalysis.* London: The Hogarth Press.

Galin, D., and R. Ornstein 1972. Lateral specialization of cognitive mode: An EEG study. *Psychophysiology* 9:412–18.

Galin, D., R. E. Orstein and J. Adams. 1977. Midbrain stimulation of the amygdala. *Journal of States of Consciousness* 2:34–41.

Galin, D., R. E. Ornstein, J. Herron, and J. Johnstone. 1982. Sex and handedness differences in EEG measures of hemispheric specialization. *Brain and Language* 16(1):19–55.

Gallup, G. G. 1977. Self-recognition in primates: A comparative approach to the bi-directional properties of consciousness. *American Psychologist* 32:329–38.

———. 1979. Self-awareness in primates. *American Scientist* 67:417–21.

Garcia, J. 1989. Food for Tolman: Cognition and cathexis in concert. In *Aversion, avoidance, and anxiety,* ed. T. Archer and L. Nilsson. Hillsdale, NJ: Erlbaum.

Garcia, J., and R. Koelling. 1966. Relation of cue to consequence in avoidance learning. *Psychonomic Science* 4:123–24.

Gardner, H. 1983. *Frames of mind.* New York: Basic Books.

Gay, P. 1989. *Freud: Life and work.* New York: Doubleday.

Gibson, J. J. 1960. *The perception of the visual world.* Boston: Houghton Mifflin.

Goethals, G. R., and R. F. Reckman. 1982. Recalling previously held attitudes. In *Memory observed,* ed. U. Neisser. San Francisco: W. H. Freeman.

Goldsmith, H. H., A. H. Buss, R. Plomin, and M. K. Rothbart. 1987. Roundtable: What is temperament? Four approaches. *Child Development* 58(2):505–29.

Coleman, D. 1984a. Denial and hope. *American Health* 3:54–61.

———. 1984b. To dream the impossible dream. *American Health* 3:60–61.

———. 1985 *Vital lies, simple truths: The psychology of self-deception.* New York: Simon and Schuster.

———. 1989. What is negative about positive illusions? When benefits for the individual harm the collective. *Journal of Clinical Psychology* 8:190–97.

Gould, S. J., 1987. *The panda's thumb.* New York: W. W. Norton.

Gould, S. J. 1979. *Ever since Darwin*. New York: W. W. Norton.

Gould, S. J., 1990. The view of life: An earful of jaw. *Natural History* 100 (March):12–23.

Gould, S. J. 1989. This view of life: Through a lens, darkly. *Natural History* 99 (September):16–24.

Gross, C. G., C. E. Rocha-Miranda, and D. B. Bender. 1972. Visual properties of neurons in inferotemporal cortex of the macaque. *Journal of Neurophysiology* 35:96–111.

Haith, M. M. 1980. *Rules that babies look by: The organization of newborn visual activity*. Hillsdale, NJ: Erlbaum.

Haldane, J. B. S. 1986. *On being the right size*. London: Oxford University Press.

Hecaen, H. and R. Angelergues. 1962. Agnosia for faces (prosopagnosia). *Archives of Neurology* 7:92–100.

Hilgard, E. R. 1977. *Divided consciousness: Multiple controls in human thought and action*. New York: Wiley-Interscience.

———. 1978. Hypnosis and consciousness. *Human Nature* 1:42–51.

Hobson, A. 1988. *The dreaming brain*. New York: Basic Books.

Hudson, W. 1960. Pictorial depth perception in sub-cultural groups in Africa. *Journal of Social Psychology* 52:183–208.

Isen, A. M. 1984. Affect, cognition, and social behavior. In *Handbook of social cognition*, vol. 3, ed. R. S. Wyer and T. K. Srull. Hillsdale, NJ: Erlbaum.

Isen, A. M., M. M. Johnson, E. Mertz, and C. F. Robinson. 1985. The influence of positive affect on the unusualness of word associations. *Journal of Personality and Social Psychology* 48:(6):1413–26.

Isen, A. M., and P. F. Levin. 1972. Effect of feeling good on helping: Cookies and kindness. *Journal of Personality and Social Psychology* 21(3):384–88.

Isen, A. M., T. E. Nygren, and F. G. Ashby. 1988. Influence of positive affect on the subjective utility of gains and losses: It is just not worth the risk. *Journal of Personality and Social Psychology* 55(5):710–17.

Iwata, J., and J. E. Ledoux. 1988. Dissociation of associative and nonassociative concomitants of classical fear conditioning in the freely behaving rat. *Behavioral Neuroscience* 102:(1):66–76.

James, W. [1890] 1970. *The principles of psychology*. Vol. 1. Reprint. New York: Dover.

————. [1917] 1980. *The varieties of religious experience.* Reprint. New York: Longmans Green.

Johnson-Laird, T. N. 1983. *Mental models.* Cambridge: Harvard University Press.

————. 1988. *The computer and the mind.* Cambridge: Harvard University Press.

Just, M., and P. A. Carpenter 1980. A theory of reading: From eye fixations to comprehension. *Psychological Review* 87:329–54.

Kahneman, D. 1973. *Attention and effort.* Englewood Cliffs, NJ: Prentice-Hall.

Kahneman, D., and A. Tversky. 1973. On the psychology of prediction. *Psychological Review* 80:237–51.

Kahneman, D., P. Slovic, and A. Tversky. eds. 1982. *Judgment under uncertainty.* New York: Cambridge University Press.

Keyes, D. 1982. *The minds of Billy Milligan.* New York: Bantam Books.

Klein, G. S. 1959. Consciousness in psychoanalytic theory: Some implications for current research in perception. *Journal of American Psychoanalysis* 7:5–34.

Kornhuber, H. H. and L. Deecke. 1964. Hirnpotentialanderungen beim Menschen vor und nach Willwegnugen dargestellt mit Magnetbandspeicherung und tsanalyse. *Pflgers Arch. Ges. Physiol.* 261:52.

Kosslyn, S. M. 1986. *Image and mind.* Cambridge: Harvard University Press.

Kosslyn, S. M., J. D. Holtzman, M. J. Farah, and M. S. Gazzaniga. 1985. A computational analysis of mental image generation: Evidence from functional dissociations in split-brain patients. *Journal of Experimental Psychology* 114(3):311–41.

Lamark, J. B. [1809] 1951. Evolution through environmentally produced modifications. In *A source book in animal biology.* M. Allman, ed. London, Longhmans.

Langer, E. J. 1975. The illusion of control. *Journal of Personality and Social Psychology* 32:311–28.

Lawren, B. 1986. Brain launching body. *Omni* 8 (March):20.

Ledoux, J. E., J. Iwata, P. Cicchetti, and D. J. Reis. 1988. Different projections of the central amygdaloid nucleus mediate autonomic and behavioral correlates of conditioned fear. *Journal of Neuroscience* 8(7):2517–29.

Ledoux, J. E., D. A. Ruggiero et al. 1987. Topographic organization of convergent projections to the thalamus from the inferior colliculus and spinal cord in the rat. *Journal of Comparative Neurology* 264(1):123–46.

Lettvin, J. Y., H. R. Maturana, S. W. McCulloch, and W. H. Pitts. 1959. What the frog's eye tells the frog's brain. *Proceedings of the Institute of Radio Engineers* 47:140–51.

Libet, B. 1978. Neuronal vs. subjective timing for a conscious experience. In *Cerebral correlates of conscious experience,* ed. D. Buser and A. Rouseul-Buser. Amsterdam: Elsevier.

———. 1985. Subjective antedating of a sensory experience and mind-brain theories: Reply to Honderich. *Journal of Theoretical Biology* 114(4):563–70.

———. 1985b. Theory and evidence relating cerebral processes to conscious will: Author's response to peer commentary on Libet (1985). *Behavioral and Brain Sciences* 8:558–66.

———. 1985c. Unconscious cerebral initiative and the role of conscious will in voluntary action. *Behavioral and Brain Sciences* 8:529–66.

Libet, B., W. W. Alberts, E. W. Wright, Jr., and B. Feinstein. 1967. Responses of human somatosensory cortex to stimuli below thresholds of conscious sensation. *Science* 158:1597–1600.

———. 1972. Cortical and thalamic activation in conscious sensory experience. In *Neurophysiology studied in man,* ed. G. G. Somjen. Amsterdam: Excerpta Medica.

Libet, B., C. A. Gleason, E. W. Wright, Jr., and D. K. Pearl. 1983. Time of conscious intention to act in relation to onset of cerebral activity (readiness-potential); Part 3: The unconscious initiation of a freely voluntary act. *Brain* 106:623–42.

Libet, B., and S. Mochida 1988. Long-term enhancement (LTE) of postsynaptic potentials following neural conditioning, in mammalian sympathetic ganglia. *Brain Research* 473(2):271–82.

Libet, B., E. W. Wright, Jr., B. Feinstein, and D. K. Pearl. 1979. Subjective referral of the timing for a conscious sensory experience: A functional role for the somatosensory specific projection system in man. *Brain* 102:193–224.

Libet, B., E. W. Wright, Jr., and C. A. Gleason. 1982. Readiness-potentials preceding unrestricted spontaneous vs. pre-planned voluntary acts. *Electroencephalography and Clinical Neurophysiology* 54(3): 322–35.

————. 1983. Preparation or intention-to-act in relation to pre-event potentials recorded at the vertex. *Electroencephalography and Clinical Neurophysiology* 56(4):367–72.

Livingston, M. S., and D. H. Hubel. 1987. Psychophysical evidence for separate channels for the perception of form, color, movement and depth. *Journal of Neuroscience* 7:3416–68.

Locke, J. 1670. *An essay concerning human understanding*. New York: Meridian.

Loftus, E. F. 1978. Shifting human color memory. *Memory and Cognition* 5:696–99.

————. 1980. *Memory*. Menlo Park, CA: Addison-Wesley.

Loftus, E. F., D. G. Miller, and H. J. Burns. 1978. Semantic integration of verbal information into a visual memory. *Journal of Experimental Psychology* 4:19–31.

Loftus, E. F., and J. C. Palmer. 1974. Reconstruction of automobile destruction: An example of the interaction between language and memory. *Journal of Verbal Learning and Verbal Behavior* 13:585–89.

Loftus, G. R., and E. R. Loftus. 1974. The influence of one memory retrieval on a subsequent memory retrieval. *Memory and Cognition* 3:467–71.

————. 1975. *Human memory: The processing of information*. New York: Halsted Press.

Lovejoy, C. O. 1981. The origin of man. *Science* 211:128–30.

Luria, A. R. 1968. *The mind of a mnemonist*. New York: Basic Books.

McClelland, J. L. 1976. Preliminary letter identification in the perception of words and non-words. *Journal of Experimental Psychology: Human Perception and Performance* 2:80–91.

————. 1985. Putting knowledge in its place: A scheme for programming parallel processing structures on the fly. *Cognitive Science* 9:113–46.

Marr, D. 1982. *Vision*. New York: W. H. Freeman.

Miller, N. 1939. Discrimination without awareness. *American Journal of Psychology* 52:562–78.

Miller, G. A. 1981. *Language and speech*. San Francisco: W. H. Freeman.

Nickerson, R. S., and M. J. Adams. Long-term memory for a common object. *Cognitive Psychology* 11:287–307.

Nisbett, R. E., and L. Ross. 1980. *Human inference: Strategies and short-comings of social judgment*. Englewood Cliffs, NJ: Prentice-Hall.

Ornstein, R. 1969. *On the experience of time*. London: Penguin Books.

———. 1976. *The mind field*. London: Octagon Press.

———. 1986*a*. *Multimind*. Boston: Houghton Mifflin.

———. 1986*b*. *The psychology of consciousness*. 3d ed. New York: Penguin.

Ornstein, R., and P. E. Ehrlich. 1989. *New world, new mind*. New York: Doubleday.

Ornstein, R., J. Herron, J. Johnstone, and C. Swencionis. 1979. Differential right hemisphere involvement in two reading tasks. *Psychophysiology* 16(4):398–401.

Ornstein, R., and D. S. Sobel. 1987. *The healing brain*. New York: Simon and Schuster.

———. 1989. *Healthy pleasures*. Reading, MA: Addison-Wesley.

Ornstein, R., R. Thompson, and D. Macaulay. 1984. *The amazing brain*. Boston: Houghton Mifflin.

Ornstein, R., ed. 1973. *The nature of human consciousness*. San Francisco: W. H. Freeman.

Pavlov, I. P. 1927. *Conditioned reflexes*. London: Oxford University Press.

Penfield, W. 1975. *The mystery of the mind*. Princeton, NJ: Princeton University Press.

Pfurtscheller, G., and A. Berghold. 1989. Patterns of cortical activation during planning of voluntary movement. *Electroencephalography and Clinical Neurophysiology* 72:250–58.

Poppel, E., R. Held, and D. Frost. 1973. Residual visual function after brain wounds involving the central visual pathways in man. *Nature* 243:295–6.

Rechtschaffen, A. 1978. The single-mindedness and isolation of dreams. *Sleep* 1:97–109.

Rock, I. 1985. *Perception*. New York: Scientific American.

Rockstroh, B., T. Elbert, N. Birbaumer, and W. Lutzenberge. 1982. *Slow brain potentials and behavior*. Baltimore and Munich: Urban and Schwarzenberg.

Rosch, E. 1973. Natural categories. *Cognitive Psychology* 4:328–50.

———. 1975. Cognitive representation of semantic categories. *Journal of Experimental Psychology* 104:192–233.

Rumelhart, D. E., and J. L. McClelland. 1986. *Parallel distributed processing: Explorations in the microstructure of cognition*. Cambridge: MIT Press.

Sackeim, H. A., I. K. Packer, and R. C. Gurr. 1977. Hemisphericity, cognitive set and susceptibility to subliminal perception. *Journal of Abnormal Psychology* 86:624–30.

Sanders, M. D., E. K. Warrington, and J. Marshall. 1974. "Blind sight": Vision in a field defect. *Lancet,* 707–08.

Schacter, D. L. 1989. Memory. In *Foundations of cognitive science,* ed. M. I. Posner. Cambridge: MIT Press.

Scheier, M. F., and C. S. Carver. 1985. Optimism, coping, and health: assessment and implications of generalized outcome expectancies. *Health Psychology* 4(3):219–47.

Segal, M. H., D. Campbell, and M. J. Herskovits. 1963. Cultural differences in the perception of geometric illusions. *Science* 139:769–71.

Shah, I. 1970. *Tales of the dervishes*. New York: Dutton.

———. 1971. *The pleasantries of the incredible Mulla Nasrudin*. New York: Dutton.

———. 1971. *The Sufis*. New York: Anchor Books/Doubleday.

——— 1986. *The exploits and subtleties of Mulla Nasrudin*. London: Octagon Press.

Shallice, T., and J. McGill. 1978. The origin of mixed errors. In *Attention and performance 7,* ed. J. Requin. Hillsdale, NJ: Erlbaum.

Sherry, D. F., and D. L. Schacter. 1987. The evolution of multiple memory systems. *Psychological Review* 94:439–54.

Shevrin, H., and P. Rennick. 1967. Cortical response to a tactile stimulus during attention, mental arithmetic and free association. *Psychophysiology* 8:149–62.

Silverman, L., and J. Weinberger. Mommy and I are one: Implications for psychotherapy. *American Psychologist* 40(12):1296–1308.

Small, M. A. 1990. Political animal: Social intelligence and the growth of the primate brain. *The Sciences*: 176–9.

Smith, G. J. W., and M. Henrikkson. 1955. The effect on an established percept of a perceptual process beyond awareness. *Acta Psychologica* 2:346–55.

Tellegen, A., D. T. Lykken et al. 1988. Personality similarity in twins reared apart and together. *Journal of Personality and Social Psychology* 54(6):1031–39.

Todman, M., Jr. 1989. Some observations upon perceptual organization and the mere exposure effect. *Perceptual and Motor Skills* 69:147–60.

Tomkins, S. S. 1962. *Affect, imagery, consciousness.* Vol. 1, *The positive affects.* New York: Springer-Verlag.

———. 1963. *Affect, imagery, consciousness.* Vol. 2, *The negative affects.* New York: Springer-Verlag.

Treisman, A., and S. Gormican. 1988. Feature analysis in early vision: Evidence from search asymmetries. *Psychological Review* 95:15–48.

Tversky, A., and D. Kahneman. 1973. Availability: A heuristic for judging frequency and possibility. *Cognitive Psychology* 5:207–32.

Washburn, S. 1960. Tools and human evolution. *Scientific American* 203(3):67–73.

Weiskrantz, L. 1986. *Blindsight.* Oxford: Clarendon Press.

Wenegrat, B. 1984. *Sociobiology and mental disorder: a new view.* Menlo Park, CA: Addison-Wesley.

Zuckerman, M. 1960. The effects of subliminal and supraliminal suggestion on verbal productivity. *Journal of Abnormal and Social Psychology* 60:404–11.

INDEX

Robert Ornstein is president of the Institute for the Study of Human Knowledge. He teaches at the University of California Medical Center in San Francisco, and at Stanford University. He has done extensive research on the human brain and is the author of *The Psychology of Consciousness* and *Multimind* and coauthor of *The Amazing Brain*, *The Healing Brain*, *Healthy Pleasures*, and *New World, New Mind*, among his twenty books.